32-page Championship Series Guide & full-color poster in center of paper

EWS
PAPER
Tuesday, October 10, 2000

STIC

ON PAGES 2 & 3

DAILY NEWS
New York's Hometown Newspaper
Wednesday, October 18, 2000

ALL ABOARD!

2000

Yanks clinch, meet Mets Saturday

DAILY NEWS

RACING ★ ★ ★ ★ FINAL

Sports
Sunday, October 12, 1986
Sports starts on Page 64

ANGELS TAKE 3-1 LEAD

Grich's RBI single beats Bosox in 11
Bill Madden, Page 70

NAILED!

Lenny Dykstra, the Met they call "Nails," is mobbed by his teammates after hitting 2-run HR in bottom of 9th yesterday to give Mets a 6-5 victory in Game 3 and 2-1 lead in the NLCS. Coverage begins on Page 64

COLLEGE SCORES		
Alabama 37	Memphis St. 0	UCLA 22
Army 35	Tennessee 21	Oklahoma 47
Auburn 31	Vanderbilt 9	Princeton 30
Michigan 27	Michigan St. 6	Miami 50
Pittsburgh 10	Notre Dame 9	Penn St. 23
Washington 34	Stanford 14	Texas Tech 17

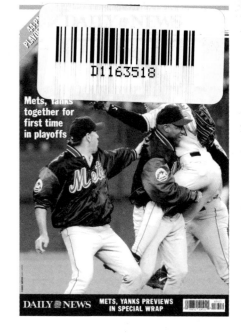

D1163518

Mets, Yanks together for first time in playoffs

DAILY NEWS   **METS, YANKS PREVIEWS IN SPECIAL WRAP**

NAL

EM

...s fallen heroes as they cover hearts with ...ball's layoff. Mets won, 4-1.   **P. 92-94**

SPORTS ★ ★ ★ ★ FINAL

CLEMENS FINED $50G FOR BAT TOSS

DAILY NEWS
New York's Hometown Newspaper
Wednesday, October 25, 2000

SUBWAY SERIES!
32-PAGE SECTION WRAPS MAIN PAPER

MET LIFE!

Mets
50

Beat Yanks 4-2; trail in Series, 2-1

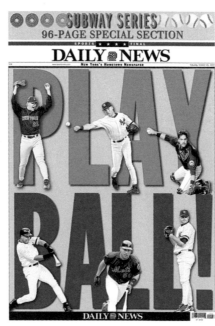

○○○○ **SUBWAY SERIES**
96-PAGE SPECIAL SECTION
SPORTS ★ ★ ★ ★ FINAL

DAILY NEWS
New York's Hometown Newspaper
Saturday, October 21, 2000

PLAY BALL!

DAILY NEWS

FINAL   # DAILY NEWS
NEW YORK'S PICTURE NEWSPAPER ®

New York, N.Y. 10017, Thursday, July 10, 1969

SEAVER PERFECT TILL 9TH
QUALLS GETS ONLY CUB HIT

Jerry Grote reaches home as Seaver's second inning single, Randy Hundley awaits ball.

So? Who's Perfect?

Cub manager Leo Durocher sits glumly in the dugout...

CUP!
soccer's big party: **P. 80-83**

EWS

David busts out as Mets down Yanks to even Subway Series

GHT CK!

...bers, 5-3, last night at Citi Field to even Subway Series ...gs — and Jason Bay, who goes 4-for-4 and scores three Subway Series coverage on Pages 50-57

FINAL   # DAILY NEWS
NEW YORK'S PICTURE NEWSPAPER ®

Vol. 56, No. 85   New York, N.Y. 10017, Tuesday, October 2, 1979   **10¢**

METS DO IT!
Beat Cubs 6 to 4 for East Flag; Meet Reds in Playoff Saturday

Yogi Berra, (r.) who was once heading for managerial showers, gets lift from (l. to r.) Ken Boswell, Dally Dyer and Jerry Grote.

Badillo Set to Endorse Beame Today
Story on Page 3

SPORTS ★ ★ ★ FINAL

DAILY NEWS
Sports
Tuesday, October 28, 1986   World Series Special

OH, SHEA CAN YOU SEE? Good lookin game for the Met fan.

GOOD KNIGHT

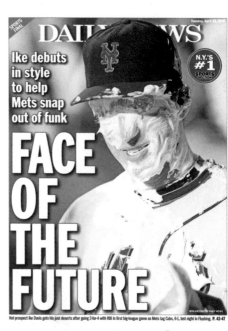

SPORTS FINAL   # DAILY NEWS
Tuesday, April 13, 1982

N.Y.'s #1 SPORTS SECTION

Ike debuts in style to help Mets snap out of funk

FACE OF THE FUTURE

Hot prospect Ike Davis gets his just deserts after going 2-for-4 with RBI in first big-league game as Mets tag Cubs, 6-1, last night in Flushing.

the *Mets*

A 50th ANNIVERSARY CELEBRATION

DAILY NEWS

the Mets

A 50th ANNIVERSARY CELEBRATION

Foreword by
RON DARLING

By Andy Martino and Anthony McCarron

Stewart, Tabori & Chang
NEW YORK

Published in 2011 by Stewart, Tabori & Chang
An imprint of ABRAMS

Library of Congress Cataloging-in-Publication Data

Martino, Andy.
  The Mets : a 50th anniversary celebration / Andy Martino and Anthony
McCarron.
      p. cm.
  Includes bibliographical references and index.
  ISBN 978-1-58479-914-6 (alk. paper)
  1. New York Mets (Baseball team)—History. 2. New York Mets (Baseball
team)—History—Pictorial works. I. McCarron, Anthony. II. Daily news
(New York, N.Y. :
1920) III. Title.
  GV875.N45M375 2011
  796.357'64097471—dc22   2010044004

Editor: Jennifer Levesque
Designer: Kara Strubel
Production Manager: Jules Thomson
Photo Editor: Shawn O'Sullivan

Text research by Deanna Harvey and Kyle Rinck
Photo captions by Joe Belock and David Green

The text of this book was composed in Apollo MT and Archer.

Printed and bound in China

10 9 8 7 6 5 4 3 2 1

Stewart, Tabori & Chang books are available at special discounts when
purchased in quantity for premiums and promotions as well as fundraising
or educational use. Special editions can also be created to specification.
For details, contact specialsales@abramsbooks.com or the address below.

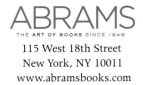

THE ART OF BOOKS SINCE 1949
115 West 18th Street
New York, NY 10011
www.abramsbooks.com

CONTENTS

FOREWORD

by Ron Darling

To be honest, I had never given the New York Mets much thought before they traded for me in 1982. Historically I had the vaguest of notions that they had posted the worst record in baseball history with 120 losses in their very first season in 1962, but had in their eighth season won their first World Championship.

I found my way to Shea Stadium as a player, but it was a very circuitous route. And now, thirty years after I was traded from the Texas Rangers to the New York Mets for their most popular player (I was one of the two minor leaguers traded for Lee Mazzilli), I have the honor of opening a book that details their fabulous and unique fifty years in the National League.

The spring in 1982 had been perfect. I was pitching in big league camp with the Texas Rangers. I had been their number-one draft choice in the summer of '81, and as spring training closed I was being told by their manager, Don Zimmer, that I was only a few Triple-A starts from wearing a major league uniform. The day was April 1, and the trick was anyone who thought that an Ivy League athlete could never pitch at the highest level. I got into my car in Pompano Beach, Florida, for the four-hour drive to Plant City to join the Oklahoma City Triple-A squad. Bereft of beaches, Plant City was famous for—of all things—strawberries. When I got to my room at the Holiday Inn, the message light was on. The flashing light usually meant good news, but this time the operator informed me that I needed to return a call to Lou Gorman. I knew Mr. Gorman; he had been a fixture in Northeast schoolboy baseball where I cut my teeth, but I had no idea why he had tracked me down in Strawberryville.

"Congratulations, Ron, you have just been traded to the New York Metropolitans." Whoa. I have been *what*? And who are the Metropolitans? (My initial thought was Bingo Long and his traveling All-Stars, that somehow I had been traded to a barnstorming team!)

I was stunned, floored, and discouraged. I had been the Rangers' top choice and had been paid a healthy bonus, and now they did not think enough of me to keep me an entire year. That trade nearly killed my career, but how was I supposed to know at the tender age of twenty-one that I had been saved? The trade brought me to New York and gave me a whole new life and an entirely different worldview. Things are always different in New York; there's more on the line, and I had been preparing for this moment my entire life. When I was at Yale, I would routinely take the Metro North train (next stop: Bridgeport) to visit and learn—almost like New York was a place to visit but not a place that could welcome a small-town kid. I would always mutter, "I would give anything to get one chance to work and live in this city." I had my chance.

My debut was in September of 1983, and my first three hitters were Joe Morgan, Pete Rose, and Mike Schmidt (I told you this New York thing wouldn't be easy!). I felt embraced by

Mets fans from day one. They had been lovable losers from 1973 (last play-off experience), but Mets fans were loyal. Expecting little but always hoping something amazing would happen that day. Every game was a fresh start, and every win could jump-start a streak. My first full year in 1984 saw a bunch of youngsters win ninety games and throw our hats into the stands after the last home game. I had never seen anything like it. We hadn't done anything yet and they enjoyed our abilities and effort.

The real foundation of my love affair with Mets fans came during my first off-season. I treated myself to a fifth-story walk-up on 53rd Street and set out to learn about the city. I started working on the lecture circuit to pay the rent and did everything: bar mitzvahs, little league banquets, and Chamber of Commerce dinners. With my trips around the city, there was a real connection to the fans. They were starving for a winner, and I took it all in. I learned why Bronxville was different from Manhasset, and just how far Staten Island was from Astoria. I learned the difference between a Brooklyn accent and a Bronx accent. I learned what it meant to cross the George Washington Bridge into New Jersey during rush hour and to catch the leaves changing along the Palisades Parkway on the drive to Bear Mountain on a crisp November morning. I learned where to find the best pizza, the best pastrami, the best bagels. I went to the library to read about Robert Moses and to study how the suburban sprawl of the metropolitan area came about. I became a New Yorker and a Met at the same time . . . and I never looked back.

And now here I am, thirty years later and still lucky enough to have affection from Mets fans wherever I go. But my perspective has changed. I went from being a player—knowing that the business of baseball could send me packing at any moment—to being a lifer. Without realizing it, I've shed my boyhood connections to New England teams and traded it in for the Mets colors of this slaphappy band of devoted followers. Mets fans are

part Chicken Little, part Charlie Brown, and part *Candide*. Hoping for the best with the worst around the corner. When is one of our great pitchers going to throw the first no-hitter, or when is a homegrown everyday player going to live up to his promise?

One of the things I miss most about Shea Stadium is a small platform behind the Ralph Kiner TV booth where I could secretly watch Mets fans filing in for another home game. It was my very favorite time to be in the stadium. The fans who were coming in were my audience—more than ever before—more than when I was a player. Mets fans aren't bandwagon types; it's not part of their DNA. They are in for the duration. They're invested. And now, so am I.

To this day, whenever I am preparing for a game and I see the Mets all-time leaders list flash on the scoreboard, I still get a thrill. Wins, strikeouts, innings pitched . . . my name is right up there with Tom Seaver, Jerry Koosman, and Dwight Gooden. I'm not delusional though: My numbers are not in the same league—it's kind of like being the fourth Charlie's Angel or the fifth Beatle—but I will take it anyway, because it's the New York Mets and their pitching rich culture. It means something, and it means I am part of something.

So, for me, being part of the Mets now means watching all these good people come to the games. Couples arm in arm. Fathers holding their sons' hands. Lifelong buddies settling in for another fun outing on a long list of many. They all have their little rituals, these fans, just as I now have mine as a broadcaster, and I find these moments inspiring. They remind me that ballplayers come and go—and that I have come a long way from my time as a player, when you are taught not to look in the stands and that our world is defined by what happens inside the lines, not outside the lines or in the stands.

But we had it all wrong. The game might be played between the lines, but it lives and breathes outside the lines and in the stands. The fans do matter. They do. In fact, they matter most of all.

INTRODUCTION

My introduction to covering the New York Mets came in the summer of 2008, as the team attempted to recover from a historic collapse the year before that left them stunned and out of the playoffs. Manager Willie Randolph was about to be fired, the clubhouse was fractious, and the horrid bullpen was preparing to spoil another pennant race and sink the team further into its malaise.

I watched as the next several seasons brought more misery in Flushing, as the era defined by general manager Omar Minaya fell steadily from its exuberant beginning. An unreal plague of injuries, the failure of Randolph's replacement, Jerry Manuel, stars accused of rape and domestic assault, longtime clubhouse manager and player favorite Charlie Samuels caught betting on baseball and hobnobbing with mobsters . . .

What is it with these Mets, this franchise that seems perennially derailed by woe? Their most promising stars, from Darryl Strawberry to Dwight Gooden to Johan San-

tana, are so often shaded by scandal. Their large-market advantages have delivered just two championships in fifty years and created decades of disappointment. Hell, they began as the worst team in baseball history, finishing 40-120 in their inaugural season of 1962.

But if 1962 introduced the Mets as hapless, it also introduced the oversimplified myths about the team that continue to persist, and prevent us from seeing the true reason for their struggle. The falsehoods began with Casey Stengal's lovable losers in '62 and their symbol, first baseman "Marvelous" Marv Throneberry.

Throneberry's image was that of a fumbling, bumbling castoff, endearing because of his ineptitude. Everyone, fans and media, seemed to buy into that persona, because the team wasn't winning, and what else was there to pay attention to? One problem: Throneberry didn't think it was very funny, and in fact was hurt by the portrayal. He wanted to win and succeed just as badly as any of us do, and he was instead considered a fool.

Still, that '62 image persisted for the franchise in Queens, even as it won the World Series in 1969 and 1986. The Mets were a blue-collar, outer-borough alternative to the wealthy Yankees and their Wall Street fans. Mets fans at dumpy Shea Stadium were not able to watch as much winning baseball as their counterparts in the Bronx cathedral, but they could take pride in their loyalty to an underdog.

The only problem with all that? At best, it's only partially true (except the part about Shea being dumpy). Generalizations, when examined, rarely prove adequate. The Mets have never been underdogs. They have always been owned by moneyed, New York elite; have often boasted high payrolls; and always enjoyed every built-in market advantage that the Pittsburgh Pirates, Oakland Athletics, and Tampa Bay Rays must live without. They have always wanted to win and have never embraced the snuggly loser image. So why hasn't the franchise been successful, save for a few outlier years?

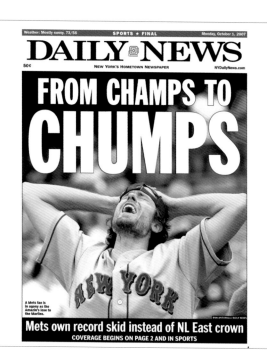

Front page from the October 1, 2007, edition of the *Daily News* featuring a disbelieving Mets fan following the Amazins' loss to the Marlins, completing an epic collapse that cost the Mets the NL East crown.

As I learned from researching and charting the team's history, a pattern emerges from study of the Mets' five decades: A general manager works to turn a flailing team into a contending one and enjoys a brief flash of success. Then, invariably, underlying flaws ruin the hopefulness of an era and lead to another long period of struggle.

It happened after Bing Devine assembled the pitching staff that won a World Series in 1969 without a particularly deep or complete roster. It happened after Frank Cashen spent the first half of the 1980s constructing the strongest team in Mets history, then watched helplessly as alcohol, drugs, and decline sank everything too soon. It happened when Steve Phillips made several high-profile acquisitions and helped bring a Subway Series to New York in 2000. Phillips lost his job before reaching the playoffs again, and Minaya swept in with ambitious plans and dramatic acquisitions; he saw one postseason, two stunning collapses, and two losing seasons before ownership dismissed him in 2010.

So far, that has been the Mets' story—disappointment and frustration interrupted often by hope and occasionally by success. Rife with human drama and fascinating characters, though, it is a story worth telling and enjoying. Uninterrupted success is boring, and the up-and-down (okay, mostly down) history of the Mets is nothing if not compelling. This is a team that has always obliged New York's desire for big stories, wild characters, crime, sex, drugs, and headlines.

—*Andy Martino*

I've been watching the Mets since I was a kid in the 1970s, when a pair of tickets sitting on my father's bureau meant nights spent dreaming of Shea Stadium until we actually walked the concourses of the Mets' former home and saw the green splendor of the field—and, mostly, a terrible team—for ourselves.

I remember a day when Dave Kingman hit a home run so far I swore I saw it take a gigantic bounce off the asphalt in the parking lot. I once stood in the Shea lobby clutching the photo album given to fans on photo day that held within its pages a serious prize—Tom Seaver's autograph.

That was the same day I was in a group of kids around Craig Swan, looking for another signature, and he grabbed my pen, signed some other kid's album, and thrust the pen back at me. I was so stunned I just stood there holding the pen, its cap off. Swan turned and inadvertently brushed against it, leaving a trail of blue ink on his shiny pink silk shirt. I know Swan didn't disappoint this autograph-hungry kid on purpose, nor did I wreck his disco-era threads by design.

I have fond memories of the team of my youth, but once I became a sportswriter, I put all that, plus any affection for the team, aside. There were new reasons to appreciate the Mets, anyway. They are newsmakers.

From their flawed stars to their occasional playoff runs to their silly dramas, the Mets have always provided good theater, even during some mirthless, pathetic years. They were born into it, perhaps, because they were the National League replacement for two beloved New York teams, and they are perennially competing on the same block with the baseball-and-myth-making juggernaut from the Bronx.

—*Anthony McCarron*

1960s

DAILY NEWS

NEW YORK'S PICTURE NEWSPAPER ®

★★★★ FINAL

MORE THAN TWICE THE CIRCULATION OF ANY OTHER PAPER IN AMERICA

New York, N.Y. 10017, Friday, October 17, 1969

104

METS ARE NO.

Big Hits by Donn, Ron, We... Leave Birds for Dead, 5-3

Forty thousand new fans lined lower Broadway to see a team that had not yet played in their city, but as they screamed, cheered, and affectionately insulted the New York Mets, the people knew one thing: Five years after the devastating loss of the Brooklyn Dodgers and New York Giants, the National League was back in New York.

It was April 12, 1962, the morning before the Mets' first home game. Reams of paper and ticker tape fell from the buildings as the team proceeded in slow-moving convertibles to City Hall, donning uniforms that nodded toward the future while suggesting the past. There was blue to comfort those still mourning their beloved Dodgers, and an orange interlocking NY on the players' caps that honored the Giants.

Then there was Casey Stengel, the seventy-one-year-old "Old Perfessor," as he was known, who lent credibility from his seven World Series titles with the Yankees, and entertainment value, to the newborn franchise. The Mets' skipper was unshaven, having stolen just three hours of sleep after the team arrived late from losing its first-ever game, in St. Louis the night before, but he bellowed encouragement to the assembled masses when he stood on the steps of City Hall.

"We hope to build this Met team better than the Yankees—and put that down in your hat!" Stengel roared, with his typical balance of nonsense and charisma.

This was exactly what the crowd needed to hear. The National League was baseball's senior circuit,

and no city enjoyed a longer-lasting and more deeply rooted connection to the game of baseball than New York. When the Giants and Dodgers fled to California in 1957, stunning a citizenry who felt more intimately connected to those teams and their players than most modern fans can imagine, New York was left with only the Yankees. And if you weren't a Yankee fan to begin with, if you weren't the type to stand in awe of the pinstripes and worship at the baseball cathedral in the Bronx, you weren't likely to suddenly become one.

The Dodgers and Giants had enjoyed long periods of excellence at different junctures, but the National League teams fostered an underdog mentality among their fans. This was particularly true in Brooklyn, where decades of losing created the mostly affectionate designation of the team as "Bums," despite their regular World Series appearances in the late 1940s and 1950s.

Despite all those National League championships, though, the Dodgers were only once able to stage a successful coup against Yankee royalty. They won the

Mets manager Casey Stengel parading through Queens with borough president Mario Cariello prior to Opening Day 1962.

World Series in 1955, inspiring wild celebrations in the streets of Brooklyn.

Two years later, the Dodgers and Giants were gone, leaving a painful void, but also leading to the joyous parade on April 12, 1962.

The story of the Mets, which began in earnest with that 1962 parade, had its roots in the dual losses of the Dodgers and Giants. In the mid-1950s, Dodgers owner Walter O'Malley began to consider the move west that had tempted so many other Americans for more than a century. Seeing the potential for riches in California, O'Malley convinced Giants owner Horace Stoneham to venture there with him. With Stoneham on board, the Dodgers could retain a natural rival and reduce travel costs to road games.

It was a decision made by the wealthy and powerful, leaving the public helpless to do anything but watch it unfold. New York fans felt a deep connection to their athletes. Many Boys of Summer, as those old

Dodgers were later nicknamed by author Roger Kahn, lived among their fans in Brooklyn communities, as the Giants did in upper Manhattan and other neighborhoods. The income disparity that later opened between players and spectators was not nearly as wide then, which helped to foster intimacy between public and team that is difficult to imagine today.

So when O'Malley and Stoneham calculated that a better business model awaited out west, they left their fans to feel a piercing void. Sensing this feeling, New York power brokers almost immediately saw the potential for profit in filling that void

In late 1958, Mayor Robert Wagner assembled the Mayor's Baseball Committee, consisting of department-store mogul Bernard Gimbel; onetime postmaster general Jim Farley; and Clint Blume, a real-estate tycoon.

Assigned to lead the group was William A. Shea, a politically connected and self-made New Yorker. Shea was born in 1907 in upper Manhattan, and his childhood spanned the three boroughs later affected by all the National League upheaval: he attended elementary school in Brooklyn, and high school in Queens and Manhattan. The Great Depression devastated Shea's previously middle-class family, and he later worked his way through law school at Georgetown University.

Once Shea returned to his native city and began work as an insurance industry lawyer, he used his natural charm and ambition to build a powerful network of friends in New York and Washington. At various junctures, Shea included among his circle New York governor Nelson Rockefeller, Connecticut senator Prescott Bush, and future president Lyndon Johnson when Johnson was the Senate majority leader from Texas.

A college athlete himself, Shea remained engaged in sporting endeavors. He married Nori Shaw, whose father, Tom Shaw, had once lent Wellington Mara five hundred dollars to launch the New York football

Giants. In 1935, Shea began working for the law firm Cullen & Dykman, which represented the Brooklyn Trust Company, the bank that controlled the bankrupt Brooklyn Dodgers

That job deepened the connections in sports and politics that would ultimately help Shea spearhead an effort to create the Mets. It paired him with bank president George McLaughlin, who himself was close to onetime New York governor and presidential candidate Al Smith, and also to the premier power broker himself, legendary urban planner Robert Moses.

In his capacity overseeing the Dodgers, McLaughlin—who fast became Shea's mentor—hired iconic front office executive Branch Rickey to run the team. (In addition to inventing the concept of a farm system, Rickey would later become responsible for the most important moment of social conscience in American sports history—he recruited and signed Jackie Robinson to play for the Dodgers and break baseball's color barrier in 1947.) McLaughlin also arranged for Walter O'Malley, one of his protégés, to buy the ball club.

When O'Malley later moved the team to Los Angeles, McLaughlin felt hurt and betrayed—he had never intended for the Dodgers to leave New York, and could not accept tht his former friend had engineered the loss. Shea, by all accounts a loyal man, wanted to heal McLaughlin's hurt, and restore baseball to a city that had gone abruptly from three teams to one.

Shea and his committee first attempted to persuade Major League Baseball to expand, but it was unwilling. They then tried to lure an existing major league team to New York, but the National League held only eight National League clubs at the time, and all were firmly entrenched in their respective hometowns.

Undeterred, the New Yorkers presented a backup plan: To create an entirely new league that would compete with Major League Baseball. If that concept could be realized, Shea was the right man to make it happen. He began by tapping his political connections

to build support for overturning baseball's long-held exemption to the Clayton Antitrust Act.

The sport treasured a quixotic 1922 U.S. Supreme Court ruling that baseball was not involved in interstate commerce and could therefore operate as a monopoly, and it was loath to see that threatened. Shea was prepared to use the act as leverage; if Major League Baseball attempted to quash Shea's new league, he planned to cite abuse of the antitrust exemption, figuring that no one in the game would care to see that questionable benefit carefully examined.

True to character, Shea built broad and relevant connections in sports and politics to create support for what he called the Continental League. He pitched his idea to powerful senators and congressmen whose constituencies lacked big-league baseball, most notably Lyndon Johnson, still the Senate majority leader. Not coincidentally, Shea planned for Continental League franchises in Dallas/Fort Worth and Houston.

As he worked his government connections, Shea also recruited potential owners for baseball teams in Washington, D.C. (Edward Bennett Williams); Toronto (Jack Kent Cooke—a Canadian loyal to Shea because Shea had once tapped his government connections

The Brooklyn Dodgers at Ebbets Field as they prepare to face the Yankees in the 1955 World Series.

to secure U.S. citizenship for Cooke); Denver (Bob Howsam, the son-in-law of a Colorado senator and future general manager of the Cincinnati Reds); and Minneapolis/St. Paul (Wheelock Whitney). Shea also worked to establish franchises in Miami, New Orleans, Indianapolis, San Diego, Portland, and San Juan.

Some of the potential investors in Shea's Continental League were naturally skeptical of the viability of a challenge to baseball's long-established American League/National League system. Those fears, though, were quickly assuaged by a smart alliance forged via George McLaughlin. Rickey, perhaps the most noteworthy and respected figure in the game, partnered with Shea and lent him instant credibility. Rickey

had been muscled out of Brooklyn by O'Malley, and shared McLaughlin's bitterness toward the man; those feelings made him all the more eager to demonstrate that a new baseball team in New York could succeed.

To own New York's Continental League franchise, the men sought heiress Joan Whitney Payson. Born in 1904 into the Whitney family, a prominent American clan since the seventeenth century, Payson had long included sports in her diverse portfolio of interests. She was a noted art collector, counting works by Manet, Ingres, Matisse, and Cézanne among the highlights of her collection. She was an active philanthropist and sports executive. Payson was deeply involved in Thoroughbred racing, and also once sat on the board of her beloved New York Giants. In 1957 hers was the lone dissenting vote against relocating the team to San Francisco.

So while Payson was firmly entrenched among the city's elite, she was also just another New Yorker heartbroken by the loss of the National League. Still, she was unsure about investing in the nascent and risky Continental League—until, that is, she received a frank assurance from Rickey, who traveled to Florida to tell Payson that he and Shea did not expect the league to come into being. They simply hoped to use it as a threat to the antitrust exemption that would muscle Major League Baseball into expanding.

National League owners, they reasoned, would be glad to award New York with an expansion franchise as an alternative to the Continental League. If and when that happened, Rickey told Payson, she would own New York's National League replacement for the Giants and Dodgers. Impressed, Payson invested $4 million, for an 80 percent interest in the team. Her stockbroker, M. Donald Grant—who would later become a central figure in Mets history—split the other 20 percent with Herbert Walker, a relative of future presidents George H. W. Bush and George W. Bush.

The plan worked perfectly: Major League Baseball blinked, and allowed expansion teams in New York and Houston. Shea and Rickey scrapped plans for the Continental League, and the Mets were born.

After Shea and Rickey successfully created the franchise, Payson and Grant began to build it. Major League Baseball teams require tremendous infrastructure, from the general manager to the scouting department to the manager, coaches, and players—and that is merely on the baseball operations side. The Mets were in a race to build the organization that would prepare them to field a team in 1962.

The new ball club, already created as a reaction to loss, would find still more castoffs eager for another chance in baseball. Rickey's contractual demands were too high for Payson, and she sought another man to assemble her team. Payson made Grant president of the team, and accepted Rickey's recommendation of his nephew, Charles Hurth, to become general manager.

Hurth's tenure, though, turned out to be a fast blip in Mets history. The early years of the franchise were altered dramatically by upheaval in the Bronx—in October 1960, after losing the World Series to the Pittsburgh Pirates on a game-winning home run by Bill Mazeroski, the Yankees fired manager Casey Stengel. Shortly thereafter, they cut ties with general manager George Weiss.

The two men most responsible for the Yankees' dominance during the Eisenhower era were suddenly available. Weiss, a shy and reserved man, had overseen the Yankee farm system, helping to build legendary organizational depth that had made it possible for the Yankees to win year after year (though piles of money also had contributed to the sustained success).

Weiss had been with the team since 1932, when then owner Colonel Jacob Ruppert noticed and envied the revolutionary farm system that Branch Rickey had created with the St. Louis Cardinals. With the Great Depression squeezing the budget of even the perennially privileged Yankees, Ruppert wanted to explore the more cost-effective strategy of developing players. He assigned Weiss, a successful minor league executive, to do it.

Weiss replaced Larry MacPhail as general manager in 1947, and oversaw ten American League Championships and eight World Championships in twelve seasons. Known for his quiet demeanor and obsessive work habits, Weiss did nothing to deserve a firing; he was simply the victim of a corporate shakeup. Yankee co-owners Dan Topping and Del Webb prepared in the early 1960s to sell the franchise—they eventually did so in 1964, when the CBS broadcasting company purchased the team and led it into an extended period of darkness—and they wanted to pare down

Casey Stengel
instructing Shea
Stadium usherettes
on the finer points of
baseball during the
Mets' first season at
Shea, in 1964.

the infrastructure. So Weiss was out, left seeking a job for the first time since Babe Ruth and Lou Gehrig played for the Yankees.

At sixty-six years old, Weiss accepted the position as Mets president in 1961. He sought an even older man to be the public face of the franchise: Charles Dillon Stengal, who at seventy had long since established himself as an icon in the game. Stengel's stock was much lower back in 1949, when Weiss made the controversial choice to hire him as manager of the white-collar Yankees. Born in 1890 in Kansas City, Missouri, Stengel was viewed more as a goofball than genius for most of a long career in baseball. As a player, he broke in with the Brooklyn Dodgers in 1912, and went on to appear in games with four other clubs: the Giants, Pirates, Phillies, and Braves.

Called before Congress with other baseball dignitaries in 1958 to discuss the anti-trust exemption, Stengel summarized his playing career to Senator Estes Kefauver of Tennessee this way: "I had many years that I was not so successful as a ballplayer, as it is a game of skill." Indeed, Stengel was perhaps best known as a player for a 1919 incident in Brooklyn when he responded to fan taunting by trapping a sparrow in his cap and releasing it.

His early managing career was also, at least on the surface, defined by a comic persona more than baseball acumen—but that perception by belied by an acute and constantly developing understanding of the game. In stints managing the Dodgers in the mid-1930s and the Boston Braves (also then known as the Boston Bees) in the late 1930s and early 1940s, though, Stengel failed to lift those teams out of the second division (the bottom four teams in an eight-team league). He was then relegated to years of minor league managing jobs.

But through all that time, Stengel fostered innovative ideas that would later serve him at the game's highest level, including forward-thinking uses of platooning and pinch-hitting. Once with the Yankees, Stengel would succeed in achieving balance with a roster loaded with talent that did not always fit perfectly. Weiss provided his manager with a plethora of talented veterans and products of the farm system, and the manager excelled at placing all of those players in a position to succeed.

The "Old Perfessor" wiped away decades as a middling player and losing manager by commandeering the Yankees' most recent golden age. Stengel managed the Yanks from 1949 to 1960. Weiss's decision to hire him before the 1949 season was criticized by fans and the press, many of whom viewed Stengel as a clown and loser. But paired with a legendary group of players that would ultimately include Joe DiMaggio, Mickey Mantle, Whitey Ford, Billy Martin, and Yogi Berra, among many other franchise notables, the manager found success.

Stengel's tenure with the Yankees began with a remarkable string of five consecutive World Championships, from 1949 to 1953. The Yanks missed the World Series—and even the American League pennant—in 1954, then quickly recovered to return the following year. They won World Championships under Stengel in 1949, 1950, 1951, 1952, 1953, 1956, and 1958.

But championship runs often create impatience, and by 1960 the Yankees had gone three seasons without a World Series win. Never mind that the Bombers had thoroughly outplayed Pittsburgh in a seven-game loss; Mazeroski's Series-determining shot over the left-field wall at Forbes Field sealed the aging Stengel's status. He was soon dismissed, replaced by Ralph Houk.

Weiss still valued Stengel, though, and thought he would be perfect for the Mets. Just as Branch Rickey had granted William Shea instant baseball credibility several years earlier when he agreed to join the effort to create the Continental League, Stengel would bring an impressive résumé to the new team.

And despite his keen strategic mind, Stengel was far better known for his outsized persona. The manager understood the value of self-promotion, and he was always a media favorite during his years with the Yankees. His manner of speaking—best defined as gibberish rich with rewarding insights for those who listened closely enough—captivated writers and readers.

In building the Mets, Weiss knew that Stengel's personality would be needed more than it ever was with the Yankees. The team president was shrewd enough to understand that he could not build a winning baseball team right away, but needed to produce a likable and entertaining product immediately, to satisfy the fans left lonely since losing their Giants or Dodgers.

Who better to distract the public from horrible baseball than Casey Stengel? This was the man credited with the sayings "All right everyone, line up alphabetically according to your height," "Being with a woman all night never hurt no professional baseball player. It's staying up all night looking for a woman that does him in," and "If we're going to win the pennant, we've got to start thinking we're not as good as we think we are."

Olympic champion Jesse Owens hurdles a bat held by Yogi Berra (left) and Met general manager George Weiss in 1965. Owens was hired by the Mets as a running instructor during spring training sessions.

1960s

Stengel was a character, but Yogi Berra he was not. While the longtime Yankee catcher tended to stumble into his famous catchphrases such as "It ain't over till it's over," Stengel knew exactly what he was doing: amusing himself, and distracting the press and public from more serious concerns about his team. As long as Stengel was rambling in charming and humorous fashion, he was providing a diversion—and Weiss knew that the Mets' new fans would need a diversion.

The problem was, Stengel did not know if he wanted to manage anymore. He spurned the Mets' initial offer, but Weiss and Joan Whitney Payson persisted, and ultimately held a negotiating advantage—Stengel was a baseball lifer, and could not resist the call of another job in the game.

"It's a great honor for me to be joining the Knickerbockers," Stengel told reporters.

A franchise that came to include Tom Seaver, Dwight Gooden, Darryl Strawberry, Keith Hernandez, and David Wright began with Hobie Landrith. The National League expansion draft to establish the rosters for the Mets and Houston Colt .45s, on October 10, 1961, offered little in the way of exciting talent. Other teams made mostly retreads available, all but ensuring that the new teams would struggle in their early years.

Weiss, who had hired Stengel as much to entertain and divert as to manage, decided on a similar strategy with his first roster. Seeing little if any high-ceiling talent in the draft, Weiss decided to select familiar veterans; it was better to lose with fan favorites than with nobodies.

As such, Weiss drafted or otherwise acquired veterans Richie Ashburn, Frank Thomas, Gil Hodges, Don Zimmer, Roger Craig, and Clem Labine. When the nascent team assembled the following February in St.

Petersburg for spring training, it featured far more name recognition than potential for winning baseball—although for New Yorkers missing their Dodgers and Giants, the warmth of familiarity might have been the most generous gift that George Weiss could have given them.

On March 1, Stengel scribbled the first-ever Mets lineups for an 11:00 A.M. intrasquad exhibition. While doing so, the manager remarked that he did not expect to send a copy to the Baseball Hall of Fame in Cooperstown.

The game pitted regulars against scrubs. This was the batting order for the big league squad:

Ashburn CF
Zimmer 3B
Bell RF
Thomas LF
Marshall 1B
Mantilla SS
Lepcio 2B
Landrith C
Craig P
Daviault P

Gil Hodges, a former Dodger star now a rickety thirty-seven years old, asked not to play in that first game, fearing that he would pull a leg muscle. Assessing his team during the early workouts that day, Stengel took advantage of the date to express traditional spring training optimism. "Some of them look awful now, but in thirty days they'll know," the manager said. "It's like taking dancing lessons, and I don't mean that new dance they're doing these days."

During that inaugural exhibition, which ended in a 4–4 tie, the *New York Daily News*'s Dick Young recorded several franchise firsts:

First pitch: Thrown by Craig Anderson to Richie Ashburn, who tapped it foul down the third-base line.

First base runner: Ashburn, who walked shortly thereafter.

First putout: Don Zimmer grounded softly to Marshall Hamilton (said Zim of his dribbler: "That sunofagun's trouble in the Polo Grounds").

First base hit: Gus Bell's sharp single to right, scoring Ashburn with the first Met run.

When Ashburn returned to the bench, Hodges quipped, "You just made history."

Another veteran, Frank Thomas, added, "We'll give you a ticker tape parade when we get to New York."

The Mets made franchise history again—not a difficult feat in a team's first days of existence—on March 5, when the donned white home uniforms for the first time. Endorsement money, a strong motivating factor for athletes even in 1962, was the reason. The Mets took much of that day off from baseball activities to allow several camera crews into their spring training facility. In the dugout, Stengel filmed an advertisement for a headache remedy; someone was overheard to remark that the manager should demand a year's supply of the product, rather than cash payment for his work.

The field and clubhouse swarmed that day with cameras and ad men in gray flannel overcoats; one of those Madison Avenue characters sat in the dugout with Gil Hodges, showing him penciled storyboards for a spot promoting a "thinking man's cigarette."

Still more cameramen stood on the pitcher's mound and behind the batting cage, filming a promotional film titled *Meet the Mets*.

From left to right, Rod Kanehl, Jim Hickman, Gil Hodges, Frank Thomas, and Charlie Neal, who belted a pair of home runs, celebrate the Mets' first victory at home, an 8–6 comeback win over the Phillies, April 29, 1962.

1960s

Beyond all the celluloid novelty was excitement about the new duds. During the ensuing decades, the Mets have experimented with various uniform tweaking, but the basics of the outfit that debuted on March 5, 1962, have remained unchanged. A simultaneous homage to the Giants (orange) and Dodgers (blue), as well as to New York's City's orange, blue, and white flag, the suits also nodded to New York's American League team.

In Young's sardonic description, "They are pinstripes, obviously designed to frighten the daylights out of the N.L., as the Yankee pinstripes have for years. Across the chest, in large script, blue letters with orange trim, is spelled 'Mets.'"

Four days later, the team played its first exhibition game against an opposing team. The afternoon foreshadowed the upcoming season, as the Mets lost 8–0 to the St. Louis Cardinals. But, as they would throughout the dismal season, the fans showed up and offered sarcastic support. A sellout crowd of 6,872—others were turned away—watched the listless Mets, who played poorly enough to inspire mock cheers when they recorded a routine out. The team managed four hits and allowed twelve.

During that first spring, the Mets were joined by several broadcasters who would later become franchise legends in their own right. Though the on-field roster lacked pizzazz, the Mets' booth featured three future Hall of Fame announcers: Lindsey Nelson, Bob Murphy, and Ralph Kiner. Of the three, Nelson, forty-two, was the best known at the time, having already announced the baseball *Game of the Week* for NBC, along with NCAA football and the NFL.

Kiner, thirty-nine, was a former Pittsburgh Pirates slugger with minimal television experience. He had spent just one year doing radio broadcasts for the Chicago White Sox, but his work there and in a World Series wrap-up television show in Pittsburgh in 1961 had impressed executives in the business. Several teams sought his services that winter, but Weiss won because Kiner was interested in working in the nation's largest media market.

Murphy, thirty-eight, first broadcast major league baseball with the legendary Curt Gowdy, spending six years with Gowdy in the Boston Red Sox booth. He then moved to Baltimore for two years to work for the Orioles before applying for the Mets position. Murphy's application was one of about two hundred, and he was the only one chosen from that group, as Weiss had recruited Nelson and Kiner.

The trio, who earned about $100,000 combined that first season, would endure far longer than any of the franchise's inaugural players. Nelson remained with the Mets for seventeen seasons before moving on to other prominent positions in sportscasting. Murphy found a home in New York and remained there for the rest of his career; by the time he retired in 2003, Murphy called games from a booth at Shea Stadium named after him, as the radio booth at Citi Field would be when that building opened in 2009.

Kiner, meanwhile, would outlast both of his 1962 counterparts. The man who had hit 369 home runs in a relatively brief yet brilliant career in Pittsburgh and later with the Cubs and Indians followed that with an extended tenure in his adopted city. The year 2010 marked Kiner's forty-ninth season employed by the team. Though his airtime was limited by age and Bell's palsy that slurred his speech, Kiner still appeared on selected telecasts with the Mets' current team of Gary Cohen, Ron Darling, and Keith Hernandez.

In spring training of '62, those announcers were surely savvy enough to understand that the flawed roster would struggle. Their boss, Joan Whitney Payson, did not yet seem to grasp that when she first saw the team play on March 17. Sitting in the front row behind home plate, Payson watched the Mets and pitcher Roger Craig lose to Philadelphia, 3–2. Afterward, she remained upbeat about the look of her new team.

"I don't really know enough about it," Mrs. Payson said. "I don't think they played badly. I think Craig went real well."

As that first spring training progressed, that loss to the Phillies represented the general tone: The Mets were not successful, but they were not embarrassing themselves as they later would during the regular season. On March 20, they dropped their sixth consecutive spring training game, but it was the third straight one-run loss. Two days later, they won a game that held meaning for Stengel, against the Yankees.

More than thirty years later, the Mets and Yankees would face one another many times in interleague play, and in the 2000 World Series. But the two teams had never seen one another on March 22, 1962, when they squared off in St. Petersburg. After the Yankees lost the 1960 World Series, the team replaced Stengel with Ralph Houk, a former catcher for the team. Though the spring training game was technically meaningless,

it offered Stengel the opportunity to perform in front of the employers who has decided that he was no longer capable of success.

The Mets won, 4–3, prompting effusive postgame comments from Stengel. "Oh, it was just lovely," he said. "It's terrific. This should be very good for my players. This will make the Mets believe that if you can beat a great team like the Yankees, you should be able to beat numerous clubs in our league."

One could hardly blame Stengel for seizing the rare chance to espouse a sprinkle of positivity, but the game was more a personal victory for the manager than it was a predictor of any success for his team. After decades presiding over terrible clubs and championship ones, Stengel must have known that his roster, formed by a weak expansion draft, was full of has-beens and never-will-bes.

But he did not yet know that his team would be historically bad. On March 24, the Mets defeated the

Kansas City A's in West Palm Beach, to extend their winning streak to four games. Joan Whitney Payson spent her second game in the stands that day, improving her record as a spectator to 1-1, and lifting the Mets to 7-7 in their exhibition schedule.

By the end of camp, though, ominous signs predicted the future more accurately. For some strange reason, the franchise—despite periods of success and World Series titles in 1969 and 1986—has often endured bad luck, particularly with injuries. That extended all the way into the 2009 season, when the team lost nearly every member of the opening day lineup to one injury or another, and it began in earnest on April 8, 1962.

Pitcher Sherman "Roadblock" Jones has the distinction of suffering the first-ever Metsian injury. Set to begin the season as the number-two starter in the rotation behind Roger Craig, Jones burned his eye in a strange fashion. As Dick Young described it in the *Daily News*:

"Jones was lighting a match when the phosperous head flew off and entered his right eye. He rubbed his eye in pain, and as he did he accidentally pushed an eyelash into the burned orb. Trainer Gus Mauch, who removed the lash, noticed a plainly visible scar on the pupil about the size of a match."

After all the heartbreak in New York over the loss of the Giants and Dodgers, after William Shea and Branch Rickey worked first to create the Continental League and then to create a new National League franchise for the city, the Mets were scheduled to begin their competitive existence on April 10 in St. Louis, but that game was postponed by rain.

With no baseball to watch, the team could retain, for one more day, its spring training optimism. "If we can make the few moves I expect, I believe we have

the chance of playing .500 ball," George Weiss said, going on to express excitement over his new job. "It's quite a thrill. I've never been president of a ball club before. The telegrams have been streaming in, wishing us well."

The next night, all that enthusiasm dampened somewhat after a dreary 11–4 loss to the Cardinals, but a more exciting debut remained. After that game, the team flew to New York, where they would ride up Broadway in that inaugural ticker tape parade. The makeup of the team's roster was clearly secondary to the city's excitement to see the senior circuit return.

That enthusiasm was, in true New York fashion, undercut by heavy sarcasm. Infielder and former Brooklyn Dodger Don Zimmer reported hearing a man shout, "Zimmer, you're still a bum. You'll strike out 114 times."

Another man, this one in a construction worker's helmet, yelled, "You guys better do better than you did last night!"

Because their new stadium in Flushing, Queens, was not nearly ready, the Mets would play in the Polo Grounds, the upper Manhattan former home of the Giants. After the parade, the team rode uptown for a workout at its temporary ballpark. Once they were there, Met luck persisted.

Preparing for their workout, the team changed into its uniforms, and then discovered that their shoes were missing. It took more than an hour for the spikes to arrive. Over on the visitors' side, the Pittsburgh Pirates arrived to find that their clubhouse floors were being sanded. That forced the team to cancel its off-day workout because they could not change or shower. "Uh-oh," Stengel said. "They'll be mad at me. I told them they could use the field."

The next day, in front of 12,447 fans on a cold and rainy afternoon, the Mets lost 4–3 to Pittsburgh. Still, as Young wrote, the day had a National League vibe. "The fans had that old N.L. feeling," he wrote. "So did the game. It tingled with repeated tensions; it had incredibly classy plays, considering the Polo Grounds was one big mud pie."

The New York fans craved a reminder of better days in their baseball history. Gil Hodges was unavailable with a swollen left knee, but that did not prevent the crowd from chanting incessantly, "We want Hodges." They stomped, they whistled, and one even blew a foghorn, but Hodges was too old and broken down to make an appearance.

In the team's next game, Hodges was again unable to conjure the old magic. The Mets' only true chance to break through against Pirate junkballing lefthander Vinegar Bend Mizell came in the first inning. They loaded the bases with two outs, bringing up Hodges and his history of fourteen career grand slams.

The crowd of 9,234 implored him to create the franchise's first memorable moment, but the veteran could only bounce out to third. Hours later, the Mets wrapped up a limp 6–2 loss, and left a frustrated Stengel to say, "Imagine not being able to hit the junk that fellow through up there. We didn't even hit any balls vicious."

Two days later, the Mets remained cold and unlucky, missing two opportunities to earn their first win. A doubleheader against Pittsburgh was scheduled on April 16, and a Felix Mantilla leadoff home run in the first game gave the Mets the first lead of their existence. But that only lasted until the third, when the Pirates tagged Roger Craig—the ostensible ace—for five runs and went on to win, 7–2.

Their fortune appeared to have turned in the nightcap, when they led 2–0 in the third; but Met luck being what it was, a heavy, wet snow began to fall, forcing cancellation of the game before enough of it had been played to count. The Mets were 0-4, but their fans still turned out in decent numbers, despite the weather and lack of initial success. "They are strange, wonderful people, this new breed," Dick

Young wrote. "They cry out in hunger—the five-year hunger for N.L. ball."

For five more games, they continued to wait for a win. The fifth loss came in the eleventh inning against their fellow neophyte team, the Houston Colt .45s. That spoiled an exciting day; after the Mets were shut out through eight innings, Gus Bell tied the game with a ninth-inning homer. Houston's Don Buddin countered with a three-run shot in the ninth, making the Mets 0-5.

New York lost 15–5 to St. Louis the next day, playing before a significantly smaller crowd of 4,725. "The fans at several points were more derisive of the Mets," wrote Jim McCulley in the *Daily News*. When the team dropped its seventh straight game the next day, Young wrote, "The Mets completed their successful home stand yesterday; nobody got killed."

Left fielder Frank Thomas was one of the only bright spots, hitting two home runs in the 9–4 loss to St. Louis, his third and fourth of the young year. But the Mets' cast of retreads was stumbling badly, and on April 22 would tie a National League record by dropping a ninth straight game to begin the season. The historic failure came in the form of a 4–3 loss to the defending-champion Pirates, whose 1960 hero tormented Casey Stengel once again.

Bill Mazeroski, the generally light-hitting but defensively brilliant second baseman, had ended Stengel's Yankee career the previous October with a World Series–winning home run over the left-field wall at Pittsburgh's Forbes Field. Six months later, the Mets were 0-8, and tied 3–3 with the Pirates in the eighth inning when Mazeroski batted with Roberto Clemente on third and Don Hoak on first. Mazeroski tripled, driving in Clemente (Hoak was thrown out at home), and providing the difference in yet another loss.

By the time the Mets finally won the following day, their status as laughingstocks had already congealed.

1960s

Branch Rickey used the occasion of the team's 9–1 win over Pittsburgh to rip the league for its expansion process and to express sympathy for Joan Whitney Payson. Rickey believed that the Continental League would have been a preferable method of expansion to the drafting system that was used; essentially, the existing teams had made lackluster players available in a draft to the Mets and Colt .45s, and then sent the new clubs the bill for the players they selected.

A sophisticated baseball mind, Rickey knew that the system created an untenable situation for the expansion teams, dooming them to several years of losing. On April 23, Rickey shared his views in the *Daily News*, calling Payson a "victim."

"There is a feeling of uncontrolled futility in this arrangement," Rickey said. "It is wrong, utterly wrong,

this idea of 'give me two million dollars for the players I don't want, then play me for the championship with them.' . . . I feel sorry for Mrs. Payson. She is victimized. She is such a fine woman, such a genuine sportswoman, and she is victimized."

Rickey added, with a large dose of sarcasm, "From a business standpoint, the owners are to be congratulated."

Despite the futility that faced them, the Mets did manage to win a game in convincing fashion that evening in Pittsburgh. The victory contained several positive franchise firsts, not a difficult feat for a team that had yet to win. Before that game, they had never before scored six runs, had never batted around in an inning—they did so in the second that night—and they had never knocked an opposing pitcher out of a game, as they did to the Pirates' Tom Sturdivant. Jay

Mrs. Charles Payson, owner of the Mets, throws out the first ball on Opening Day 1965.

Hook was the winning pitcher for the Mets, and he also knocked a two-run single.

The following day, natural order was restored as the Mets lost 7–3 to Cincinnati. The team then resumed its preordained path, losing far more than it won, losing at an historic pace. The Mets would finish 40-120, the worst major league record in the modern era, but they would charm their fans with a bumbling but lovable image—though that media-created reputation might not have been accurate or fair.

The cuddly loser persona of the 1962 Mets arose from a complicated set of circumstances. Though the image sold tickets, held public interest in a team that did little well on the field, and endured for decades, it left many of the players feeling belittled. It is worth reexamining.

The creation of the Mets coincided with a new era in sports journalism, which evolved from a romantic notion of the athlete-as-hero to something very dif-

ferent. No team represented that change in the way it was covered more than the 1962 Mets.

During the so-called Golden Age of Sports, a term often used to describe the 1920s, many athletes were portrayed in glossy fashion, including Babe Ruth by the New York press. "The media began casting professional baseball players as heroes," said Michael Oriard, an English professor at Oregon State University and noted historian of American sports and sports journalism. "Babe Ruth, we know now, had these rather unsavory habits, but we didn't read about them."

Though many Golden Age writers oversimplified Ruth, perhaps none did so as enthusiastically as Dan Daniel, who wrote for several New York newspapers and the *Sporting News*. Daniel covered the Yankees during Ruth's heyday—and spent a great deal of time with the hard-partying, womanizing slugger.

In 1930, Daniel published a book titled *Babe Ruth: The Idol of the American Boy*. The foreword, ostensibly written by Ruth, offers the Bambino's tips for young boys, which he calls the "Boys' Bible." Ruth advises, "Get at least eight hours of sleep, and realize that early to bed and early to rise is still sound advice," and "do everything in moderation."

Daniel's first four chapters enthusiastically justify the $80,000 contract Ruth signed with the Yankees in 1929. He compares Ruth's salary to that of actors and other athletes, and quotes Ruth saying, "Yes, $80,000 is quite a bit of money—but it must be conceded that I am quite a ball player."

The modern reader may wonder why Daniel was so eager to advocate for his subject. In the book *No Cheering in the Press Box*, an older Daniel tells author Jerome Holtzman:

"I signed Babe Ruth for eighty thousand dollars. I made the deal with him. He was holding out in St. Petersburg, Florida . . . this was 1930." Daniel went on to describe how he acted as the intermediary between Ruth and Yankee ownership; *Idol of the American Boy* was published later that year, and made no mention of its author's work as Ruth's agent.

Grantland Rice, dubbed the "dean of American sportswriters," was another key figure in the Golden Age. On October 24, 1924, Rice, covering an Army–Notre Dame football game for the *New York Herald Tribune*, began his story:

"Outlined against a blue-gray October sky, the Four Horsemen rode again. In dramatic lore, they are known as Famine, Pestilence, Destruction and Death. These are only aliases. Their real names are Stuhldreher, Miller, Crowley and Layden."

Longtime *New York Times* sports columnist Robert Lipsyte, who covered the 1962 Mets beginning in spring training, says that no matter how fawning such Golden Age portrayals may have seemed, they were dehumanizing to athletes. "They mocked players by making them Greek heroes," he says. "It was such bullshit. How much of that comes out of whatever mix of hero worship and resentment they felt toward these athletes?"

As the sportswriters of Rice and Daniel's generation faded, changes in American society created an opening for journalists to challenge the concepts and formulations of the Golden Age. The results would be groundbreaking, flawed, and short-lived.

During the 1960s, of course, many American values and traditions were challenged, including those in journalism. At the beginning of that decade, the press boxes and sports departments in New York were becoming populated with young sportswriters, many of whom were consciously reacting against the tone of Golden Age writing, according to writers who worked during this era.

Some of these writers were saddled with the nickname "Chipmunks," intended as an insult but worn as a badge of honor, recalls George Vecsey. Vecsey, a sports columnist for the *New York Times* whose career began at *Newsday* in 1960, does not consider himself a true Chipmunk—he was a bit too young—but worked at the newspaper that was central to the movement.

He remembers that the nickname was coined when sportswriter Jimmy Cannon, whose work the Chipmunks generally admired, referred to young Phil Pepe of the *Daily News* as a "chipmunk," because Pepe's front teeth were large. Pepe, along with Stan Isaacs of *Newsday*, and Leonard Shecter, Larry Merchant, and Vic Ziegel of the *New York Post*, among others, wrote about baseball with irreverence and humor, in work free of allusions to mythology, and did not mind the humorous nickname given them.

Vecsey recalls the conditions at *Newsday* that helped to foster a sense of creative freedom. The late Jack Mann, sports editor at *Newsday* from 1960 to1962, encouraged young reporters to cover athletes more critically. "Jack had a crabby, outsider's view of the world," Vecsey says. "He was saying, 'Hey, we don't need to make heroes out of these guys. Don't be afraid to say who is acting out.'"

The Chipmunks' coverage of Mickey Mantle and Roger Maris's pursuit of Ruth's single-season home run record in 1961 provided evidence of the new tone. "Mantle was complicated," Vecsey says. "He had a hilarious country humor. I wrote a lot of stuff about him as a funny, bawdy guy. When he was miserable, we wrote about that, too. We never portrayed him as being a blonde god."

Maris, Vecsey recalls, "was not nearly the grump or misanthrope that he sometimes came across as. He was easier to talk to than Mantle. He was blunt, honest."

As the decade progressed and issues such as civil rights and the conflict in Vietnam consumed the nation, other sportswriters advanced the practice of portraying athletes as complex humans by covering race, politics, and other issues. Lipsyte wrote about Muhammed Ali, Kareem Abdul-Jabbar, and other outspoken athletes. He credits Dick Young, whose career began in the late 1930s, as pioneering a less reverent tone in covering athletes, and the Chipmunks for helping to further diffuse the hero-making impulse. Changes in sports culture—particularly diminishing access to players, and the ascension of television as more culturally relevant than print—also contributed to the change in tone.

"Here's a sportswriter no longer riding the train with athletes, playing cards, talking. He's left with picking up the crumbs," Lipsyte says, noting that by the 1960s, the age of Dan Daniel had ended, forcing sportswriters to rethink their role. "Everything changed. Once you couldn't damage your access by writing a negative story, it became more adversarial."

Though the Chipmunks have been rightly credited as pioneers, they were not above oversimplifying athletes, Lipsyte says. Instead of creating heroes, they often mocked their subject, as they did in portraying the hapless 1962 Mets, and their first baseman Marv Throneberry, as clowns. "I don't see much difference between that and what Grantland Rice did," Lipsyte says.

Throneberry presents an interesting case study in Mets myth versus reality, courtesy of the Chipmunks' work covering the 1962 Mets. The first baseman imagined himself as anything but a cuddly, bumbling loser—at one point, in fact, Throneberry was supposed to be the next Yankee legend. As an eighteen-year-old, Throneberry signed with New York's American League club for a $50,000 bonus in 1952, a high number at the time. The Yankees outbid the Phillies, Tigers, Cubs, Browns, and Red Sox for the teenager from Tennessee.

Hall of Fame Yankee catcher Bill Dickey placed both thrilling expectations and an unfair albatross on Throneberry when he watched the young slugger and said, "Mickey Mantle is the only man on this Yankee club who can hit better."

Throneberry performed well during his first several seasons in the minor leagues, hitting 42 home runs and 145 runs batted in 1956, and winning American Association MVP honors. Through much of the 1950s, Throneberry attended spring training with the Yankees, and Stengel, but was always blocked by the team's major league talent. He began to age, and tire of minor league life, and in 1959 was traded to the Kansas City Athletics in the deal that made Roger Maris a Yankee. The A's later moved him to Baltimore, who traded him to the Mets in May 1962.

Throneberry made his New York debut on May 11 and immediately began to fumble at first base. In that first game, Denis Menke of the Milwaukee Braves sent a foul pop-up toward the first-base stands. Throneberry pursued it tentatively, did not reach it in time, and allowed the catchable ball to fall on the field.

He hit well enough that year—well enough, that is, for a first baseman on a second-division team, finishing with sixteen home runs, second on the team to Frank Thomas—and batting .244. But Throneberry's defense was, by all accounts, atrocious. He signature play was the ground ball through his legs, but he also had a knack for clutch hits in the rare situations that required them during that 120-loss season.

Without a decent team to write about, the Chipmunks constructed a legend of Throneberry. The *New York Post*'s Leonard Shecter coined the nickname Marvelous Marv, and the first baseman initially embraced it, even hanging a sign with the nickname over his locker at the Polo Grounds, replacing the nameplate that simply said "Throneberry."

As Lipsyte recalls, Richie Ashburn also assisted in the creation of the Marvelous Marv persona, and with the Mets' reputation in general. The All-Star player was soon to become a legendary broadcaster for the Phillies, and was more sympathetic to the media's needs than most players. "Richie Ashburn

was very savvy," Lipsyte recalls. "You could almost see him making the transition from player to media that year."

But Throneberry would never be a member of the media. He was a twenty-nine-year-old balding former standout prospect who had once modeled himself on Mantle. While in the Yankee system, Throneberry mimed Mantle's batting stance, even wore his socks like his hero. He came up expecting to be a star, not a joke.

"I never realized how he felt until I went back to interview him years later," Lipsyte says. "There was a part of him that was hurt by the portrayal."

That was the reality of the 1962 Mets—despite the charming manager, the bumbling roster, and record futility, these were professional athletes, most near the end of middling careers and some near the end of spectacular ones. Losing in goofy fashion was not a joke to them, but it served a press and public that craved diversion and entertainment.

The Throneberry legend endured for decades, but his time with the Mets was brief. He played fourteen games for the team in 1963 before being demoted to

Triple-A Buffalo. For a time, some of the New York newspapers published reports of his play in the minor leagues, but Throneberry soon faded from public consciousness and never again appeared in a major league game.

How long did it take for the lovable losers to become mere losers? Sports fans, after all, are looking to back a winner, and would not support a hapless team indefinitely.

At the beginning, Casey Stengel proved a brilliant hire by ownership and George Weiss, and not because of his on-field moves. Aging and saddled with a deeply flawed roster, the manager was powerless to help the team in a meaningful way. A brilliant baseball man, Stengel had left his prime years by the time he arrived at the Polo Grounds, and was known to snooze on the dugout bench during Met games.

But the Mets did not need a tactician, or a leader of men. They needed a diversion for the fans and press,

Met center fielder Duke Snider gets a warm welcome from loyal young fans prior to the opener at the Polo Grounds in 1963.

By the early 1960s, though, Snider was in deep decline, and had been pushed aside in L.A. in favor of younger outfielders. For a time, he appeared headed to the Bronx as a bench player for the Yankees, but that deal was never consummated. So, late in spring training of 1963, the Mets purchased Snider from L.A. for about $40,000. This caused great excitement among a certain segment of the fan base—the Dodger fans, of course—and many turned out for early games that year holding banners that welcomed Snider back to the city where he had once been baseball royalty.

Not that it really mattered to a team destined for last place, but the thirty-six-year-old Snider embodied the Mets' strategy during those early years. He was sentiment and entertainment over winning, a once-great player no longer his best self. Snider's very appearance advertised his decline: slow from bad knees, doughier than he had been in Flatbush, a white head of hair under his cap, the Duke was in his final days. He had a modicum of pop left in his bat that year, and managed 14 home runs for the Mets while hitting .243. He spent one season in New York before returning west to finish his career with the Giants in 1964.

If there was one on-field area of optimism for the 1963 Mets, it was twenty-two-year-old rookie second baseman Ron Hunt, the team's first All-Star. He was known more as a "grinder"—a Pete Rose–type player whose hard work and aggressive style keyed his success, more so than superlative natural ability—and this allowed him to enjoy a respectable twelve-year career in the majors with the Mets, Dodgers, Giants, Expos, and Cardinals.

Originally in the Milwaukee organization, Hunt was not enough of a prospect for the Braves to hold on to; they sold Hunt to the Mets for $25,000 before the 1963 season. His primary talent was getting hit by pitches, and he set a major league record at that time when it was done to him fifty times in 1971, while playing for Montreal.

and Stengel remained a masterful talker. During those early years, he served to remind New Yorkers of winning baseball while making them laugh. He drank with and charmed the press, ensuring that a sizable chunk of the articles would be about him, not the players, team, or standings.

Seeing that a contending team was nowhere near possible in 1963, the front office again focused on pleasing its fans and appealing to nostalgia to sell tickets. Their big move that off-season was to lure Duke Snider from Los Angeles.

Not long before, New York baseball fans argued over whether Brooklyn Dodger Snider, New York Giant Willie Mays, or Yankee Mickey Mantle was the greatest center fielder in town. Snider was an icon at Ebbets Field, and unlike many of the Boys of Summer, he made the trip to Los Angeles and continued his career with the Dodgers.

For the Mets, Hunt represented a player who was neither novelty nor washed-up legend. He was a moderately talented youngster. After purchasing him from the Braves, the Mets had thirty days in spring training to decide whether to pay the price or return him. During that time, Hunt endeared himself to Stengel with his toughness and hustle, and the Mets decided to keep him.

After a few itchy weeks on the bench, Hunt talked his way onto the field, and made his major league debut on April 16, collecting three hits. That came during another bleak April for the Mets, this one devoid of any welcome parades or fans exulting the return of National League baseball to their city.

The Mets dropped their first eight games of 1963, and faced the Braves at the Polo Grounds on April 19. The fiery Hunt saw an immediate opportunity to exact revenge on the organization that had rejected him when he batted in the bottom of the ninth with two on, two out, and his team trailing 4–3. Hunt doubled in both runs, making him an instant favorite among fans eager to see a quality baseball player in a Met uniform. The following year, with the All-Star Game staged at the new Shea Stadium, Hunt would be the only Met on the squad.

The other young player of note during those early years would become a much more significant name in the franchise's history, because he would hang around far longer than Hunt.

Ed Kranepool was a cocky seventeen-year-old from the Bronx who had ditched class in 1962 to attend the first-ever Met game at the Polo Grounds. A few months later, he graduated from James Monroe High School to become the Mets' first-ever highly touted and well-paid prospect. The team outbid all other comers by offering Kranepool $85,000. The brash teenager blew threw three minor league levels that summer and made his major league debut on September 22. Kranepool collected three hits for the team

Ed Kranepool.

that year, the same one that began with him as a high school senior sitting in the stands.

And so began a very long run with the team for Kranepool, who would retire a Met after the 1979 season. He was young and ridiculously inexperienced in 1963, but the Mets had few viable alternatives. So when they opened the season at the Polo Grounds, Kranepool was in right field.

Though neither he nor Hunt would ever be a superstar, they did provide the Mets and their fans with some hope for the future in 1963—though his rough rookie season was defined by setbacks. Batting .190 on July 10, Kranepool was demoted to Buffalo, and would not return until the major league rosters expanded on September 1.

Another one of the team's most talented players, pitcher Roger Craig, endured a far more miserable and hopeless campaign. Another of the former Brooklyn Dodgers brought in by the Mets in 1962, the thirty-two-year-old Craig was the team's best pitcher—in

truth, its only solid starter—that inaugural season, though the team's futility left him with a 10-24 record. Craig projected to be the "ace" once again in 1963, and generally pitched decently that year. But Craig was a victim of his abysmal offense and defense, and lost 18 straight decisions between May 4 and August 8. Craig finished the year 5-22, and his more-than-respectable 3.78 earned-run average tells all anyone needs to know about the rest of his team.

For his part, Craig never complained during the streak. He went on to pitch three more seasons in the majors for St. Louis, Cincinnati, and Philadelphia, then became a respected pitching coach and manager. Craig's ultimate legacy was a Johnny Appleseed of the split-fingered fastball, that downward-diving pitch that has baffled hitters for decades as a weapon of Bruce Sutter, Roger Clemens, and others. Craig was proficient at throwing the pitch, and later prolific at teaching it. His coaching career culminated in a managerial stint with the Giants from 1987 to 1992, a tenure that included a World Series visit in 1989.

Amid all the losing and the slowly waning charms of futility, the 1963 season included one poignant and transitional moment. Gil Hodges, another Brooklyn Boy of Summer, was never able to contribute much to the Mets as a player. From the beginning of spring training in 1962, Hodges' knee left him unable to offer much beyond serving as another reminder to fans of the Ebbets Field glory days. At age thirty-eight he played in just fifty-four games in 1962, batting .252, with nine home runs.

Hodges hobbled through the first eleven games of the 1963 season before realizing that he was done as a player. His knee still hurting, Hodges went on the disabled list on May 9, with the team wondering if he would return. He had long been seen as a future manager, and perhaps he could lead the Mets sooner than later, with Stengel aging and still catching regular catnaps on the bench during games.

Traffic backs up as
cars stream to Shea
Stadium for Opening
Day 1964.

Before that could transpire or be seriously discussed, the Washington Senators swooped in and
offered their managerial position to Hodges. On May
22 the Mets granted Hodges his release, so the New
York baseball legend could begin a new phase of his
life and career. Before the decade was over, a dramatic
and triumphant return would be among his final acts.

Robert Lipsyte recalls 1964 as the definitive end of
the endearing Marvelous Marv, cute loser Mets.
After two years of bad baseball, the act simply ceased
to charm most people. "By the time they were at Shea
Stadium, that was totally over," Lipsyte said.

Shea Stadium, the shiny new ballpark in Flushing,
Queens, became the Mets' longtime home in 1964.
Designed by a team spearheaded by Robert Moses,
the stadium was very much of its time, offering hints
of suburbia and sprawl while still in an urban setting.

Moses was the legendarily powerful city planner
who had built highways and parks and who did all
he could to make the tristate area more automobile-

friendly. In most cases he succeeded, splitting the
Bronx with the Cross Bronx Expressway, and Brooklyn with the Brooklyn-Queens Expressway. He even
desired at one point to demolish much of Greenwich
Village and SoHo to make room for a highway, though
community activists stymied him in that project.

Though located in the ethnically diverse and primarily urban borough of Queens, Shea Stadium was
less a part of its city than the other New York ballparks. Most people walked or took the subway to
Ebbets Field, the Polo Grounds, and Yankee Stadium;
while the No. 7 train ran to Shea, the ballpark was also
accessible by highway from Long Island, that postwar
capital of urban flight from New York City. The parking lot contained more than twenty thousand spaces.

The people who ventured to the new park that
season saw the team go 53-109, finishing forty games
behind the St. Louis Cardinals, who would win the
World Series. But as the Mets advanced from the early
1960s to the middle of that decade, from the Polo
Grounds to Shea, they slowly began to lay a foundation for better things. It took years to improve upon a
roster assembled by the flawed process of an expansion

draft, but the team was slowing doing so. In August 1964, for example, the team signed an amateur pitching prospect named Jerry Koosman, who later became a central figure in Mets history.

That month also led to the arrival of an even more important—though far less known—addition, a man who would become perhaps the most pivotal figure in the franchise's turnaround. Bing Devine was a lifelong baseball man who had served as general manager of the St. Louis Cardinals since 1957. He constructed a roster that included Bob Gibson, Tim McCarver, Lou Brock, and many other legends, and one that would win World Championships in 1964 and 1967 and a National League title in 1968.

But that first championship did not seem likely in August 1964, when the Cardinals seemed hopelessly buried under manager Gene Mauch's Philadelphia Phillies in the standings. An impatient ownership fired Devine that month, then watched the players he chose overtake the collapsing Phils to win the pennant and eventually the World Series against the Yankees.

St. Louis's rash decision was the Mets' gain; the team hired Devine as part of its front office, with the expectation that he would eventually take over from George Weiss. He became general manager of the Mets in 1966, and returned to St. Louis the following year. But while he had long departed by the team's unlikely championship year in 1969, Devine has done much to make it possible.

As a member of the Mets' scouting department, Devine helped to spearhead an organizational shift toward young talent, while the major league roster slowly shed the Duke Sniders, Frank Thomases, and Roger Craigs of its formative years. Devine helped to scout and sign a teenage pitcher named Nolan Ryan, talked Weiss out of cutting Koosman loose when the prospect was struggling in the minor leagues, and convinced team brass to give Tom Seaver a $50,000 bonus. By 1965, youngsters such as Tug McGraw and Ron Swoboda also were on the roster.

The signing of Seaver—one of his nicknames was "the Franchise," after all—was the most impor-

1960s

Rookie righthander Nolan Ryan (left) with 1967 NL Rookie of the Year Tom Seaver during spring training in 1968.

tant move. A righthander born in Fresno, California, Seaver was brimming with talent, and available to the Mets through a lucky set of circumstances. After an excellent first season at the University of Southern California in 1965, Seaver was drafted by the Los Angeles Dodgers, of whom he asked $70,000. The Dodgers thought that price too high, and passed.

The following year, the Atlanta Braves made Seaver a first overall draft pick, and successfully signed him for $51,500. That should have doomed the Mets to more failure, and boosted a rival franchise for years to come, but New York was saved by a controversial

decision by Major League Baseball. On March 2, Commissioner William Eckert ruled the contract invalid because USC had played two exhibition games before Seaver signed with the Braves. Seaver had not appeared in those games, and his father threatened to sue Major League Baseball.

As a compromise, Eckert backtracked somewhat and decided that any team willing to pay Seaver as much as the Braves could enter a lottery for the right to do so. In the Flushing offices of the Mets, there was much internal debate over whether to pay one player what then was an extreme sum. Devine advocated for doing so, noting the team was woefully light on pitching, and would never improve without a major effort to address that.

Devine won the argument, and the Mets, Phillies, and Cleveland Indians notified the league that they were interested and willing to pay. On April 3, 1966, the commissioner put those names in a hat and drew New York.

Before Seaver or any other of those promising players arrived at Shea, the central character of those early seasons would abruptly leave. Stengel's departure was necessary for the organization to move forward, and the aging manager's decline had become obvious by 1965. He was seventy-five years old that year. Because he had charmed and coddled the press, many in the media were reluctant to criticize Stengel. One iconoclastic newcomer took the opposite approach.

A born contrarian and self-styled truth teller, Howard Cosell would become a major narrator of the Muhammed Ali saga, an original *Monday Night Football* broadcaster, and generally an omnipresent figure in sports of the late 1960s and the 1970s. But in the mid-1960s, Cosell was still building his career, and hosted the Mets pre- and postgame radio show on WABC in New York.

He used that platform to lambaste Stengel, calling him old, racist (Stengel was known for unevolved attitudes on race, once reportedly saying of catcher Elston Howard, the first black Yankee, "They finally get me a nigger, I get the only one who can't run"), and overrated. "I'm suspicious of anything that causes kids to fall in love with futility," Cosell once said of Stengel's work with the Mets.

Many of the newspapermen pushed back at Cosell's criticisms, defending Stengel. But the aging skipper truly was in decline, and the Mets were beginning to

ascend. The team still lost most of its games, but owned more talent than it ever had. That talent needed to be nurtured and developed. Decades earlier, Stengel was a master teacher; after disastrous tenures managing the Braves and Dodgers, he had resurrected his career as minor league skipper in the late 1940s.

But in his midseventies, Stengel was not the man to lead the Mets into a hopeful new era. When the franchise was in its infancy, he had served brilliantly as entertainer and lender of instant credibility. Because of that, and because George Weiss recalled the public relations fiasco that ensued after the Yankees dis-

Mr. Met bicycles down the Grand Concourse during a parade celebrating the Bronx's fiftieth anniversary as a county in 1964.

did not announce it at the time, Stengel would never manage again.

Succeeding him on an initially interim basis was a man mostly forgotten in Mets history, Wes Westrum. The forty-three-year-old former catcher had been a Mets coach since 1964, and a coach for the Giants before that. Westrum became the Mets' pitching coach during the 1964 season after the Mets' awkward experience with Hall of Famer Warren Spahn.

Spahn was yet another washed-up legend recycled by the Mets. After a twenty-year career pitching for the Braves, Spahn signed with the Mets in 1964 as both starting pitcher and pitching coach. The problem was, he could no longer pitch effectively. Embittered by this, he was unwilling to devote adequate attention to the rest of the staff. The Mets released Spahn in August and made Westrum the pitching coach.

Temperamentally, he was Stengel's opposite. Shy and not nearly as quotable and garrulous with the press, Westrum—though a respected baseball man—was the perfect symbol for the years between the Mets' Polo Grounds years and their World Championship season in 1969. With all novelty drained from the team, Westrum steered them blandly through the next several years.

Under the surface, of course, things were not that simple, or boring. Starting that first season, Westrum granted playing time to several promising youngsters. In September, Bud Harrelson, Ron Swoboda, Cleon Jones, and Ed Kranepool all appeared at Shea Stadium. They hinted at better times, but would not deliver them anytime soon.

missed Stengel in 1960, the Mets were in an awkward situation with their declining skipper.

After the first year at Shea Stadium, Stengel was initially uncertain of his plans for the 1965 season. He ultimately elected to return for what would likely be one final year, though he did not last even that long.

Following the Mets' Old Timers' Day festivities on July 26, 1965, Stengel went to a late-night party at Toots Shor's, the Manhattan restaurant that had long served as a favorite watering hole for the city's sports elite. In the men's room at one point in the evening, Stengel slipped and fell on his hip, though he remained at the gathering. Later, a friend drove him home, and Stengel fell on the same hip while getting out of the car. The following day, he went to the hospital and underwent surgery. Though he

Despite continued losing, the mid-to-late 1960s were a transitional time for the franchise. With the Stengel era over, and players such as Richie Ashburn, Marv Throneberry, Duke Snider, and Warren Spahn

long gone, the Mets continued to acquire and develop young talent. Under a front office led by Bing Devine, and including future Hall of Fame manager Whitey Herzog, the Mets slowly became a solid organization.

Seaver was the most significant piece. After a year in the minor leagues following the lucky lottery in 1966, the big righthander registered an immediate impact in 1967 with the Mets. Though the team finished in last place once again, Seaver managed to win 16 games, including 18 complete games, 170 strike-outs, and a 2.76 ERA. All of those numbers set franchise records, and Seaver made the National League All-Star team and won N.L. Rookie of the Year honors. The Mets had never before had a bona fide phenom,

and Seaver became an instant sensation in New York, a reason for optimism, and an opportunity for fans to see athletic greatness instead of more bumbling.

Seaver won 16 games again in 1968, and topped 200 strikeouts. Those accomplishments were enough to help lift the Mets out of last place and into ninth—though other young players contributed to the slight improvement. It was essentially the same cast that would lead the way to an unlikely title in 1969.

The Mets finished 73-89 in 1968, the year before they would post a 100-62 record and win the World Series. In some ways, worst-to-first campaigns like that rely on luck, other teams failing, and career-making performances from otherwise ordinary players. But the

Tom Seaver delivers a pitch during his near-perfect one-hitter versus the Cubs on July 9, 1969. The Mets won the game, 4–0.

1960s

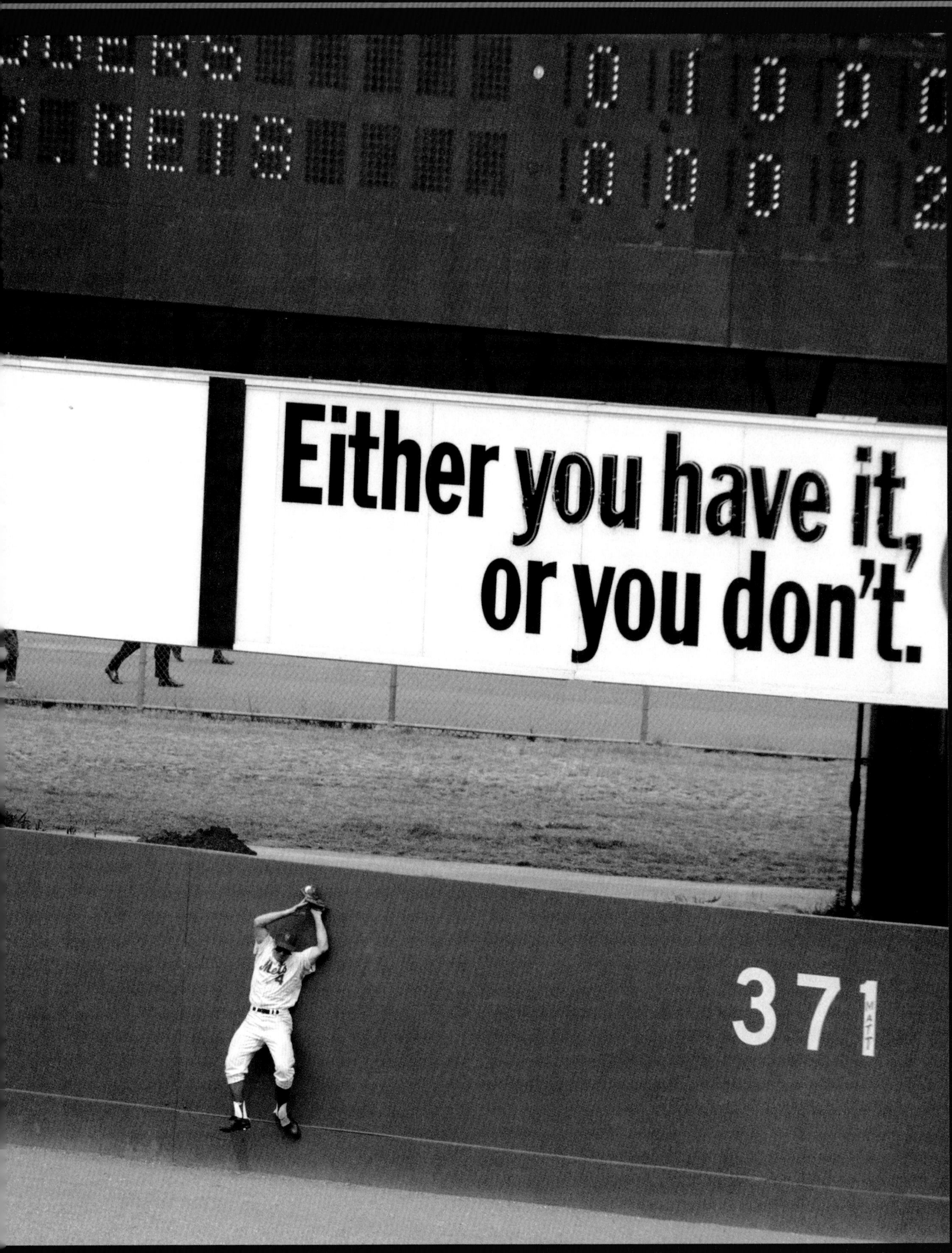
METS
Either you have it,
or you don't.
371

Mets' leap also can be attributed to the improvement of several key players who had been with the franchise during the last of the woeful years.

No factor led more directly to the Mets' startling leap in 1969 than the pitching staff. For several years the organization has successfully scouted, signed, and developed a group of key arms. Seaver was most essential, a talent profound enough to lend the team instant credibility, lasting enough to build a team around. From the beginning of his major league career, Seaver began to fulfill his promise.

Tug McGraw's path was not nearly as direct. A product of Vallejo, California, and Solano Community College, he signed with the Mets way back in 1964 and alternated showing exciting potential and puzzling inconsistency. Known for a garrulous, outgoing personality and a plethora of quirks that extended to his name (legend was that Frank McGraw became "Tug" when still breast-feeding, when his mother labeled him a "littler tugger"). Though he merited only a modest $7,000 signing bonus, McGraw made a fast ascension through the minor leagues, making the team in 1965 without ever appearing in Double-A or Triple-A.

He spent the first half of that season as a reliever, and performed well, going 0-1, with a 3.52 earned-run average in that role. That earned McGraw a promotion to a rotation role, and he made his first major league start on July 28 at Wrigley Field. It did not go well: McGraw allowed three runs and failed to last through the first inning. Success, however, found him soon after; in McGraw's third start, he defeated Sandy Koufax and the Dodgers, 5–2.

That first big league year was a microcosm of McGraw's development: the righthander was talented but spotty, and shuffled between the bullpen and rotation. The Mets could not yet decide how best to use McGraw, and their optimism about him waned over the next several seasons.

Met pitcher Tug McGraw shows off his acrobatic skills, performing a handstand in the Met locker room.

In 1966, the pitching-starved team again slotted McGraw into its starting rotation. The results were abysmal: a 2-9 record, and 5.52 ERA. After that, he was banished to the minor leagues for most of the next two seasons, forcing him to revisit a development cut short by the fast promotion in 1965. The organizational pitching depth that developed during the mid-to-late 1960s resulted in a solid rotation by 1969, leaving McGraw without a spot. That turned out to be a blessing, finally forcing him into the role to which he was best suited, reliever.

Late-inning relief pitching was developing greater prominence in the late 1960s, and McGraw's timing in assuming that role was fortuitous. The 1969 season

Jerry Koosman delivers a pitch during his 2–0 victory over the Pirates. It was Koosman's seventh shutout of the 1968 season, tying a record for shutouts by a rookie.

brought the save rule, created by Chicago baseball writer Jerome Holtzman. That statistic created a way to recognize, and ultimately compensate, relievers to a greater extent than before.

For much of baseball history, pitching staffs were designed far differently than they are today. The best arms started games, with the lesser talents relegated to the bullpen. Starters threw many more complete games and innings than they do now, creating far fewer opportunities for relievers to appear in key situations.

The bullpen was viewed as a lesser role, quite different from the contemporary game. Now, baseball relief corps are filled with often well-compensated specialists. Teams build their bullpens around the closer, and seek dominant seventh- and eighth-inning setup men, right-handed and left-handed specialists, and long men. But until the late 1960s, most bullpens were merely a place to put a team's worst pitchers.

The save rule began to change that, because it lent new status to a relief job. In the ensuing decades, Hall of Fame closers such as Rollie Fingers, Bruce Sutter,

and Dennis Eckersley would take advantage of this change. McGraw was one of the first, returning to the Mets in 1969 from his time in the minors to finally find his niche as a high-impact reliever.

That move was made possible not only by Seaver, but also by the rotation depth that began with Jerry Koosman. Koosman's talent as a starter fell somewhere between Seaver's and McGraw's. A righthander from Minnesota, Koosman signed in 1964, and needed a few years in the minor leagues to convince the team that he was worth retaining. After a few up-and-down years in the Mets' farm system, Koosman led the International League in strikeouts in 1968, and was poised to join the Mets' rotation the following year. He did so, and enjoyed a successful rookie campaign, going 19-12, with a 2.08 earned-run average and 178 strikeouts.

That was the year of the pitcher, when Bob Gibson and other top hurlers dominated the game to an extent not seen since the dead-ball era. Surrounded by dignified mound company, Koosman was a standout, making the All-Star team, besting Seaver's franchise records for wins, ERA, and strikeouts—all set in 1967.

It is not possible to build a team around one ace pitcher; Seaver could only help the Mets on his turn in the rotation. But once an organization begins to accumulate two or more quality young arms, they become more difficult to contend with. Koosman's emergence gave the Mets an excellent top of the rotation, and provided Seaver with a strong number two. And the farm system was ready to produce still more exciting arms, including Nolan Ryan and Gary Gentry.

Of the two, Ryan clearly enjoyed the more distinguished career—but Gentry appeared to hold more promise, or was at least more fully developed, by 1969.

With a scorching fastball, the Texan would eventually set a major league record by throwing seven no-hitters, make eight All-Star teams, and strike out 5,714, the most in history. He would become a franchise icon for both the Houston Astros and the Texas Rangers, and an easy choice for the Hall of Fame.

But as a recent high school graduate out of Alvin, Texas, in 1965, Ryan was an unpolished twelfth-round draft choice for a Mets organization that would never quite figure out what to do with him. He made a brief big league debut in 1966, then suffered health and performance setbacks in 1967.

The following year, the Mets granted Ryan a chance in their starting rotation, but the twenty-one-year-old did not meet the challenge. Still learning how to control his superlative pitches, Ryan went 6-9, and could not crack the rotation the following year.

But in 1969, Ryan proved a useful, even essential bullpen piece, particularly during the postseason. Though he would eventually leave the Mets in 1971 for the California Angels in a long-bemoaned trade to bring in third baseman Jim Fregosi, Ryan made an important mark on his first organization, which might not have won its initial World Championship without him.

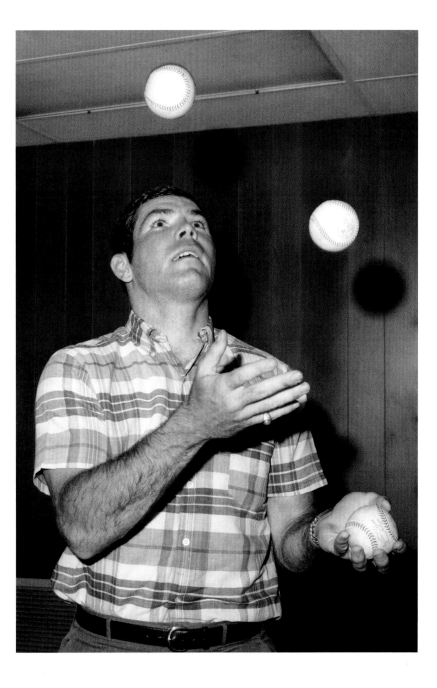

Ron Swoboda shows off his juggling skills.

While Ryan's New York stint would ultimately represent a mere blip in a transcendent career that lasted into the 1990s, Gentry's arc was the complete opposite. Full of potential and at twenty-two years old more polished than Ryan in 1969, Gentry was good enough to make the Mets' rotation as a rookie, and contribute significantly throughout the season and postseason. But those Met triumphs would turn out to be his brightest moments; Gentry suffered a serious elbow injury in 1972 and was gone from the game three years later.

Cleon Jones slides
into home as the
Cards' Tim McCarver
awaits the throw.

Though he would later become known for a spectacular and crucial World Series catch, Swoboda was no defensive whiz; his nickname, "Rocky," was a result of his shaky fielding. Swoboda came up as a left fielder, but the Mets moved him to first base in 1967 to accommodate new acquisition Tommy Davis. That position does not require stellar defensive capabilities, but it was too much for Swoboda to handle, and he soon moved to right field.

After a disappointing 1966 season, in which he batted just .222 with eight home runs, Swoboda also stabilized at the plate in 1967. The next season, he continued to blossom, not as an All-Star, but certainly as a solid player. He led the team with six triples that year and drove in fifty-nine runs, the most of his career. And despite his lack of range in the outfield, he displayed a strong arm, registering fourteen outfield assists that year.

Outfielder Cleon Jones made his Mets debut way back in 1963, after signing with the team as an amateur free agent. A Mobile, Alabama, native and football and baseball star at Alabama A&M University, Jones was two for fifteen that year in a September call-up. He spent most of the next two seasons in Triple-A Buffalo, and became the Mets' center fielder in 1966, when he batted .275, with eight home runs, and finished fourth in National League Rookie of the Year voting.

Before the 1968, season, a significant trade further bolstered the Mets' roster and pushed Jones to left field and added his childhood friend to the team. Tommie Agee, who played high school baseball with Jones in Alabama, had gone on to receive a $60,000 bonus from the Cleveland Indians before the 1962 season.

Later sent to the Chicago White Sox as a key cog in a blockbuster trade that involved pitcher Tommy John, Agree won American League Rookie of the Year honors with the White Sox in 1966. Batting .273 that season, with twenty-two home runs and eighty-six runs batted

The 1969 lineup was certainly more solid than it had been for most of the decade. And while it was not mighty, it was enough to back the talented pitching staff.

Ron Swoboda would ultimately become known for a defensive contribution, a quirky twist to a career defined far more by modest hitting talent. Signed for a $35,000 bonus in 1963 after one year at the University of Maryland, he made his Mets debut in 1965. In his second major league at-bat, Swoboda launched a pinch-hit, eleventh-inning home run against the Houston Astros; he ended the first half of that season with fifteen homers, the most ever for a Mets rookie before he All-Star break. Though Swoboda slowed in the second half and finished with nineteen, that remained the Mets' rookie record until Darryl Strawberry hit twenty-six in 1983.

in, Agee also won the Gold Glove Award and was the White Sox' lone representative at the All-Star Game.

Young, promising, and gifted at the plate and in the field, Agee was not the type of player who appeared on those early Met teams. He perfectly represented the improvement that began in the middle of the decade.

The Mets were able to acquire him because a dip in production in 1967—he batted .234 that year—temporarily decreased his value and made him expendable to the White Sox. After finishing in fourth place that year largely because of a weak offense, Chicago looked to acquire an established hitter. The Mets offered outfielder Tommy Davis and others for Agee and Al Weis—remember that name—and the White Sox agreed. The outfield that would win the World Championship in 1969 was thus assembled.

Jerry Grote was another key member, whose skills fit perfectly with the theme of those Mets. Known as a top defensive catcher and handler of the pitching staff, Grote produced only scant offense. With a young and talented staff, though, his receiving skills were of paramount importance, and so highly regarded that in 1968 he became just the second Met after Ron Hunt to start an All-Star Game.

Grote's career began with the Mets' expansion sisters, the Houston Colt .45s, and he was traded to the Mets after the 1965 season. Known for a prickly personality and sharp competitive nature, Grote was not well liked throughout the league—but he was the perfect leader and mentor to the Mets' talented and still developing staff in the mid-to-late 1960s.

Wes Westrum was by all accounts a good man, but not a championship manager. Shy and prone to malapropism, Westrum's shortcomings as a public figure were magnified by the unfortunate luck of fol-

lowing Casey Stengel as the Mets' skipper. Never comfortable or totally happy in New York, Westrum finally resigned on September 21, 1967, after the San Francisco Giants offered him the third-base coaching job.

This created an opening for a choice that would excite fans looking for both Brooklyn Dodger nostalgia and a chance to win. Gil Hodges had worked as manager of the Washington Senators since leaving the Mets as a creaky-kneed first baseman in 1963, and ownership saw a chance for him to return. The Mets paid Washington $100,000 and midlevel pitching prospect Bill Denehy for the right to Hodges, and the Mets moved still closer to their first taste of success.

Sister Francis Consuelo shows off her handmade sign supporting Mets star Cleon Jones.

1960s

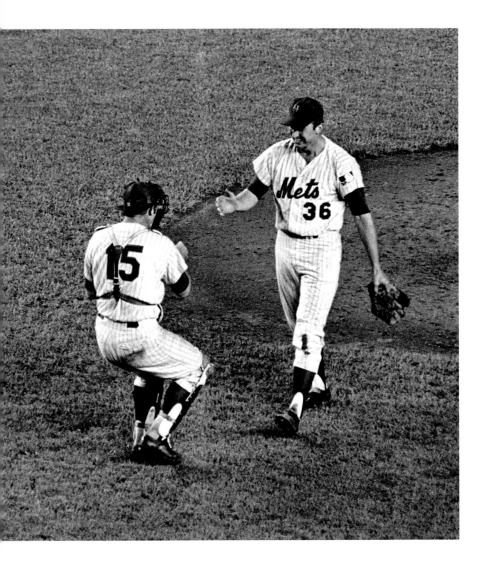

Jerry Grote congratulates Jerry Koosman after the Mets knocked off the Chicago Cubs, 3–2, on September 8, 1969.

The Mets' miracle run in 1969 came during one of the country's most turbulent and interesting epochs, a time defined by cultural forces apart from sports. When the Mets came into being in 1962, New York and America were still in their buttoned-down, post-1950s, *Mad Men* phase, with underlying tensions yet to explode. By the end of the decade, the Vietnam War had become the most controversial conflict of the century, and long-simmering racial tensions had boiled. The Mets won the World Series during the summer of Woodstock, and Neil Armstrong and company walking on the moon.

The Mets were not immune to these strong societal forces, but they also operated somewhat apart from them—a complex formula for a complex time. Several players, including infielder Bud Harrelson and pitcher Jerry Koosman, spent time in the military during their playing careers. Tom Seaver at one point pledged to purchase a newspaper advertisement protesting the war.

Lipsyte, the columnist for the *New York Times* whose sports coverage often leaned toward sociological topics, recalled the 1969 Mets as a unifying force. "People came to Shea, and they were excited about the Mets," he said. "They were excited about the Mets everywhere that summer. Sure, among a lot of us there was this feeling of, 'there's a war going on, who cares about the pennant?,' but it also brought some people together. You have to be careful about oversimplifications."

Indeed, 1969 was a complicated and unpredictable year. Certainly no one in baseball expected the Mets to conquer the league just seven years after stumbling into existence. The 1968 season concluded on a promising note, with the young rotation coalescing. Seaver finished that season 16-12, with a 2.20 earned-run average. Koosman was even better, winning 19 games and losing 12—not an easy record to achieve on a 78-89 team—and a 2.08 earned-run average. Gentry was primed to debut the following year.

But as the franchise gained a tough, demanding, and soon-to-be successful manager, it lost an even more important leader. Bing Devine's trouble in St. Louis several years before had created a fateful opportunity for the Mets to acquire a savvy designer of quality baseball teams. But the general manager's family had never left St. Louis, and New York had never felt like home.

Before the 1968 season, when Stan Musial resigned as the Cardinals' GM, ownership tried to lure back Devine. It was not a difficult sell, and Devine returned home. Though he would be working for a competitor two seasons later, Devine watched as the Mets—who he led out of the deep wilderness of perennial last-place finishes—would accomplish what no one thought they could so soon after setting a record for futility in 1962.

The timing was fortuitous for the Mets to develop such talented arms. Across the major leagues in 1968, pitchers dominated and hitters struggled; there was perhaps never a better time in baseball history to have a team defined by pitching.

The Mets most certainly were not defined by thunder in their lineup; they batted .228 as a team in 1968. That is why few expected them to fare much better in 1969. With no brand-name hitters, the team appeared destined to lose close games all season.

It did not seem to improve their prospects when Hodges suffered a heart attack late in the 1968 season. The gritty manager was back at work in November at the team's instructional camp in Florida, and reported on time to spring training having quit smoking. He

and the Mets appeared ready to go, far from a complete roster but more promising than they had ever been.

A decision beyond the team's control would also prove beneficial. The 1969 season brought more expansion, divisional realignment, and an additional playoff round. The Montreal Expos and the San Diego Padres joined the National League. To accommodate the larger league, owners created the N.L. East and the N.L. West, categorizing teams in ways that defied logic: St. Louis and Chicago joined the Mets in the East, while Atlanta and Cincinnati went to the West. Though it was impossible to know in advance, those odd decisions set up a thrilling pennant race later in the year.

But when the season began, hope quickly turned

The Mets' starting outfield, from left to right, Cleon Jones, Tommie Agee, and Ron Swoboda, in 1965.

Met manager Gil Hodges relaxes in his office during the 1969 World Series.

OPPOSITE: Tug McGraw, a member of the Marine reserves, does pull-ups as part of weekend drills during the 1969 season.

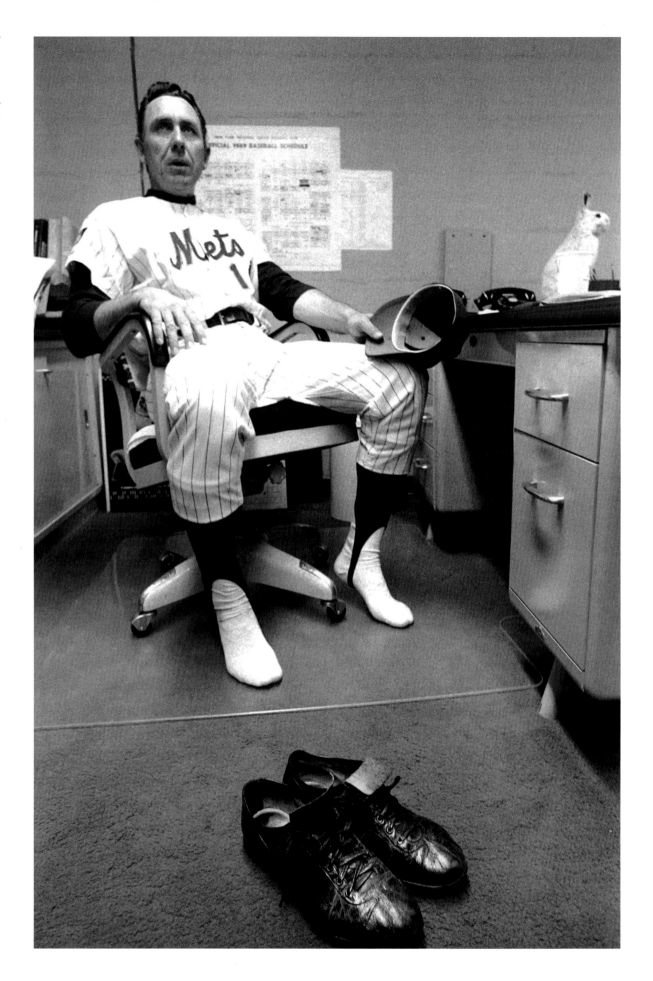

to disappointment. Opening Day appeared to present an opportunity for the Mets to begin the season well, as they were set to face the expansion Expos. The Mets had never won a season opener, but finally they could prey on a franchise newer than they were.

The day before that game brought another health scare for Hodges, who missed the team's workout at Shea Stadium and skipped the welcome home banquet. Returning from spring training with a 102-degree fever, Hodges called a doctor to his home at two thirty in the morning, but managed to show up for the opener on April 8. He was not able to help the team avoid yet another defeat, in front of 44,541 cautiously optimistic fans in Flushing. They would witness the first international game in major league history.

Seaver started but did not pitch like an ace. He allowed five runs in 5 1/3 innings, and the bullpen surrendered six more. The Mets scored four in the ninth but ended up losing, prompting a cranky Hodges to exclaim, *"Mon Dieu, c' était terrible!"* (My God, that was terrible) in his postgame press conference.

The following day was better, as Tug McGraw, beginning to settle into his new relief role, led the way to a 9–5 win over the Expos. It had been a trying few years for McGraw, who followed that 1965 win against Sandy Koufax—the first time the Mets ever beat the legendary lefty—with struggle. On April 10, 1969, when summoned into a bases-loaded, no out jam created by starter Jim McAndrew in the second inning, McGraw had not earned a major league win since 1966.

McGraw managed somehow to escape that sticky frame without allowing a run, and continued to post scoreless innings until the eighth, when Nolan Ryan relieved him. The day promised better things for the twenty-four-year-old McGraw, still young despite being in his fifth professional season.

Elbow injuries slowed his development, but allowed McGraw time in the minor leagues to develop

a so-called screwball, a potentially baffling breaking pitch. Before that, his only weapons were an average fastball and good curveball; the "scroogie," as it was called, changed McGraw, and was on display during those 6 1/3 dominant innings of relief against the Expos.

It was a good sign for the Mets, as was the following day's game, when Gentry flashed his potential in earning his first major league win. Tommie Agee's two home runs provided all the necessary help for Gentry, who allowed just four hits in eight innings, and did not walk a batter until the eighth. After the game, both Hodges and Jerry Grote praised the rookie's ability and steely mound presence.

"He's right in there with the other good young pitchers we've had the last couple years," Hodges said.

Added the catcher: "He's got the poise, and as for speed, he, Koosman, and Seaver are all together."

After two straight days of positive signs, though, the Mets began to struggle. They lost the next day to St. Louis, when Brooklyn native and future Met manager Joe Torre blasted Koosman and two relievers for a home run, double, and single and got an intentional walk. The performance helped to vindicate a trade by Bing Devine; once re-installed in his old post with the Cardinals, Devine dealt Orlando Cepeda to the Atlanta Braves for Torre.

As promising at McGraw's and Gentry's early outings had been, Koosman's season debut raised concerns. He had suffered from a sore arm throughout spring training, and his loss to St. Louis did nothing to placate fears that his 1969 would be more challenging than the year before.

Two days later, Seaver also became a source of consternation, falling to 0-2 on the season. After the rocky outing on Opening Day against the ragtag expansion Expos, Seaver fared better against the Cardinals, but lost 3–1 to Bob Gibson. It was the Mets' third straight loss, dropping them to 2-4.

The unfortunate April continued, threatening the cautious optimism the Mets had felt in spring training. When thirty-seven-year-old former Phillies ace Jim Bunning, now with the Pirates, three-hit the Mets and the Bucs beat Koosman 4–0 on April 17, the Mets had lost six of their previous seven games and were 3-7 overall.

The following day, a frustrated Hodges shook up his flailing lineup, benching Tommie Agee and Rod Gaspar, and moving Amos Otis from third base to center field. Gaspar, a phenom who had won the right-field job over Swoboda after a strong spring training, endured predictable rookie struggles.

After carrying the spring training hot stretch into early April and batting .412 during the regular season's first week, Gaspar went two for twenty-two and saw his average drop to .221. Agee also began the year well, then went into a two-for-twenty-eight slide that sunk his average way down to .195.

Despite Hodges's focus on squeezing more production from what had fast become an anemic lineup, he and his team won the following day because of the squad's strength pitching. In St. Louis, Seaver had the difficult assignment of facing Bob Gibson, whom the Mets had not beaten in two years.

In what Dick Young referred to as "a battle of non-scoring wonders," Seaver bested Gibson, and the Mets won, 2–1. The pattern that would solidify and characterize the team all summer and fall was already apparent: These Mets would live and die by their pitching, with minimal help from the offense. In that win against Gibson, neither of the Mets inserted in the lineup contributed to the just-enough scoring, leaving Hodges to once again wonder how to reshuffle the deck chairs he had been dealt.

Six days after that win, Koosman's continued arm trouble darkened a victory led by the team's lone hot bats, Jones and Swoboda. As the Mets defeated Pittsburgh, 2–0, Jones had three hits and an RBI single,

which lifted his batting average to .444. The streaky Swoboda already had ten runs batted in, and he singled in the Mets' other run that day.

Jones's average led the National League at that early juncture, and he boasted that pitchers' new-found desire to throw at him was evidence that he was becoming an offensive factor. Jones, who batted .246 in 1967, improved to .297 in 1968, and would go on to post a career-high .340 in 1969, said, "About the end of last season, that's when they started throwing at me. I guess I was hit more times those last couple months than ever before."

As Larry Fox of the *Daily News* noted on April 25, Jones's assertion jibed with the facts. Opposing pitchers plunked Jones five times in 1968, all after July 30. It was perhaps no coincidence that Jones was batting .223 on June 1, then heated up, toward what he saw as his true potential.

OPPOSITE: Arnold and Kevin Pratt cheer on the Mets during the 1969 World Series victory parade.

Mets pitcher Jerry Koosman celebrates his eleventh victory of the 1968 season, a five-hit, 11–2 defeat of the Houston Astros.

"I would like to be known as an accomplished .300 hitter," Jones said that April. Ultimately, he would not see that wish fulfilled. In a career that spanned from 1963 to 1976, Jones batted over .300 for a full season just twice, and never again would approach that .340 mark from the Mets championship season. As must happen with players on any team that makes a profound leap in the standings from one year to the next, Jones enjoyed a career year at exactly the right time for his run-starved club.

In that 2–0 win over Pittsburgh, Koosman pitched brilliantly, hurling a shutout for his first win of the season after two losses, but his postgame comments were ominous. After an ineffective spring training and those two defeats, Koosman said that despite the win he was not entirely healthy.

"I didn't feel I had a good fastball at all," he said. "It was cold out there, and I didn't seem to be able to get my shoulder loose. My fastball had no tail; it was straight most of the day. I had to rely a lot on my curveball."

That same mixed equation—Met optimism over Jones marred by worry about Koosman—lingered through the end of that season's first month. Jones's torrid pace continued, and he knocked a game-winning home run against the Cubs on April 27. But the young righthander Koosman was still sore a few days later, clouding another win for the team, as Kranepool's two home runs defined a 2–0 victory over the Expos.

Working on a two-hitter with one out in the fifth inning, Koosman removed himself from the game, saying that his arm "felt like a rubber band stretching . . . I felt like I couldn't lift it."

Though he felt better later in the day, lifting said arm and declaring himself ready to pitch, Koosman's April remained a source of anxiety for a team reliant on its impressive young rotation.

The following day, the team sent Koosman to an orthopedic specialist in Manhattan. "There's no use taking chances with our second-best pitcher," said general manager Johnny Murphy, who had succeeded Bing Devine.

Though Koosman remained generally optimistic about his long-term prognosis, his performance so far had been a downgrade from a very promising 1968 season. He was 1-2, after beginning the previous season 4-0. Before that, he allowed eight runs in eight spring training innings. After his win over Montreal, the pitcher said that "suddenly, it felt like everything tore loose in my shoulder and my arm was just hanging there. It felt like the arm was hanging to the ground. It was numb."

As he said those foreboding words, though, Koosman was smiling in the Mets' clubhouse and eating cold cuts from the postgame spread. Somehow he felt fine, without knowing why. That would be the story of Koosman's season, as the shoulder trouble came and went without explanation, contributing to a slow start for the Mets but clearing in time for the strong finish.

The visit to team physician Peter Lamotte proved encouraging. "Dr. Lamotte says he could find absolutely nothing wrong with the arm," trainer Gus Mauch said that day. Any encouragement caused by that development withered the following day, when Koosman halted his bullpen session after three pitches, saying his shoulder felt "tender." The seesaw news continued the next day, when Koosman took to the bullpen mound again and felt better.

The issues clouding the Mets' promising pitching staff did not clear immediately, however. On May 3, with the 9-13 Mets in fourth place in the National League's Eastern Division, Gary Gentry suffered his first career loss after beginning the season 2-0. The rookie took a shutout into the fourth inning against the Cubs at Wrigley Field, but allowed home runs to Ron Santo and Al Spangler in that four-run frame.

The team was starved for positive pitching, and hungry for an early-season strike against the first-place Cubs. They received both on May 4, in front

Jerry Koosman
working on a shutout
in 1968.

of more than forty thousand hostile and enthusiastic fans who turned out for a doubleheader at Wrigley Field. The Chicago faithful was excited about its team, and surely not threatened by the Mets and that franchise's brief and remarkable history of losing.

But the Mets of the early and mid-1960s did not have Tom Seaver. The young righty beat the Cubs 3–2 in the first game, and Tug McGraw won by the same score in the nightcap. Both starters went nine innings, and showed the ability to tune out adversity and pressure that would later lead them to a World Series title. The screaming Cub fans chanted "We want a hit" in unison for many of the eighteen innings, and some threw oranges and hard-boiled eggs onto the field from the upper deck. The Mets were unfazed, and picked up two games in the early-season standings in one successful day.

McGraw was showing consistency for the first time in his career, and credited his newfound success to married life. McGraw and his wife, Phyllis, wed on

June 1, 1968, and moved into a basement apartment in Flushing. The Mets were growing up, more focused and settled, and McGraw's personal changes were emblematic of that shift.

"Mostly it's being married," McGraw said a few days after that complete-game win over the Cubs. "I have a lot more time to think about baseball than when I was single. I used to go out and fool around quite a bit. Now I come home to Mama. We have more serious things to talk about."

He elaborated that he was better able to throw strikes because of added weight due to Phyllis's home cooking. "When I first joined the Mets, I weighed 165," he said. "Last year, before I was married, I weighed 170. Now I weigh 190. It's not fat at all, but good, solid weight. Phyllis is a tremendous cook."

Whatever the reason for McGraw's increased focus and command, he was becoming a valuable asset to the Mets' pitching staff, alternating between the bullpen and rotation early in the year.

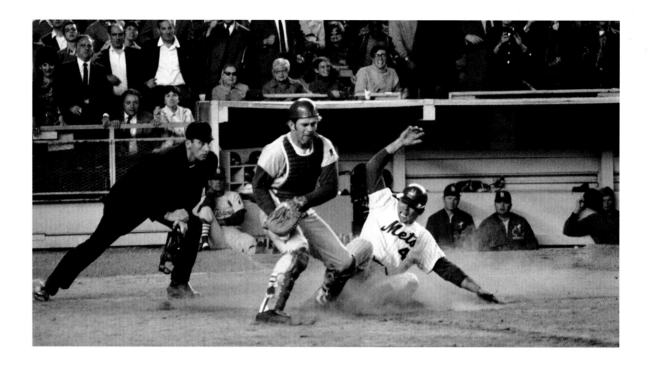

After the somewhat bumpy April, Seaver had also recovered his stature as the pitching staff's most exciting young talent. He four-hit the Astros on May 11 at Shea Stadium, winning 3–1. That lifted Seaver's record to 4-2, a marked improvement from his 1-3 start in 1968.

The ace's reemergence, combined with a decent May for the team, left the Mets optimistic about their pitching and team. On May 20, Jerry Koosman successfully completed a rehabilitation start for the Mets, as they played an exhibition against their Texas League affiliate in Memphis. After five innings and no reported shoulder pain, Koosman was exuberant about his team's chances.

"We have a pennant contender," he said of his team, 17-18 at the time and in second place in its division, six games behind Chicago. "All we need is to have Nolan to come back [Ryan was on the disabled list with a pulled groin], and we'll give those Cubs a battle."

Three days later, the team made a significant move toward that goal. Since the very beginning in 1962, the Mets had never had even a .500 record; they had been a losing team for every moment of their existence.

That changed on May 23, 1969, in a game pitched— appropriately—by the man who led the Mets out the darkness, Seaver, who beat the Braves, then brashly downplayed the significance of being 18-18.

"We haven't done anything yet," the pitcher said, rightly noting that winning teams are hardly content with such a win-loss record. "You go get Marv Throneberry and Richie Ashburn and the rest of those original Mets and have a champagne celebration with them, then come back in September when we clinch first place and celebrate with us."

As it turned out, that winning record lasted only a day, anyway, and the team would go on to lose five straight games, its longest slump of the season to date. They lost four straight on a road trip, and returned to Shea Stadium on May 27 to lose, 3–2, to the Padres.

A healthy-again Koosman finally pulled them out of the slump the following night, in a game that illustrated as well as any other what was strong and weak about those Mets. Koosman tied Nolan Ryan's franchise record by fanning fifteen Padres. The problem was, that fifteenth strikeout came in the tenth inning of a 0–0 ball game. That night and for much of the summer, the Mets could pitch but struggled mightily to score.

On this occasion, after McGraw walked two but pitched a scoreless eleventh, Bud Harrelson drove in Cleon Jones for a game-winning hit. They won again the next night, as Seaver beat the San Francisco Giants in front of an oddly large and enthusiastic crowd.

Willie Mays was the only remaining holdover from the Polo Grounds, and the Giants traveled to New York

only once a season, so his return might have accounted for some of the more than fifty thousand spectators at Shea Stadium that evening. But despite their recent losing streaks, the Mets were becoming increasingly popular and interesting to New Yorkers, who could see a quality game in Flushing for the first time.

Strangely, thousands of people lined up outside Shea that night, backing up the line so many of them remained in the line when the game began at eight-fifteen. The walk-up customers ultimately equaled the advance ticket sales of twenty-five thousand. It was Memorial Day weekend, with a thrilling summer about to begin.

It was a novel way for the Mets to arrive at June, just three games under .500 and possibly on an up-swing. The team was not accustomed to the mere sug-

gestion of relevance, but they did not shrink at the challenge, winning their first two games of the month to sweep that home series against the Giants.

The Dodgers were next in town, and the Mets were back to within a game of .500. They evened their record at 23-23 with a win in the series opener, and the following night Seaver led them to a totally unfamiliar place: the Mets had a winning record for the first time ever. After Seaver beat Los Angeles, Hodges said quietly, "They are playing ball the way I thought they might be able to."

Asked if he thought there was a chance the Mets would end their season with a champagne celebration after all, the manager—and member of the '62 Metsha—smiled and said, "Maybe there will be a time soon to consider it."

Tom Seaver pitching during game one of the 1969 World Series versus the Baltimore Orioles.

1960s

Excited young fans getting a close look at their heroes on Opening Day 1964.

By that point in the 1969 season, the tone of newspaper coverage also was different than it had ever been. If gentle—some would say condescending— mocking characterized those first seven years of writing about the Mets, the New York writers were beginning to wonder in print whether the current version was capable of something more. In retrospect, the early June date and the team's middling record make that shift seem premature, but as a June 1 *Daily News* headline put it, "Never, but Never, Have Mets Been So Good, So Late."

The next day's headline made reference to the team's newfound position in second place. "Mets Sitting on Cloud 2 . . . but for How Long?" it read.

"Second place," Joe Trimble wrote, unable to shake his memories of the pathetic Mets from earlier in the decade. "Have they gone nuts?"

The craziness lasted for the remainder of the home stand, and the Mets flew to San Diego on June 6 for the beginning of an eight-game West Coast swing, having won seven in a row. They were 23-25, in second place but 8 1/2 games behind the Cubs.

After that streak stretched to ten, Dodger manager Walter Alston note the club's maturation. "They've grown up," Alston said. "They no longer beat themselves. They hold on to one-run leads, and they make the big plays."

After receiving that compliment, the Mets won again, beating the Giants 9–4 on two home runs by Agee and one by Jones. It was the longest winning streak in the major leagues that season, the longest in franchise history, and the longest ever by an expansion club.

To date, 178 players had appeared in games for the Mets, and the team that began in such lowly fashion, mocked by fans and newspapers, was suddenly receiving more respect than ever. Wrote Trimble, "The Mets simply have matured to become the best expansion club ever."

Even losses were covered differently now. When the Mets finally dropped a game the next day, the *Daily News* headline read, "Can't Win 'Em All!"

The extended winning streak placed the Mets in a most unfamiliar position leading up to the trade deadline, which in those days was in mid-June (it has since been moved to the end of July to give teams more time to assess whether they should be buyers or sellers in a given season). The pitching, though troubled in the early going, had begun to fulfill its potential, and on June 15 the Mets remained in second place, with a 29-25 record, 8 1/2 games behind the Cubs.

They were far from guaranteed to remain in contention for the rest of the season, and they would probably need help in the lineup if they wished for continued success. Though the rotation and bullpen were among the best in baseball, the Mets' offense struggled to support the pitchers. The team's need was glaring and clear: upgrade the lineup, and try to do it without trading away one of the pitchers.

"I've talked to a couple of clubs," general manager Johnny Murphy said on June 14. "But it's the same old story. They want our young pitchers, and we'll stand pat before giving up any of them. One club I've talked with is Montreal. I was interested in Donn Clendenon, but they wanted four players for him, and two had to be pitchers. No chance."

It is a yearly tradition, baseball executives postured and negotiating through the media. Murphy had identified the player he wanted, Expo first baseman Donn Clendenon, and he was working on a reasonable package. The very next day after the Mets' GM made those firm comments in the newspaper, he acquired Clendenon for four minor leaguers, managing not to sacrifice any top pitcher or other contributor to the big league club.

Hodges said that Clendenon would begin by platooning at first with Ed Kranepool, and the new acquisition was thrilled to play for a man he called his "idol." Clendenon never forgot a gesture by Hodges several years earlier, when he was playing for Pittsburgh and Hodges was managing the Washington Senators.

Clendenon was struggling in the field, and he saw an opportunity to ask the formerly smooth-fielding Hodges for advice. "Before an exhibition game, I got the guts to go over and ask him to help me," Clendenon said. "I think that no right-handed first baseman could find a better fielder to copy himself after. Gil is the kind of man who won't walk over and offer advice. But if you ask it, he will give you all the help he can. I was having trouble because I had 'stiff hands.' I had been told to use both hands in taking the throw.

"Gil said that wasn't necessary. He showed me how to relax my hand and catch the ball with the glove. And I hope that I'm not enough of a nut at thirty-three to think he can't help me some more. I'm sure

he can teach me more than I know now, and I want to keep learning from him."

With the lineup improved, the Mets' pitching continued to cruise. On June 18, Koosman four-hit the Phillies, shutting them out 2–0 for the team's fourteenth win in their past eighteen games. Seaver won the next day, and the team rolled back into Flushing for a home series that saw growing excitement from a fan base hungry for winning.

On June 22, a total of 55,862 fans packed Shea Stadium to see the Mets sweep a doubleheader over the Cardinals behind Koosman and Gentry. The latter allowed a first-inning run in the first game, the first and final time St. Louis would score that day. The surging Mets had now won eighteen of twenty-three, and were just 4 1/2 games behind Chicago. It was a bit early in the season to watch the standings, but the Mets and the writers who covered them could not help themselves; the team had never before been so relevant, so late.

As June ended, the mystery surrounding the team was simple: How good were these Mets? Were they too young to hang in the pennant race all summer and into the fall? Would their young pitchers tire down the stretch? Was the offense too meek?

The roster was far from stellar, or complete. The team was playing over its head. As spring turned to summer, the Mets and their fans wondered if the exuberance could last.

July began with an improbable display of thunder from the Met lineup as they hammered the Cardinals 10–2 in St. Louis. Jerry Grote and Art Shamsky homered, and Jim McAndrew pitched a three-hitter.

As the pitching continued to excel into that first summer month, the lineup, improved with the addition of Clendenon, also enjoyed several productive games. The team mustered thirty hits in a doubleheader to beat the Pirates 11–6 and 9–2 on July 4, and two days later Clendenon had four runs batted in against the same team in an 8–7 win. That series set up the most important three games in franchise history to date.

The first-place Chicago Cubs, five games ahead of the Mets, were on their way to Shea. They would face Koosman, Seaver, and Gentry, giving the Mets an opportunity to defeat their chief rival with the best of their young arms.

It was telling that the Cub series meant so much more to Hodges than the event scheduled for the day before, which in previous years would have been one of the more interesting events of the Mets' summer. In those days, the Mets and Yankees played a yearly exhibition called the Mayor's Trophy, and that 1969 game was scheduled for July 7. Rain postponed the event, an afterthought for the Mets that summer, and Hodges expressed relief that none of his players would be subjected to the risk of unnecessary injury. After all, they were in a pennant race.

Veteran third baseman Ed Charles said the young team was confident going into the series. Baseball history is dotted with inexperienced clubs who find themselves in contention without knowing enough to be intimidated—the 1950 "Whiz Kids" Phillies come to mind, as do the 2008 Tampa Bay Rays. The 1969 Mets were perhaps the strongest example, too green and excited to know what they were facing.

"This club is as loose as it can be," Charles said the day before the Cubs came to town, and Clendenon agreed. "We'll give 'em hell," he said, and his performance lent credibility to his words—at that point, Clendenon had eleven RBIs in his short time as a Met.

An energy previously unseen before a Mets game buzzed in Flushing on July 8. Buses lined up in front of the stadium, and a thick crowd of fans—more than fifty-five thousand—milled in the parking lot before the game. "You felt the tingle of excitement that had been missing in this town for too many years," wrote Phil Pepe in the *Daily News*. "It was only July, but it sounded like September."

Koosman started and pitched well, but the Mets trailed 3–1 in the ninth. In previous years, the team might have folded, but on this night they treated their frenzied fans to a thrilling comeback. Ken Boswell began it with a leadoff double, and Clendenon later moved him to third with a one-out two-bagger. Cleon Jones drove both runners in with yet another double, which tied the score at three runs apiece. Swoboda's two-out single to left drove in Jones to win the game and make a statement to the Cubs: Forget your assumptions about the Mets, because this team will not die easily.

If that series opener presented high drama, the next game provided a spectacle still more sublime. A crowd of 59,083, the most substantial in the history of Shea Stadium, arrived to watch Seaver. Though he was fighting midseason shoulder stiffness, the young ace gathered all his talents to offer one of the finest performances of his Hall of Fame career.

Fans gave Seaver a loud, standing ovation when he batted in the bottom of the eighth, because they appeared poised to witness baseball history: The pitcher had not yet allowed a base runner. Just three outs separated him from a perfect game, against the team the Mets were chasing, in front of a newly exuberant fan base.

So it seemed hardly believable, a gross injustice, when Jimmy Qualls, a backup outfielder playing in his eighteenth big league game and batting .243, knocked a clean single into left center with one out in the ninth. Despite achieving a complete-game one-hitter and second consecutive victory, the loss of a perfect game left Seaver and the Mets with an unsatisfied craving for more—more than likely a good thing for a team in July of a surprisingly interesting season. Still, that night made the possibilities of 1969 feel potentially limitless, breathlessly exciting.

Apart from its meaning in the 1969 standings—or, to a degree, because of it—the game still stands as the most noteworthy of an odd quirk in Mets history. The

franchise, for whatever reason, seems incapable of producing a no-hitter, and has brought its fans tantalizingly close with a remarkable thirty-five one-hitters through the 2010 season.

Al Jackson had the first, way back on June 22, 1962, against the Mets' brothers in expansion, the Houston Colt .45s. Seaver's was the third (he would, of course, pitch his only no-hitter in 1978, while a member of the Cincinnati Reds), with rookie Jon Niese and veteran knuckleballer R. A. Dickey providing the most recent, in 2010. The list also included likely names—Gentry, Nolan Ryan, Dwight Gooden, Tom Glavine, Pedro Martinez—with more obscure ones such as Pete Schourek, Aaron Heilman, Shawn Estes, Steve Trachsel, and Bobby J. Jones.

Seaver's masterpiece had immediate negative ramifications, however. The shoulder stiffness he felt during that start lingered, and he would lose four of his next five decisions. The summer brought other dark moments, including a doubleheader loss to Houston on July 30 by a combined score of 27–8. Though a 9–5 win over Chicago on July 16 pulled the Mets to 3 1/2 games behind the division leader, they would trail by 9 1/2 on August 19. It was then, though, that they began a run that would end in the World Series.

By September 4, the Mets trailed by five games, and would play teams in their division for the remainder of the regular season. If they continued winning, they could make the playoffs.

The following day, a healthy Seaver, who had recov-

Winning pitcher Jerry Koosman gets a cold drink from Ed Charles after defeating the Cincinnati Reds.

ered his top form of the early summer, began that
stretch run by setting a Mets milestone. By defeating
the Phillies 5–1 at Shea Stadium, Seaver became the
first pitcher in franchise history to win twenty games
in a season. When the Mets beat Philadelphia 9–3 two
nights later, the set up an exciting event: The Cubs
were coming to New York for two games, up 2 1/2 in
the standings.

Chicago appeared headed in the wrong direction.
Since August 14, when they had a 9 1/2-game lead,
Chicago had gone 11-13, and brought a four-game losing streak into Shea. They were primed for a streaking
club to take advantage of them.

The Mets won the first game 3–2, while showing
they would not be intimidated. In the first inning, Cub
pitcher Bill Hands threw behind Agee, leading Jerry
Koosman to drill Chicago star Ron Santo in the ribs.

Hands later tried to retaliate by throwing at Koosman's head, but he missed in repeated attempts, and
the two men shouted at one another. Agee later scored
the winning run.

"Okay," Koosman later said. "Yeah, I threw at him,
but don't make it sound like I'm bragging about it,

because I'm not. They threw at Tommie. I had to do it
to end it right there. If I don't, they keep doing it, and
they keep getting away with it."

"Our boys will take care of our boys," Hodges said.

The incident underscored the team's camaraderie,
and helped them roll into a 7–1 victory behind Seaver
in the next game, one marked by the infamous black-
cat incident.

Cub fans, who have not seen their team win a
World Series since 1908, point to several moments
as evidence of a supposed curse against the club.
There is the Curse of the Billy Goat, stemming from
the team's ejection of a goat from Wrigley Field in
1945—the last time the Cubs have even played in a
World Series.

Then there is the case of Steve Bartman, the fan
whose poorly timed reach for a ball in play contributed to the Cubs' collapse in the 2003 National League
Championship Series against the Florida Marlins. In
between those was the black-cat incident at Shea Stadium on September 9, 1969, when one of several stray
cats who lived under the ballpark got loose during
the game.

Unfortunately for the Cubs, the cat was black, a
traditional symbol of bad luck, and it ran right into
the visiting team's dugout. The team was already on
a losing trajectory, sinking in the standings, while
the upstart Mets caught a wild wave of momentum. It was baseball, not the whims of fortune, that
buried them—but the black cat nonetheless stood as
a symbol of the franchise's sour conclusions to every
postseason hope.

By this point, the Mets appeared unstoppable, all
their elements solidifying simultaneously, and at the
perfect time. They moved into first place—first place!—
on September 10, and continued to build the lead.

There were still shaky moments, the most notable
when Pirate pitcher Bob Moose pitched a no-hitter
against the Mets on September 20, extending a losing

streak to three games. But optimism still reigned, as the Cubs lost again, reducing the Mets' magic number to clinch the division (that means any combination of Met wins and Cub losses) to six.

New York rebounded the next day by sweeping Pittsburgh in a doubleheader, wiping that magic number down to four. The fans, who exceeded fifty thousand nearly every day and night at Shea Stadium, anticipated what had once seemed impossible. It became real on September 24, when Gentry went eight shutout innings and beat St. Louis, 6–0. The Mets had won their division, and were headed to the first-ever National League Championship Series.

In a preview of a rivalry that would again become manifest thirty years later in a thrilling 1999 NLCS, the Mets drew the Atlanta Braves as their first post-season opponent. Inexplicably assigned to the new National League West, where they would remain for decades, Atlanta finished the season 93-69, well behind the Mets' 100-62, which left New York eight games ahead of the Cubs.

Atlanta's roster was full of veteran players, whose name recognition and experience far outdistanced those of their playoff opponents. Sluggers such as Hank Aaron, Orlando Cepeda, Rico Carty, and Clete Boyer presented a formidable challenge to the Mets' young pitchers. But Seaver, Koosman, and company had completed a dominant season: the latter finished 25-7, with a 2.21 ERA, the former 17-6 with a 2.28 ERA. They highlighted a staff that, with Ryan, McGraw, and Gentry, was as deep as it was top-heavy.

The first two games were played in an unlikely style, with both teams engaging in a slugfest. Counter to the Mets' pitching-centric persona, they pitched poorly but outhit the Braves. In the first game, Seaver faced knuckleballer Phil Niekro, and neither pitcher was particularly sharp. The Mets won 9–5, though, on the strength of a five-run eighth.

In the second game, the Mets attacked six Brave pitchers for thirteen hits and eleven runs. That gave Koosman what should have been a breezy afternoon, but the pitcher could not escape the fifth inning, despite enjoying an 8–1 lead at that point.

A rally that included a home run by Aaron, a double by Cepeda, a single by Felix Millan, and a double by Clete Boyer brought Hodges from the dugout with

Jerry Grote and Rod Gaspar celebrate the 1969 National League pennant by bathing New York City mayor John Lindsay in champagne.

an early hook. But the Met offense was suddenly a steamroller, and the team won 11–6 to come within one game of clinching the best-of-five series.

The team found itself in an unlikely scenario, leading two games to none after receiving disappointing outings from its top two pitchers. Strangely, that pattern would continue in the third game, and take them all the way into their first World Series.

It began with Aaron continuing to take full advantage of what would become his final playoff appearance. The eventual career home run record holder bashed a two-run shot off Gentry in the first inning. The rookie did not last through the third inning, when Hodges replaced him with Nolan Ryan.

It was the perfect button for the manager to push. Ryan struck out seven in seven shutout innings. The Mets won 7–4 and were headed to the World Series.

They had so far proved an unstoppable force, but the powerhouse Baltimore Orioles appeared to be the immovable object that would end their plucky run.

The story has been told many times, used to illustrate Baltimore's arrogance: When Mets bench player Rod Gaspar was quoted saying that the Mets would win the World Series in four games, Orioles superstar Frank Robinson reportedly declared, "Bring on Ron Gaspar!"

When fellow Oriole Merv Rettenmund said, "That's Rod, stupid," Robinson replied, "Okay, bring on Rod Stupid."

The arrogance was earned. Baltimore had won 109 games that season, and boasted a roster far more

Jerry Koosman
pitches during
game two of the
1969 World Series.
Koosman held the
Orioles hitless until
the seventh inning
in a 2–1 Mets win.

stacked then even the star-heavy Atlanta Braves. Playing for legendary manager Earl Weaver, hitters such as Boog Powell, Davey Johnson, and Frank Robinson led the attack, and supported an intimidating starting rotation of Jim Palmer, Mike Cuellar, and Dave McNally. Helping those pitchers keep their earned-run averages low was third baseman Brooks Robinson and shortstop Mark Belanger, two of the best ever at fielding their respective positions.

Because they were such heavy underdogs, it seemed that the Mets would be best served to begin the first game strongly, or risk being swept quickly away by the juggernaut Orioles. As with most things involving the team, though, reality proved far less predictable.

The Series could hardly have begun in more dispiriting fashion for the Mets. Seaver started, the ace who would theoretically have to win two or three games in the Series for his disadvantaged team to

have a chance. His second pitch of the game was a high fastball to Don Buford, who sent it over the right-field wall at Baltimore's Memorial Stadium for a home run.

Cuellar, Baltimore's game one starter, did not suffer similar difficulties, and the Orioles cruised to a 4–1 win. They appeared to have quickly snuffed the wild momentum that had enabled the Mets to charge past Chicago and Atlanta.

But the Mets were somehow not demoralized by that initial defeat. Koosman looked to redeem his NLCS dud, and took a perfect game into the seventh inning. General manager Johnny Murphy's midseason trade seemed prescient, as Donn Clendenon's solo homer in the fourth inning gave his team a 1–0 lead.

But Koosman lost the perfect game, no-hitter, and lead in the seventh. Paul Blair singled, stole second, and scored on a base hit by Brooks Robinson. That 1–1 tie held into the ninth inning, when Ed Charles

Tommie Agee makes a spectacular catch of Elrod Hendrick's deep drive in the fourth inning of game three of the 1969 World Series at Shea Stadium.

OPPOSITE: Jerry Grote (left) and Tommie Agee celebrate the Mets' 5–0 win over the Orioles in game three of the 1969 World Series.

singed to instigate a two-out rally. Jerry Grote moved Charles to third on a hit-and-run, which brought up light-hitting utilityman Al Weis.

A team such as the 1969 Mets does not win without surprise contributions from unlikely players, and here Weis produced a career-defining moment. Defying his .215 regular-season batting average, Weis banged a double off the left-field wall at Memorial Stadium to score Charles and give the Mets a two-run lead. Without that hit, and without a game two win, even those fighting Mets would almost certainly not have been able to win the World Series, having to climb from a two games to none hole against the great Orioles.

But Weis did get the hit, Koosman and reliever Ron Taylor finished Baltimore in the ninth, and the Series shifted to Shea Stadium, with the Mets having achieved a satisfying split of the first two contests.

In the third game, the Mets again relied on their formula of pitching, defense, and a modest amount

of offense. The matchup did not appear favorable as Gentry prepared to face Jim Palmer, but the Met rookie dominated in a game ultimately remembered for Agee's sparkling play in center field.

The first gem came in the fourth inning, when Elrod Hendricks sent a shot to left center. A sprinting Agee extended his glove, caught the ball backhanded, and banged into the fence. The impact threatened to disrupt the precarious catch, and the ball sat at the edge of Agee's glove, but he held on.

Then, in the seventh, Gentry lost the strike zone and loaded the bases with walks. Hodges lifted him for Ryan, who allowed Paul Blair to crush a fly ball to deep right center. Had it fallen in, the hit would have cleared the bases, and it appeared ready to do just that—before Agee dove and snagged it. Ryan remained in the game until the ninth, when he loaded the bases with two outs, then struck out Blair to win the game and give the Mets a 2-1 Series edge.

Donn Clendenon homers off Dave McNally in the fourth inning of game two of the 1969 World Series in Baltimore. Clendenon's home run gave the Mets a 1–0 lead.

Current events invaded game four. Before the Series began, Seaver said that if the Mets won, he would purchase an ad in the *New York Times*—protesting the Vietnam War.

Before the game, antiwar protesters distributed pamphlets outside Shea Stadium featuring Seaver's likeness, though the pitcher insisted he had no knowledge of, and did not endorse, those protests.

On the field that day, Seaver had a chance to redeem his game one disappointment. This time he was fully poised and ready to pitch as he had while leading the Mets to their first World Series. Needing only a second-inning home run by Clendenon, Seaver took a 1–0 lead into the ninth.

But just as game three had been defined by Agee's agile defense, this one would become memorable—more memorable than all but a handful of games in franchise history—for a thrilling outfield catch.

This time, the man who made the catch was a far less likely candidate. Ron Swoboda had always been considered a clunky defender, and it surely did not seem an advantage to have him in right field in the ninth inning of a one-run game.

That slight lead was threatened when Seaver allowed one-out hits to Frank Robinson and Boog Powell, putting runners at the corners for Brooks Robinson.

Hodges ran to the mound to assess Seaver's ability to continue, and decided to leave him in the game. He had been masterful all day, and Robinson was one for fifteen in the Series heading into that at-bat. But Seaver allowed a first-pitch fastball to get too much of the plate, and Robinson lined it to right field.

It looked like a potentially Series-tying hit, but Swoboda charged toward it, and he made a catch with his body fully extended that would forever endear him to Met fans. But while the play did prevent the

Mets from falling behind late in a crucial ball game, it could not preserve Seaver's lead, as Frank Robinson tagged and scored from third to make it 1–1.

After a moment like that, though, how could the team lose?

Seaver remained in the game through the tenth inning, as his pitch count climbed over 140. He finished by striking out Blair on three pitches, but it was clear he would not be able to return for the eleventh. To provide their gutsy starter with a well-earned win, the Mets would have to score in the tenth.

Unfortunately, the seventh-, eighth-, and ninth-place batters were due up in that frame. Facing reliever Dick Hall, Grote led off and sent an easy fly to left. Fortune being on the Mets' side all that year, Don Buford lost it in the sun, allowing Grote to land on second base instead of making the first out.

Hodges yanked his catcher in favor of pinch runner Rod "Stupid" Gaspar, and Earl Weaver elected

to intentionally walk Al Weis, creating a double-play opportunity and leading Hodges to instruct backup catcher J. C. Martin to pinch-hit and lay down a sacrifice bunt.

Weaver then summoned left-handed reliever Pete Reichert. As expected, Martin bunted, but the play took an unpredictable turn from there. Reichert fielded the ball and accidentally plunked Martin with it, allowing it to skip down the right-field line. Rod Stupid scored the winning run.

The Orioles argued that Martin was out of the baseline when the ball hit him, and should have been called out. Replays later showed that they might have had a valid point, but the umpires ruled against it.

In a best-of-seven Series, game four is crucial, particularly when one team leads two games to one. The difference between 2-2—a long, unpredictable slog to games six and maybe seven—and 3-1 is gigantic. Because of Ron Swoboda, Tom Seaver, Donn Clende-

non, and J. C. Martin, the Mets were one game away from knocking off the heavily favored Orioles.

The following day, Koosman looked to end the Series in Flushing, but he began bumpily. Home runs by Frank Robinson and pitcher Dave McNally left the Mets in a 3–0 hole after three innings.

An irate Koosman intentionally drilled Robinson in the fifth as revenge for the home run, but umpire Shag Crawford erroneously ruled it a foul ball. The ball had actually hit Robinson in the leg, and it was not the last such call that day that would go in the Mets' favor.

In the sixth inning, McNally hit Cleon Jones in the foot with a pitch—unless he did not. The ball bounced into the Mets' dugout, and reemerged with a shoe polish stain on it, apparent proof that it had grazed Jones's black spikes. At various points since, Koosman and Grote have claimed credit, or been outed, as the person who covertly rubbed the ball against his own shoe before returning it to the field. No matter what actually happened, Jones landed on first base.

Clendenon, soon to be named World Series' Most Valuable Player, followed with a two-run homer to make it 3–2. In the seventh, Weis hit a solo home run to tie it, and the Mets added two in the eighth.

Leading 5–3, Koosman went out in the ninth to try for a complete game, and finish the Mets' resurgence from laughingstocks in 1962 to World Champions by the end of the decade.

With two out and a runner on first, Koosman faced Davey Johnson, who would be back at Shea seventeen years later for the team's only other title celebration. Johnson sent a decently hit fly ball to center, presenting the brief risk of a game-tying home run. The hit died, though, on the inner lip of the warning track, and Jones caught the ball.

It was over. The Mets had won, the past was irrelevant, and the future seemed limitless. The team would not taste another championship until 1986.

Rod Gaspar scores the winning run in 1969 World Series game four as Tom Seaver and teammates look on.

1960s

ABOVE: Ed Charles bats during game five of the 1969 World Series.

BELOW: Al "Mighty Mite" Weis receives congratulations from teammates after his game-tying homer in the seventh inning of game five. He hit only two home runs during the regular season and a total of seven in his big league career.

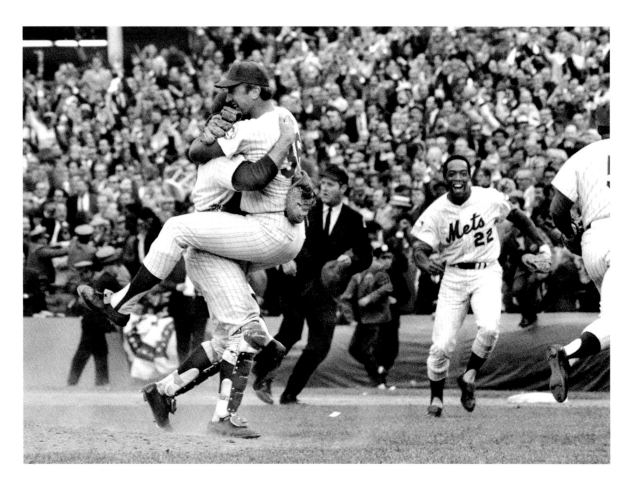

ABOVE: Winning pitcher Jerry Koosman celebrates with catcher Jerry Grote as Donn Clendenon rushes in after Mets defeated the Baltimore Orioles, 5–3, in game five of the 1969 World Series, clinching the Mets' first world championship.

BELOW: A championship pennant flies high as fans rush the field to celebrate the Mets' first World Series title in 1969.

MET MEMORIES

Ron Swoboda played six seasons with the Mets, but is best remembered for his spectacular—and uncharacteristic—defense in the 1969 World Series.

I had some problems catching fly balls. Casey tried to put a good face on it. He probably sacrificed a large measure of his legend as a true baseball guy by his relationship with the Mets, by him buying into the expansion. You were going to have to grow your own talent. He became more of an entertainment of the media. His last act was this lovable, wrinkled former Yankee who tried to find the funny side of anything. It cost him, I think, in the kind of respect he deserves. To manager into your midseventies is no small deal. The fact he was managing the unmanageable was the price he paid. He came off as a clown and he was no clown at all.

I could've been a lot smarter. I worked hard, but I didn't work smart. I could've been smarter about what my swing was about. There weren't a whole lot of swing doctors around then.

On "the catch": Over the years, having seen what it became, I joke about it. Some people had a career, I had a catch. You could sum it all up with that, but if you get a little deeper than that, it says one thing—I worked at it. I made some mistakes, but I worked at it. Coming into the World Series, conventional wisdom was that I was a mediocre to bad outfielder. I was a good outfielder and I knew that. I let one get away early in that World Series and I was embarrassed by that. Fortunately, I got a chance to make up for it. I haven't seen the right-field sign at Citi Field, the silhouette behind right field. I went wow, that's pretty cool. I can't wait to get up there and take a look at it in person. Someone sent me a picture. It's pretty cool. There's no name tag, but that's OK, I know where it came from. I know a whole lot about it. That's hugely complimentary.

AL WEIS

*Al Weis was a utility infielder who played on the Mets'
1969 World Championship team. He remained with the
club until 1971.*

I got traded to the stumbling, fumbling Mets in 1968.
In '64, we [the Chicago White Sox] lost out to the Yankees by one game. I got hurt in '67 and didn't play the
last two or three months of the season. Going from a
pennant contender to a last-place club, you're thinking right away, there go my chances of ever, ever playing in the World Series.

In 1968, we finished ninth in the league and the
next year we won the whole ball of wax. It has to
rate up there among the great sports stories. The Mets
had never won anything before in their short history.
In the beginning of the year, the oddsmakers had us
at 100–1 to win the division or whatever and even
all the games we played in the World Series, we were
never favored. It was a big accomplishment that we
pulled it off.

I was born and raised in New York. Being able to play
for your hometown team was special. Some of the
memories, I got to play quite a bit that year because
Ken Boswell and Buddy Harrelson were younger and
had military commitments. I got to play when they were
on weekend duty or whatever. That was one of the
reasons they traded for me—they knew I had my military commitments fulfilled. When those guys went, I
was able to fill in for them. Playing in front of huge
crowds at Shea, you can't really put that into words.

Playing in the World Series, I never thought I'd play
in the World Series, much less doing as well as I did.
I tell everybody that I had an average career in the
major leagues as a utility player, but I had two good
weeks of baseball and they came in the '69 World

Series. Gil Hodges, during the '69 season, we pla-
tooned. I alternated with Boswell at second, Kranepool and Clendenon at first, Garrett and Ed Charles at
third. Gil stuck with that into the World Series and
I was very fortunate that I was playing against lefties and Baltimore had two lefties—I started four of
the five games in the World Series. That's the way it
worked out.

Gil let me hit in the World Series. I was only a lifetime .215 hitter and I came up in some critical times
in the World Series and he let me hit. He instilled a
world of confidence in me. It was a fun time.

We combined everything to put it all into one group.
We did have a great bunch of guys. We all got together
really well. We were a close-knit team. Everybody knew
their job as far as what they had to do on the field. I
don't think anyone got into trouble off the field. We
were a good team. I don't think we got enough recognition for being the good team we were. Once you get
into an attitude where you know you can win, it's
contagious. Pitchers pitch better, guys hit. That year,
we beat the Cubs, we wound up beating them by nine
games. While we were winning, Philly was beating the
Cubs, Pittsburgh was beating them. We played good
baseball, we won something like nineteen of twenty-
four at the end.

OPPOSITE: Ron
Swoboda rolls
across the outfield
grass after making
a diving grab of
Brooks Robinson's
sinking liner in game
four of the 1969
World Series.

Al Weis takes some
swings.

Met catcher Duffy
Dyer fires to first
base to complete
a double play
after forcing out
Philadelphia's Larry
Bowa at home.

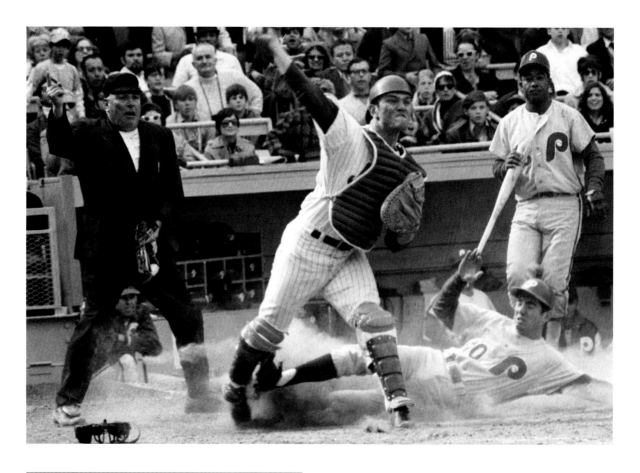

DUFFY DYER

Duffy Dyer was a backup catcher behind Jerry Grote in 1969, and hung around long enough to be a part of the 1973 team that reached the World Series.

In 1969, I was just a rookie, so I was in awe of being in the big leagues, seeing all the stadiums. First couple months, we weren't doing well. In August, we realized we had a chance and we became very confident. The most I remember about the season before we got to the playoffs, I was in awe of playing against the best players in all those stadiums. I love to study the game, so I loved to see those stadiums. But the biggest thrill was winning the World Series. Individual thrills—catching John Candelaria's no-hitter in Pitt was probably my biggest thrill. Some of the pinch hits. The teams in New York and in Pittsburgh.

I'll never forget—we had just traded for Rusty Staub and they were going to hold a press conference nine thirty to ten at Shea. I was in New York for the banquet circuit. Mets call at 8:00 A.M. I was asleep. "Duffy, we're

having a press conference, he's requested number 10," which was my number. "Would you mind giving it up?" I was groggy, said "OK." My wife asked who was it and said, "You can't do that! It's on your World Series ring." I called the Mets back and said, "Wait a minute." I kept it for another ten years. I almost screwed that up. Rusty just took number 4 and when I got traded, he took number 10.

Tears came to my eyes when the trade happened [in 1975 to Pittsburgh]. It was during the morning, during the winter, the Mets called and said, "We traded you to Pittsburgh," and said they'd call in an hour and that was all they said. I was stunned. I was on the Pirates, they were our rivals, I had been there six years, two World Series. It broke me up. Came up through the system. They had Manny Sanguillen, and I knew I wouldn't have much of a chance to play. But I loved my four years in Pittsburgh. It was a good time to be traded, because the Mets started getting rid of guys, they had just traded Tug. It was a good time to get traded, but I didn't want to.

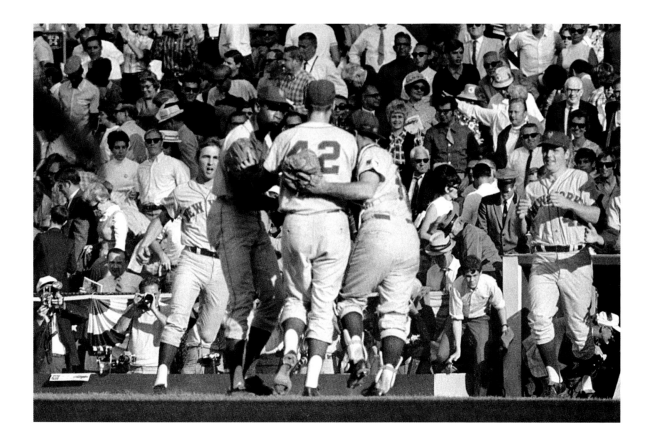

RON TAYLOR

Ron Taylor was a relief pitcher on the 1969 Mets, who later became a doctor and the Toronto Blue Jays' team physician.

When I was playing, went over to Vietnam on a USO tour with Tug after 1969 Series. We visited a lot of the hospitals and that got me interested in medicine. We had won the World Series that year and it was the same year of the Tet offensive, so there were a lot of casualties. When I finished my career in 1972, I was looking around for jobs in engineering and only jobs were sales engineering. Rather than do that, or get a PhD in engineering, I became a doctor.

I have a degree in electrical engineering. Undergraduate degree. I applied for medical school, they interviewed me, and told me they wanted to go back and take a makeup year of life science. If I got the same grades I had in engineering, they'd accept me. They said it'd be 50–50. I gambled on it and I had a very good academic [year]. I was able to reprogram myself and do it. I had been out of school eleven years, that's why they wanted

it. I wasn't in academics. Went back with a bunch of kids and competed [at the University of Toronto].

On the '69 Mets: In the playoffs I had a win and a save over Atlanta and we swept them. Against Baltimore I saved the Mets' first World Series win, game two in Baltimore. I really enjoyed the fans in New York. When we won the World Series, the ticker tape parade was overwhelming. To be out there in an open car, all the confetti coming down, the roar was amazing.

I pitched in almost 500 games. We were used differently than current closers. We were both the setup guy and the closer. Tug and I would alternate. Sometimes you pitched three days in a row. That would take its toll on you over eleven seasons. I was really lucky I got out when I did. Although I was old for medicine, I still had a chance.

When I walked in, they thought I was a repairman. It was a joke—how do you get into med school—straight A student or a washed-up ballplayer? I qualified on both counts.

1960s

TOM SEAVER

Tom Seaver was the leader of the pitching staff in 1969 and 1973, when the Mets made their first two World Series appearances.

What we did, was set a cornerstone for the franchise. It gave the franchise a, let's say, an adult reputation. It graduated. They had lived so long on the floundering Mets. By the time we got there, we didn't buy that. It wasn't fun to go out and lose, no question. Jerry Grote was the first one to say we could win and he said it in spring training. Gil would never say that, he'd never put that kind of pressure, put the relatively impossible dream in front of us. Jerry said it because he knew the pitching—Seaver, Koosman, Ryan, and Gentry. We had a whole stack of very good arms and he knew what it meant and it's exactly what happened.

I don't watch much baseball, but I read box scores. The little things count when you have good pitching—saving a base can win a ball game. Those things count because you win by one run and that's what our pitching gave the organization. And defense. It just made our pitching and defense. If the other team made a mistake, we would win. We didn't club people to death, we beat them 3–2, 2–1, with all the small-ball stuff.

[It was the] realization of a dream. Every boy that plays this game, Little League, in their town, high school, junior college, etc., you dream of the things that happened to other people. All of a sudden, you're there and you begin a journey. I was fortunate enough to play twenty years and have a World Series in the third year. It becomes far more than what you think. Your passion for what you're doing becomes far more than your relationship to the game. It evolves into an art form. That's what Gil was talking about. His demand for a level of professionalism and how to play

the game—twenty-seven outs, not twenty-three—he demanded that. The team really responded to him. We had a very good core group and we were all very focused and we loved it. It was a very hard-working group as well, as all teams usually are. Gil kept us between the ropes, headed in the right direction. There was no alternative to how he wanted you to play.

Favorite memories: It was probably the ride and the real belief that you can win. At that time, you go through a transition where it becomes an art form. It was probably just that period of time, yes, we can win, all the way through winning the division, then the pennant, and going to the World Series.

We go to Baltimore and I have a bad game, Buford hits the homer. I pitched relatively poorly. I think I came out in the fifth, sixth inning. I was in the runway, standing next to Donn Clendenon. The game was winding down and he said, "You know what? We're going to beat these guys." I was somewhat taken aback. It was just the two of us. We got our feet wet—we played poorly and we lost. They didn't run us off the field. Koosman's out there tomorrow. And then Gentry. You're in every game—the next day wasn't a soft spot for the opposition. And that's exactly the way it happened. He believed it. He wasn't just yakking. He really believed it. We had every right to say, they are the big, bad Orioles. Koosy was so overpowering, great World Series. It goes back to what Grote said in spring training—if you beat our number 1, now you have to beat 1A. We had all these number 1 pitchers.

The two great catches by Agee in the outfield, everyone was "oooh, aaah." We weren't surprised. They were great catches, but that level of play was expected. Swoboda's catch, Agee was backing him up. The runner wouldn't have gone to second.

NOLAN RYAN

Nolan Ryan is baseball's all-time strikeout leader, a Hall of Famer, and now a part owner of the Texas Rangers. He was a member of the 1969 Mets' pitching staff.

I have some fond memories. Any time you win a championship with a group of guys, you have a special relationship with those guys the rest of your life. The World Series, obviously. But I think it goes back to when we started making our move on the Cubs and just being involved in that momentum that was going and the realization that we, in our minds, were going to win.

We thought we were a better ball club in spring training, but in reality, I don't think we thought we'd win the division. As the season went on, the team started believing, though.

When I look back at it, it was my one shot at a World Series team. At that point, when it happened, probably a lot of us, if not all of us, thought that we'd be in that position again. I think it was our inexperience to not realize how hard and unique it is to get in that position. Now, there's such an appreciation.

I think it meant a lot to Met fans. It brought respectability to the organization and to a level that I don't think fans thought it was going to at that time. Up until then, they were viewed on a basis of the initial expansion team and the frustration. The organization had gone in a different direction from what they originally did—they had filled that club with veteran players who were trying to get one or two more years in on their career. They started on a youth movement and trying to built around young pitching.

On the trade that sent him to the Angels for third baseman Jim Fregosi: You know, in all trades, you

never know how they are going to play out. What you hope for is that they benefit both organizations. I understand what the Mets were trying to accomplish and what the Angels were, too. Hoping they'd get some young talent that would help.

There were two things that made a difference in my career—I went to the Angels and I had been in an army unit and went back to Houston every other weekend. The year they traded me, my obligation was over. I didn't have to do the military anymore and I could stay in the rotation. Then I went to a club that was rebuilding, trying to develop pitchers, and they knew they had to give me innings and they did. The fact that I had control issues anyway early in my career, pitching on a regular basis was probably something I needed and wasn't able to get during my time with the Mets.

JERRY KOOSMAN

*Koosman was the Mets' number two starter, and an ace
in his won right, behind Seaver. He lasted with the Mets
until 1978.*

[H]e and Nolan Ryan] are friends, but we don't keep
in touch on a regular basis. Once in a while,
I get an e-mail from him. I think about when he first
came up, all the talent he had, the great fastball, the
curveball. But he struggled throwing strikes. Everybody was aware of it, including himself. I remembered games where Gil brought him in and God, he
embarrassed the other club he was so overpowering.
When he was throwing strikes, he was untouchable.

Same thing with Seaver, we see each other in New
York. Once in a while, an e-mail. I send Nancy [Seav-
er's wife] an e-mail.

It's no doubt the highlight of my baseball life. Winning the World Series changes your life. I couldn't
begin to count up the interview requests and the
questions there's been about that year. It always stays
somewhat current in your mind because of all the conversation about it. There are things you forget, but
team things that happened, people will remember
certain instances on the field. It's always fun to hear
someone else's perspective on something.

It brings you more into the public view. You're name
is mentioned more, highlights are shown, and things
build on that. People just interested in knowing what
it was like to go through something like that. It brings
notoriety.

It's something that's so hard to achieve, winning a
World Series. Being on a team that gets there and then
have a team makeup, the chemistry molded into a
smooth-run machine, it's just an experience you never
forget. There's a closeness that comes from that, you're

kind of like brothers to every one of your teammates. You experience things together that you'd never experience. The excitement brought to the team, the fans by winning World Series, you have a much different relationship with people, something in common. The fans relate, I was there for game five, game one, or whatever. It's a great conversation piece.

On his favorite memory: Cleon Jones catching that last ball, knowing it's over and we win. There's a lot of memories, a tremendous amount. The feelings of what it was like before the game started, going through the game, the finish of it. The whole works, you're in ecstasy. For immediately after it's done, it takes some time for it to sink in.

A team has to stay healthy, you've got to have the talent, the chemistry, and you have to have the coaches and managers to bring it out. The players have to be willing to work, to be in your best physical condition. You can't have problems at home and have success on the field. The wives played a big part. There are just

so many people involved—the minor league system that helps produce players. The PR, the scouting. It takes a lot of human ingenuity to make it happen. It isn't just the twenty-five to thirty people on the field. There's a big cast of people.

On Hodges: Gil is the reason. He is the reason. First of all, he was a brilliant baseball person. His ability in managing players was, God, you can't say enough about it. Put that together with his baseball smarts and how he would stay ahead of the opposing manger. He put together a great group and kept it running.

I hear so many people saying his name. You think of '69, the first person that comes to mind is Gil Hodges. How many managers brought an expansion team that was only seven years old and developed it into a World Series winner that fast?

I imagine some of his energy was still on the team before he even got to be the manager. His energy is still there in New York, people talking about him. It'd be a joy for me to see him going in the Hall of Fame and hopefully it'll happen.

ABOVE: New York City mayor John Lindsay presents Mets manager Gil Hodges with a street sign at City Hall. A section of Brooklyn's Bedford Avenue, where Hodges lived, was renamed for the day.

BELOW: Met players and fans celebrate New York's victory over Baltimore in the 1969 World Series.

ABOVE: The field at Shea Stadium is covered by delirious Mets fans celebrating their team's victory in the 1969 World Series.

BELOW: Mets fans dancing in the streets following the Amazins' triumph in the 1969 World Series.

1970s

DAILY NEWS

NEW YORK'S PICTURE NEWSPAPER®

New York, N.Y. 10017, Wednesday, July 23, 1975

FINAL ★★★★

LARGEST CIRCULATION OF ANY PAPER IN AMERICA

100

KOOSMAN 6-HITS REDS, 3-1

YANKEES SLUG CHISOX, 11-6

Stories on Page

JERRY KOOSMAN'S STEAL WAS FIRST OF HIS CAREER-HE IS NOW 117 BEHIN LOU BROCK'S SEASON RECORD!..

NEWS photos by Gene

One of the comics o
ing the scorebo
Shea flashes th
news that Jerry
man is only 117
behind Lou Brock
son record. Jerry
off third with a l
second, and conti
third as Reds
Bill Plummer th
Jerry then so

As the 1970s dawned, the Mets were no longer cuddly bumblers, no longer the cute team prone to slapstick and hilarity and the comic relief to the buttoned-up Yankees from across town. The Mets were the defending World Champions, whether it was a miracle or not. Their yearbook cover, long a cartoonish snapshot of pipe dreams of a rosier future, had as its background in 1970 something real—a photo of the team celebrating its first division title.

Since that season's Mets were the second-youngest team in the National League and there were all those blossoming pitchers with rocket-infused arms, some believed that kind of scene could be repeated several times during the decade.

But fewer than two months after winning the title, at baseball's winter meetings in Florida, Gil Hodges craftily tempered expectations, saying he believed the Cubs would be the favorites in 1970. But the manager also made it clear that he believed the Mets could win again too, saying in the December 4, 1969, edition of the *Daily News*, "Nobody believed it when we did it once and I guess nobody will believe it when we do it again."

That was the same day the Mets completed a trade they believed would make them stronger, sending twenty-two-year-old outfielder Amos Otis, who had appeared in forty-eight games in 1969, pitcher Bob Johnson, and shortstop Teddy Martinez to the Royals for third baseman Joe Foy. Foy, a New Yorker, was supposed to be a long-term answer at third, replacing Wayne Garrett and Ed Charles, who had mostly played the hot corner during the championship season.

Foy, then twenty-seven years old, had been a starter for four seasons—three in Boston, including

on the Red Sox' 1967 American League championship club. But Boston lost him to Kansas City in the 1968 expansion draft. In 1969, Foy stole thirty-seven bases and knocked in seventy-one runs for the Royals. The '69 Mets had sixty-six steals as a team.

The trade, however, was a disaster, one that stuck in the craws of Met fans for years and may have contributed to another terrible trade, in 1971, as they tried to solve third base once again.

Only a year earlier, Otis had been considered untouchable because he was center-field insurance in case Tommie Agee followed his dreadful 1968 season with another poor one in '69. Once Agee flourished in '69, though, Otis became expendable, a chip to be used to improve the team.

Of course, Otis became a star in Kansas City, helping the Royals become one of the American League's best teams throughout the 1970s, and Foy flopped in Flushing. Foy played in only ninety-nine games for the Mets and batted just .236 with six home runs, thirty-seven RBI, and twenty-two stolen bases. The Washington Senators took him in the Rule 5 draft after the season and released him the next July and he never played in the majors again.

Over seventeen seasons, Otis was a five-time All-

OPPOSITE: Mets players celebrate winning the 1969 World Series.

ABOVE, LEFT: New Met third baseman Joe Foy, acquired in a trade from Kansas City, gets help from club general manager Johnny Murphy as he tries on his new uniform.

ABOVE, RIGHT: Met general manager Bob Scheffing watches the defending World Champs battle the Cubs for the runner-up spot in the NL East as the 1970 season draws to a close.

1970s

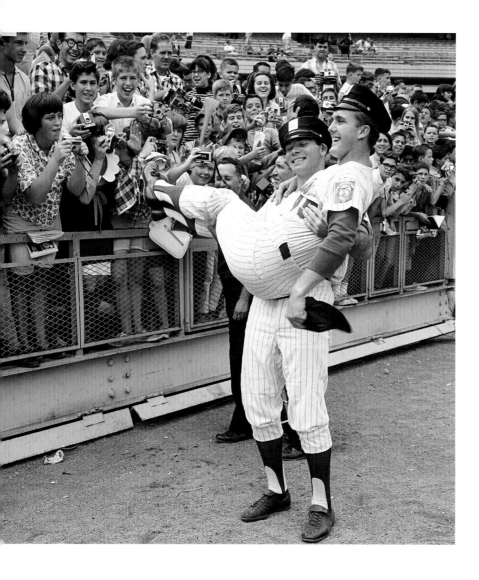

Ron Swoboda, in policeman's cap, carries Tug McGraw past eager fans on Camera Day 1965.

Star, a three-time Gold Glove winner, and finished in the top ten in American League MVP voting three times. He led the American League in doubles in his first season as a starter—1970—and won a stolen-base crown with fifty-two in 1971.

All that was in the future as 1970 began and the Mets mostly believed their future was now. They were jolted on January 14 when Johnny Murphy, their general manager since the end of 1967, died of a heart attack. Murphy helped shepherd much of the Mets' superb pitching stock through their system. He was replaced by Bob Scheffing five days after his death.

Meanwhile, the baseball world was beginning to accept the Mets as something beyond lucky. The cover of *Sports Illustrated*'s April 13, 1970, baseball preview issue read, "The Mets against the World" and showed a Walter Iooss Jr. photo of Jerry Koosman in a

circle in the middle, surrounded by the caps of baseball's other twenty-three teams.

The story inside read in part: "The Mets can run, field and bunt, and when these factors are combined with a very deep and strong pitching staff their chances of repeating must be considered good, even if not overwhelming."

It also added, "The Mets sneaked up on a lot of people who weren't looking; now they will be in the spotlight. Still, the pressure should be bearable. Most Met fans, thankful for last season, will forgive their team almost anything this time around, which could be a big psychological advantage for a team whose pitching should prevent any prolonged losing streaks."

As a team, the Mets were reveling in the closeness they had developed the previous season, something even years later players such as Tom Seaver and Koosman pointed to as part of their success.

In a dispatch from the team's spring training camp in St. Petersburg, Florida, on February 24, 1970, the *Daily News*'s Dick Young wrote, "The World Champion Mets have no Bolsheviks. They conform. More than that, they seem to enjoy it. There is a re-generation gap in the camp. The older guys work hard. The younger guys look up to the older guys. The young guys work hard. It's all very unusual these days, also very healthy."

Pitcher Gary Gentry told Young, "I'll tell you what I think it is. You go into some camps and see the older guys jake it. You see that and you do the same thing. Here, it's different.

"The older guys go out of their way to help you. Funny, they know you're after their job and still they help you. Then they turn around and try to outdo you. I don't mean just some of them; all of them. It makes the young players go harder, to try to outdo them."

There were blips of unhappiness, though, like in every camp in every pro sport. Outfielder Ron Swoboda, the man who made one of the most famous catches in World Series history in game four the previous October, signed for $42,000—$8,000 more than he had made in 1969, but $8,000 less than he had wanted from the Mets.

Swoboda was quoted in a Young story saying, "I'm sick. I'm bitter. I'm ashamed to look at my wife!" But he also added, "I'm a big enough person to go out there and give it everything I got. I told Scheffing that, too. I told him I'm not the kind to lay down. I'm ashamed and I'm bitter, but I won't let it hurt my play."

Swoboda said he agreed to the contract so as not to disrupt the team's "great feeling of togetherness."

Still, it was quickly clear this wasn't 1969, the year most everything went the Mets' way. Opening Day on April 7 provided, perhaps, an odd omen—the Mets won in Pittsburgh, beating the Pirates, 5–3, in eleven innings. It was the first time the Mets had won a season opener in their brief history.

Except for some sparkling individual performances, the Mets were just so-so early in the season. On April 18, making his first start of the season, Nolan Ryan threw a one-hitter to beat Jim Bunning and the Phillies, 7–0, at Shea. It was the first time Ryan had been on a mound since April 2, and only Denny Doyle, Philadelphia's rookie second baseman, got a hit off him, leading off the game by whacking an 0-2 pitch into left field for a single.

Ryan also established a then-Met record with fifteen strikeouts, besting by one the mark he and Seaver had shared. Ryan threw 154 pitches in the game, a number that would cause a firestorm if a twenty-three-year-old pitcher chucked that many today.

"When you consider how little work I've had and how long I've gone since pitching, I'm awfully proud of this shutout," Ryan was quoted saying in the next day's *Daily News*. Dana Mozley, who penned the article, also wrote, "The Mets should give a vote of thanks to Lou Napoli, a former featherweight boxer who now serves as press room steward at Shea and

at the Stadium for Ryan's laborious effort. Nolan had a case history of being able to pitch only six-seven innings before blisters would bloom on his fingers. Lou suggested applying olive brine and Ryan can now go nine."

Ryan walked six Phillies in the first four innings but said, "I found my rhythm about the fifth inning and everything fit into place after that. I've never thrown so many changeups and with such great success. They were particularly good against the lefthanders. And my curveball was working well, too."

Said Gil Hodges, "Rube [Walker, the pitching coach] studied him closely from the sixth inning on. The later it got, the better a pitcher Nolan was getting to be. He didn't have to rely only on his fastball . . . There was never any serious thought of taking him out."

As great as Ryan was that day, Seaver outdid him—and nearly everyone else in baseball history—just four days later, against the Padres at Shea. On the same day Seaver was presented with his 1969 Cy

Young Award plaque, April 22, he tied Steve Carlton's major league record of nineteen strikeouts in a nine-inning game and also established a mark for most consecutive strikeouts by fanning the final ten batters of the game in a 2–1 victory.

Al Ferrara, the man whom Seaver whiffed in the top of the sixth to start the streak, struck out for the final out of the game. Earlier, Ferrara's solo homer had accounted for San Diego's only run.

Seaver's dominance that day was compared to his near-perfect game against the Cubs on July 9, 1969, which he lost with one out in the ninth on Jimmy Qualls's famous single. "This wasn't quite as exciting," Seaver said of his nineteen-strikeout game in the next day's *Daily News*. "It was very exciting, but not quite as exciting as that one."

Seaver did not know how many strikeouts he was piling up until the Shea message board flashed that he had tied Ryan's team mark of fifteen. "It came as a shock," Seaver said.

"He was like a machine out there, whomp, whomp, whomp," teammate Ed Kranepool said.

Less than a month later, on May 13, Gary Gentry threw a one-hitter. As Dick Young wrote in the next day's *Daily News*, "With the flame of his fastball heating the refrigerator called Wrigley Field, Gary Gentry today came within four outs of a no-hitter."

Future Hall of Famer Ernie Banks spoiled it with a single to left that perhaps should have been caught by Dave Marshall. "It banged against the tip of my glove," Marshall was quoted saying. "I should have had the damn thing."

Still, the victory brought the Mets to within 1 1/2 games of first. After a travel day to Philadelphia, they moved to within half a game of first when Seaver threw a one-hitter in a 4–0 victory over the Phillies. Philadelphia's only hit was a third-inning single by catcher Mike Compton.

On May 19, the Mets were tied for first and held or shared the top spot from June 24 to July 10, too. The Mets were 3 1/2 games behind the Cubs when they arrived in Chicago for a five-game series in late June but left town up 1 1/2 games after a five-game sweep. The *Daily News*'s Bill Gallo drew a cartoon depicting the sweep as Chicago's greatest disaster since Mrs. O'Leary's cow started the Great Chicago Fire.

The Mets were in such a lofty spot in part because of their pitching and Gil Hodges's right-left platoon

A fan expressing his feelings toward Tom Seaver.

system, which saw Ron Swoboda and Dave Marshall sharing right field, Donn Clendenon and Art Shamsky first base, Al Weis and Ken Boswell second, and Joe Foy ceding time to Wayne Garrett at third.

"I platoon because we don't have the power other clubs have," Hodges said in a July 8 story by the *Daily News*'s Joe Trimble.

Beginning on July 10, the Mets started a five-game losing streak that took them out of first. They contended the rest of the season and even were tied for first as late as September 14. But they played poorly the last fifteen games of the season. As Phil Pepe put it in the *Daily News* when he wrote about the Mets' late acquisition of pitcher Dean Chance, "The Mets found themselves with two chances to win in the NL East—slim and Dean."

Chance, the 1964 Cy Young Award winner, saved one game and lost another, but the Mets stumbled down the stretch, going 5-10. With nine games left and pennant hopes dim, Hodges was quoted saying, "We've won nine in a row before." That, as Phil Pepe

pointed out in the September 22 edition of the *News*, was 1969. "But this isn't last year," Pepe wrote. "Not by a long shot it isn't."

Added Koosman, "I don't think things are clicking like last year."

From September 19 to 21, they lost two of three to Pittsburgh at Shea. Even the great Seaver was booed when he gave up five runs in 5 1/3 innings in the second game of a Sunday doubleheader. "Nobody likes to hear it," Seaver was quoted saying in the September 23 *Daily News*. "I guess they don't want to know about what has happened before. Only what is happening now."

Then the Pirates swept them in Pittsburgh from September 25 to 27, clinching the National League East in the final game of that series, a 2–1 victory in which Cleon Jones perhaps should have scored from second on a first-inning hit by Donn Clendenon, especially since it appeared that third-base coach Eddie Yost was waving him home.

Jones told reporters, "Ask the coach" when they

1970s

Tommie Agee shows off his 1970 Gold Glove trophy.

wondered why he didn't score. Yost answered, "Did he say that?" When Yost's reaction was carried back to Jones, Jones said, "If that's the case, somebody has to take the blame and it might as well be me, I guess. I could have scored."

It was that kind of season. On the final day, Ferguson Jenkins beat the Mets, 4–1, dropping them into third place, six games back at 83-79. The game drew 48,314—the previous day's game had drawn only 6,895—and the Mets set a club record for attendance at 2,697,479, which would stand until better days in 1985.

Tommie Agee won a Gold Glove and led the team in runs (107), homers (24), hits (182), total bases (298), and steals (31); Clendenon led in RBI with 97; Cleon Jones set a club record with a 23-game hitting streak. Seaver was 18-12 and led the National League with a 2.82 ERA and 283 strikeouts, the first of his five strikeout crowns.

The 1971 Mets finished with the same record as the previous year's team—83-79—and in the same place in the NL East—third—but there was no pennant race and not much to feel good about unless you count Seaver's spectacular season. The Met ace went 20-10 with a career-best 1.76 ERA and 289 strikeouts, winning his second ERA and strikeout crowns.

But Jerry Koosman spent time on the disabled list with a back injury and was only 6-11. The Mets were ten games out by July 11 and finished tied with the Cubs, fourteen games behind the Pirates, who went on to win the World Series.

For the Mets, the most significant event of the whole calendar year came after the season. On December 10, the Mets put Nolan Ryan in a trade package for California Angels' shortstop Jim Fregosi, who they envisioned moving to third base and becoming the man to solve the franchise's perennial aches at the hot corner. Fregosi became the forty-sixth third baseman in Met history. No wonder the *Daily News*'s Joe Trimble called it "that troubled spot" in his account of the Ryan trade in the December 11 edition.

After a disappointing 1971, the Mets had been under media and fan pressure to make a trade. Ultimately, this wasn't the right one.

Since Don Zimmer had been the first Met third baseman in 1962, the Mets never could find anyone to excel there. Joe Foy had fizzled in 1970. In 1971, Wayne Garrett, Tim Foli, and Bob Aspromonte played the position without distinction. Fregosi, Scheffing reasoned, was the answer, and he could help with the club's offense, too. More pop could mean a pennant.

During the World Series in 1971, Scheffing told reporters that the Mets' first need was a "big hitter." Scheffing tried during that winter to pry Orlando Cepeda from the Braves, Nate Colbert from the Padres, and Ron Santo from the Cubs, but those clubs asked for too much, Scheffing said.

So on the final day of interleague trading, he sent

1970s

Ryan, outfielder Leroy Stanton, righty Don Rose, and catcher Francisco Estrada west. Asked afterward if Fregosi was the "big hitter" he was looking for, Scheffing said, "Well, he was as close as I could get," according to Trimble's report. Foreshadowing for Fregosi's Met tenure, perhaps?

Lynn Nolan Ryan was a lanky eighteen-year-old from Alvin, Texas, when the Mets took him in the twelfth round of the 1965 draft on the recommendation of scout Red Murff. Little more than a year later, Ryan made his major league debut.

Ryan was a remarkable pitching package even then, with a blazing fastball and a dazzling curveball. "I think about when he first came up, all the talent he had," Jerry Koosman recalled in a 2009 interview. "But he struggled throwing strikes. Everybody was aware of it, including himself. I remember games where Gil brought him in and, God, he embarrassed the other club he was so overpowering.

"When he was throwing strikes, he was untouchable."

On the outside, Ryan was a "tough, hard-nosed Texan, all that stuff," Seaver said in a 2009 interview. But, the ace added, "Nolan has a very infectious smile and laugh. We were very good friends when we were young."

The Mets seemingly grew tired of Ryan's wildness, though. In 1971, he had been 8-4 on June 30, but dropped ten of his final twelve decisions. He set a Met record by walking nine Cardinals in five innings and 116 in 152 innings during the season. But he also showed flashes of such brilliance, including another sixteen-strikeout game on May 29, the most by a National League pitcher in 1971.

The trade to the Angels changed Ryan's career in two ways. As Seaver put it, Ryan knew "the ball was going to be in his shoe every fifth day, we don't care if you're 0-30," meaning, of course, that Ryan was going to be in the rotation whether he pitched well or not. "That's what he needed," Seaver said in a 2009 interview.

Ryan also had been fulfilling his military obligation while with the Mets, meaning that he had to travel back to Houston every other weekend to train with his unit. With that bi-weekly interruption coupled with his wildness, it was difficult for Ryan to pitch his way into a set role with the Mets. "The year they traded me, my obligation was over," Ryan said in a 2009 interview. "I didn't have to do that anymore and I could stay in the [Angels'] rotation.

"I went to a club that was rebuilding, trying to develop pitchers, and they knew they had to give me innings and they did. The fact that I had control issues anyway early in my career, pitching on a regular basis was probably something I needed and wasn't able to get during my time with the Mets."

As a fixture in the Angels' rotation, Ryan soared. He found control—some, anyway—and became a strikeout machine. In his first three seasons in California, pitching for a poor team, Ryan won 19, 21, and 22 games and struck out 329 or more batters each season, including a record 383 in 1973. He went on to throw seven no-hitters, win 324 games, and become the all-time strikeout leader.

To this day, the Flushing faithful cringe at what might have been. Ryan will always be the Pitcher Who Got Away. This was worse than Amos Otis for Joe Foy. Much worse. Imagine what the 1970s Met rotation would have been like with a developed Ryan, Seaver, Koosman, and Jon Matlack.

"He had," Seaver said in a 2009 interview, "as good stuff as anyone who ever walked to the mound."

Ryan knows his spot in Met history, though. "Probably best known for the Jim Fregosi trade," he said. "You know, in all trades, you never know how they are going to play out. What you hope for is that they benefit both organizations. I understand what the Mets were trying to accomplish and what the Angels were, too—hoping they'd get some young talent that would help."

1970s

Nolan Ryan works out at Shea Stadium prior to the start of the 1969 World Series.

Unfortunately for the Mets, 1972 was the second straight year that an off-the-field event overshadowed the season. During spring training, Gil Hodges said the team "may be the best I've ever brought out of Florida." But he didn't live to find out if that statement was true.

Hodges died of a heart attack on April 2, two days shy of his forty-eighth birthday, after playing golf with his coaches in West Palm Beach, Florida, on a spring training off-day. The team was stunned—their strong, stoic leader, the calm, compassionate man who guided them out of a history of pratfalls and baseball comedy to a world championship, was gone.

"He looked so good," Joe Pignatano, one of Hodges's coaches, told the *Daily News*'s Phil Pepe. "He was feeling so good. One minute he was having so much fun and then the next minute he was gone. Our loss is God's gain." On the charter plane back to New York that carried Hodges's body, coaches' eyes were red and puffy with grief, Pepe wrote.

"The trip home from Florida, in most years, is a joyful one. But this trip was quite something else. This is the time of year when baseball teams and baseball players are charged up with the excitement of a new season. This is the time of year when an airplane trip from Florida to New York signals a beginning. This trip was different. It was not a beginning, it was an end."

The Mets wore black armbands during the 1972 season. On June 9, 1973, Hodges's jersey number 14 was retired by the team.

Even now, Mets who played for Hodges feel his impact, and they firmly believe that Hodges—the manager, the player, the man—belongs in the National Baseball Hall of Fame in Cooperstown, New York. "He was so important to everyone," Seaver said in 2009. "He has been a part of our lives, whether he's dead or alive."

Jerry Koosman, in a 2009 interview, called Hodges "the reason, Gil is the reason" for 1969's success. "First of all, he was a brilliant baseball person. His ability in managing players, God, you can't say enough about it. Put that together with his baseball smarts, how he would stay ahead of the opposing manager. He put together a great group and then kept it running. I hear so many people saying his name. You think of '69, the first person who comes to mind is Gil Hodges.

1970s

DAILY NEWS
NEW YORK'S PICTURE NEWSPAPER ®

10¢

Vol. 53. No. 242

New York, N.Y. 10017, Monday, April 3, 1972*

WEATHER: Sunny, breezy and cool.

GIL HODGES DIES OF HEART ATTACK

Mets' Boss Stricken After Round Of Golf

Mets' manager Gil Hodges, who died yesterday of a heart attack in West Palm Beach, Fla., after a round of golf, was hugged by original Mets' skipper Casey Stengel after the Cinderella Team won World Series in 1969. Hodges, who starred with the old Brooklyn Dodgers, would have been 48 tomorrow. Gil had suffered a mild heart attack during a Mets' game in Atlanta on Sept. 24, 1968. He returned the following year to lead the Mets to championship.

Stories on pages 3 and 67; other pictures on back page

Daily News front page announcing the tragic death of Mets manager Gil Hodges.

"His energy is still there in New York, people talking about him. It'd be a joy for me to see him get in the Hall of Fame and hopefully it'll happen."

While the Mets coped with their grief, management had the task, too, of picking Hodges's successor. The day after Hodges died, team brass met at M. Donald Grant's place in Hobe Sound, Florida, about forty miles from where Hodges had died. Afterward, Grant said, "It will be somebody within our organization. You do your organization some good when you promote from within," according to Dick Young's story in the *Daily News* on April 5.

"If they name one of the coaches," Bud Harrelson added, "then Gil Hodges will be managing the Mets in 1972. That would be good. I know I don't want an outsider and I don't think the rest of the guys do."

Young wrote that seven names were under consideration at the Hobe Sound meeting—Yogi Berra, the first-base coach; pitching coach Rube Walker; bullpen coach Joe Pignatano; third-base coach Eddie Yost; GM Bob Scheffing; Hank Bauer, the former Yankee outfielder and Orioles' manager who was piloting the Mets' top farm club; and Whitey Herzog, the team's director of player personnel.

Herzog, who had been the Mets' third-base coach under Wes Westrum in 1966 before moving into the front office, was generally considered a brilliant evaluator of talent. Hodges had admired him, and when Herzog was inducted into the Baseball Hall of Fame, he told a story about how he went to congratulate Hodges on winning the 1969 World Series, Hodges leaped out of his chair and said, "I want to congratulate *you*. For three years now, every time I called you about what I need, you have sent me the right player."

Herzog called it "One of the greatest compliments I ever got in my life . . . Believe me, that went right to my heart."

Herzog sensed he had little shot at the Mets' managing job, though, in part because the organization didn't

even want him to attend Hodges's funeral. "They would not let me leave instructional league," Herzog recalled. "I was hurt because Gil and I were tight."

Herzog was also known for plain speaking. Red Foley, writing in the *News*, called him "capable and knowledgeable," but also "a rebel. He tells it like it is and will argue his blunt opinions against those of his employers if the occasion demands. Herzog will never be indicted as a 'yes' man; diplomacy is not his bag."

Needless to say, Herzog did not get the gig. But that decision turned into more Mets' "What Might Have Been?" Herzog left the organization to manage the Texas Rangers in 1973, and though he did not last the year there, he briefly managed Ryan's Angels in 1974, and in 1975 started a successful five-year run managing the emerging Royals. In 1980, he took over the Cardinals and managed them into 1990, winning three NL pennants and the 1982 World Series.

Herzog and the Mets tangled repeatedly in the mid-1980s, with St. Louis playing "Whitey Ball," a smothering mix of speed, pitching, and defense, and the Mets countering with Dwight Gooden, Keith Hernandez, Darryl Strawberry, and their cast of colorful teammates.

Had Hodges been choosing, he might have picked

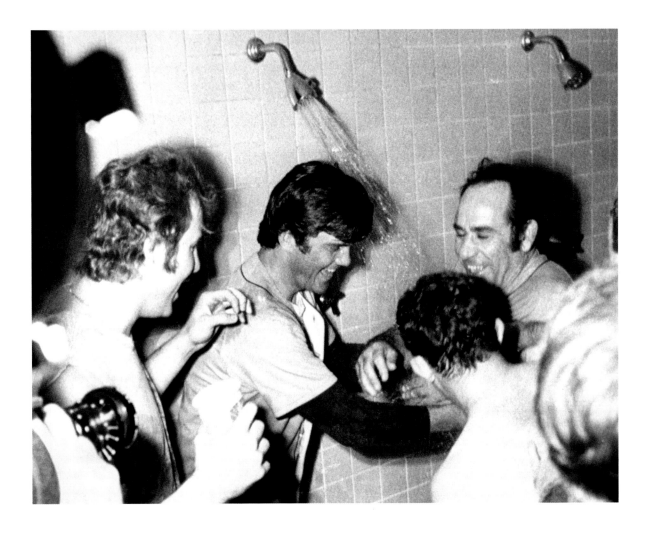

Walker. The men were teammates with the Brooklyn Dodgers, and Walker was Hodges's confidant and pitching coach in both Washington and New York. Berra, however, appeared to be the early favorite, and only he, Scheffing, and Bauer, had ever managed in the majors.

"I think the guys would accept Yogi or any of the other coaches," Harrelson told Young. "They wouldn't try to crap on him like they might do with some outsider. I think if it's Yogi, that whole four coaches will really be running the club and that means number 14 [Hodges] will be the manager, because they would do things as if he was still there."

An all-time great catcher for the Yankees, Berra also reached the 1964 World Series in his first year as a manager. But he was caught in a Bronx Zoo– like maelstrom long before George Steinbrenner even bought that team, and was fired after losing the Series to the Cardinals in seven games. He was

replaced by Johnny Keane, the man who led the Cards to the championship.

According to the *News*'s Joe Trimble, the Yankees were a team in which "the Night Riders got out of control and the Day People resented it." The team was split between carousers and serious players, and on August 19, 1964, Berra became, as the *News*'s Wes Gaffer put it, "baseball's best known music critic."

Phil Linz, one of the serious ones, made the mistake of playing a harmonica on the team bus to the airport after the Yanks had lost their fourth consecutive game. No music would soothe Berra's savage breast that night—the manager told Linz to "shove it" when Linz got to the end of "Mary Had a Little Lamb." When Linz added a final blast on the instrument, Berra slapped it out of his hand. That one incident probably didn't seal Berra's fate; the tumultuous atmosphere around the team did.

Still, the Mets believed he was the right man for the

job. So later in the day after Hodges's April 6 funeral, Grant and Scheffing announced that Berra was the new manager. All the other coaches remained. The same day, the Mets announced they had traded for Montreal slugger Rusty Staub, dealing away outfielder Ken Singleton, shortstop Tim Foli, and outfielder/first baseman Mike Jorgenson, considered by many among their best young players.

It's hard to say who ultimately got the better of the deal—all three players the Expos acquired had long, productive careers. But Scheffing may have finally found his "big hitter." Staub played in only sixty-six games for the Mets in 1972 because he suffered a broken hand when hit by a pitch thrown by future Met George Stone on June 3, but he proved to be a reliable run producer over the following three years, as well as one of the most charismatic Mets.

There were other changes to the '72 Mets, too. Fregosi was the new third baseman. Promising rookie pitcher Jon Matlack joined the rotation for good. Matlack still counts among his favorite memories the day in spring training at Miller Huggins Field in St.

Petersburg when he counted the lockers that still had uniforms inside, calculating whether he had made the twenty-five-man roster.

"I finished counting and gave a little fist pump and Gil Hodges had walked through the door and caught me," Matlack recalled in a 2008 interview. "He said, 'That's right, kid, you made it' and went on to his office. He died a few days later."

Matlack finished the season 15-10 with a 2.32 ERA and became the second Met—Seaver was the other one—to win the Rookie of the Year award.

Slugging first baseman John Milner, nicknamed "Little Hammer" because of his resemblance to Hank Aaron came up, too, and led the club with seventeen home runs.

The Mets also brought back a New York icon, acquiring forty-one-year-old Willie Mays from the San Francisco Giants for pitcher Charlie Williams and $50,000 on May 11. Mays had starred for the New York Giants before they went west, the image of him flying around the bases, his cap falling off, burned into fans' sweet memories.

Rusty Staub's three-run blast in the second inning of game three of the 1973 National League playoffs at Shea Stadium gave the Mets a 6–0 lead over the Cincinnati Reds. The Mets went on to a 9-2 win and a two games to one lead in the series.

1970s

Former Giants great Willie Mays models his new uniform as he prepares to face his old team at Shea Stadium in 1972.

When the season finally started on April 15 after a two-week delay because of a player strike, the Mets took the field wearing the black armbands on a cold, wet day. Before facing Pittsburgh at Shea, the Mets honored Hodges in a pregame memorial, including a marine playing "Taps" at home plate.

Then the Mets got off to the fastest start in club history, including a 4–0 whitewash of the Pirates, the defending division champs, on Opening Day on a combined five-hitter by Tom Seaver and Tug McGraw at Shea.

Mays's return was met by much fanfare, some of it from the "Say Hey Kid" himself. The day of the deal, Mays said it was "coming back to Paradise." Dick Young said "the wonderful thing the Mets have done is to give their fans Willie Mays in a Met uniform for however short a time, for whatever contribution he may make. Having Willie Mays to root for is something special, something that a whole generation of young fans in New York had not experienced."

Young also called the Mays acquisition a "Mother's Day present" to Joan Payson from Donald Grant.

Trimble, writing in the May 16 edition of the *Daily News*, said, "Willie's return to a New York uniform is a happening of sheer joy." Trimble wrote about a recording one heard if one called St. Patrick's Monastery on 135 West 31st Street.

A friar announced the church's address and then added: "This is the good word for today. Willie has returned and all New York rejoices. . . . New York fans never really did let Willie go . . . his return brings out the feeling that there is heart in professional sport. . . . The Mets should be proud at bringing Willie back home. Again they have shown the feeling and close personal regard that they have always shown for their players and fans." The friar went on, Trimble wrote, ending after about three minutes.

On his first day as a Met, Mays also offered some foreshadowing of the difficulties he and Berra would have in figuring out how to best use the aging star. "If used in the right way, I know I can do a good job for the Mets," Mays said. "Yogi and I will get together and I know I can help this club. You know the Mets are a very good ball club and they're not going to have me playing just because I'm Willie Mays."

1970s

Mays did not play the first game he was in a Met uniform, though 44,271 at Shea chanted "We Want Willie." And it was unclear what Mays could offer as a player. He'd never be the same superstar he was in his first tenure in New York—forty-one is old for a player in today's game, so imagine 1972.

But he showed that he still had plenty of flair for big plays. In his first game as a Mets, on Sunday, May 14, he homered in the fifth inning to snap a 4–4 tie in a game the Mets won, 5–4, over Mays's old team, the Giants.

The Mets, meanwhile, were soaring. They opened play on May 19 at 21-7, the best record in baseball. They held a 5 1/2-game lead over the Phillies and were ahead of Pittsburgh by six games.

"It is early yet," Berra said at the time. "But it sure feels good."

They had an eleven-game winning streak from May 12 to 21, matching a club record, and were 30-11 on June 1, and five games up.

But on June 3, with the Mets at 31-12, disaster struck, though they really didn't know it at the time. Staub hurt his hand, but no one realized for about a month how serious the injury was. He had broken the hammate bone, but the fracture eluded X-ray after X-ray until it was finally discovered and he had surgery in late July. He did not return until September 18.

Injuries became a theme for the Mets, and they lost Harrelson, Grote, and Cleon Jones for stretches during the season, too, and began to fade.

July 1 was the last day they held at least a share of the top spot in the NL East and they finished at 83-73, 13 1/2 games behind the Pirates. It was the Mets' third consecutive third-place finish.

As with any Met season, there were some individual achievements of note—and some nonachievements. The 1972 Mets are the only team in history to play a full season and not have a player collect 100 hits. Tommy Agee led with 96. Fregosi, injured and

ineffective, was a tremendous disappointment, hitting .232 with 5 homers and 32 RBI in 101 games.

Seaver threw the fourth one-hitter of his career in the opener of a July 4 doubleheader against the Padres, coming within two outs of an elusive no-hitter for the fourth time, too. Leron Lee's broken-bat single to center wrecked this one.

Tug McGraw was the winning pitcher in the All-Star game and established a club record with twenty-seven saves. Matlack, in addition to his Rookie of the Year award, was part of baseball history when Roberto Clemente doubled off him on September 30. It was Clemente's three-thousandth and last hit. Clemente died in a plane crash that winter while on an aid mission to help victims of a Nicaraguan earthquake.

"I had no idea he was sitting on 2,999," Matlack said. "I was just trying to win another game. When I gave up the double, there was all this hoopla, the ump presents him the ball at second, and I'm glowering. Hey, we have a ball game. I was just an oblivious rookie. I saw it on the scoreboard and then that's how I knew.

"I get autograph requests where people want me to write that down. I've had people put together collages of stuff with me in the windup, Duffy Dyer catching, Clemente hitting."

Matlack, whose 2.32 ERA was fourth in the National League, got nineteen of twenty-four first-place votes in balloting of the baseball writers for Rookie of the Year, which was announced in November. After winning the award, Matlack said, "I think Rube Walker and Tom Seaver helped me most. Rube changed my motion in spring training so that I could keep the ball down lower. My locker is next to Tom's at Shea and he advised me about diet and sleeping habits the day before I was to pitch."

According to Joe Trimble's story of the announce-

A devout fan displays her sign with Tug McGraw's catchphrase "You Gotta Bee-leeve."

ment of Matlack's award, the pitcher earned what Matlack called "a little over the rookie minimum" for the season. The rookie minimum for that season was $13,750.

A slogan was born on July 11, 1973, the day a buoyant, thigh-slapping relief pitcher in a slump came to Shea Stadium in a good mood, up after a conversation with a friend about confidence. "I'd been terrible," Tug McGraw recalled, "but that day I was all psyched up, yelling in the outfield before the game, preaching sermons."

McGraw hollered, "Ya Gotta Believe!" to teammates and fans, anyone who would listen. Later, M. Donald Grant came to the Met clubhouse looking to preach a little himself, saying, "You still have a wonderful shot. You can't lose if you won't lose."

Grant spoke for five or ten minutes, and when he left the room, McGraw shouted, "Ya Gotta Believe!" But then the fireman realized he might be in a jam worse than the bases full of Pirates—Grant hadn't actually departed.

"Omigod," McGraw said to himself, "I bet he thinks I'm mocking him." The more McGraw thought about it, the more it worried him, so he called Grant. "I'm glad you called, I did think you were gigging me," Grant said.

McGraw had picked up the phrase from Father Feehan, his baseball coach at St. Vincent's High in Vallejo, California. Father Feehan was no longer alive at the time, McGraw explained, but, the reliever said, "I talk to him in my dreams."

In the final week of the season, as the Mets were pulling off yet another miracle that would captivate the baseball world, two nuns showed up at Shea with a sign that read, "You Gotta Believe."

By the time the season was over, everyone did.

But this was different from 1969, in part because the Mets had at least played well enough to be in pennant races since their World Series win, whereas before 1969, they were only lovable losers.

But the 1973 team probably had a more difficult time in winning their National League pennant. Injuries slammed into the Mets once again, bringing back bad memories of 1972. With the way they fizzled in 1972, it's understandable that the Mets dreaded the potential havoc injuries could wreak on their roster even in the sunny, carefree days of spring training. Even spring sweat did little to wash away their wariness.

"I think we should win, but you just worry about it because you know what can happen," Bud Harrelson told Dick Young in the March 4 edition of the *Daily News*. "You've seen it happen.

"We should've won it hands-down last year. I think the whole club felt that way." But, Harrelson noted, injuries skewered the Mets: "First Rusty and then Cleon and Agee and myself and just about every other guy on the club."

Even the Mets themselves could see they were vulnerable. "We got the front line to win it, if we don't have any serious injury problems," Tug McGraw said in the same article. "I don't think we have a lot of depth. I think we're about eighteen, nineteen guys strong. I don't think we're twenty-five strong."

"If the pitching holds out, I think we'll do it because we got some guys this year who came to play," said Cleon Jones. "I think that he came to play this year," Jones added, nodding at Jim Fregosi across the clubhouse.

Fregosi, who hit just .232, and Jones, who batted .245, played poorly when they weren't hurt in '72, and the entire team viewed them as a focal point for '73. Tom Seaver fingered them by name in Young's story, noting, "If they play the way everybody knows they can play, we'll win it.

"We have the potential to win," Seaver added.

"After that, it becomes a matter of playing up to your potential, every man. That's how we did it in '69, with every man on the club giving everything he had."

As spring training opened, the Mets had two potential dramas to unravel. One was a holdout by Rusty Staub, their best slugger. The other was what to do with Willie Mays, who was entering what was likely going to be his final season. As Young wrote on March 2, "The last act of the Willie Mays story is starting here. How will it end? Happily? Flat? Dragging on and on? Sad?"

The aging Mays was unhappy that he had played so much in 1972 and had clashed with Yogi Berra over his schedule. Mays had to play more as the season went on because the Mets were beset by injuries.

Mays admitted his first season in Flushing was difficult, saying, "Honest, I didn't know the Mets' system, the guys, the manager. Now I know them. It won't be so hard to try to fit in. I'll be relaxed. I had to try to fit in. I had a tendency to hold back a little. If I started talking too much, I'd get too bad a name. I fitted in more as the year passed."

The Met players certainly respected Mays and wanted him in the lineup. "Maybe he could create that momentum for us," Tug McGraw said, "get us going. Then we would get the positive attitude and keep it snowballing."

Staub, meanwhile, ended his holdout in March, signing a three-year contract totaling $330,000. He had wanted a no-trade clause, but Scheffing refused to give it to him. According to Young's story detailing Staub's contract, Scheffing assured Staub there was every intention of keeping him at Shea, a declaration that proved to have a relatively short shelf life.

After signing the contract, Staub was immediately fined $200 by the team for reporting to camp 2 pounds over the 210 playing weight team brass had determined for him. Staub, the last Met to join workouts, took seventy to eighty extra swings in the bat-

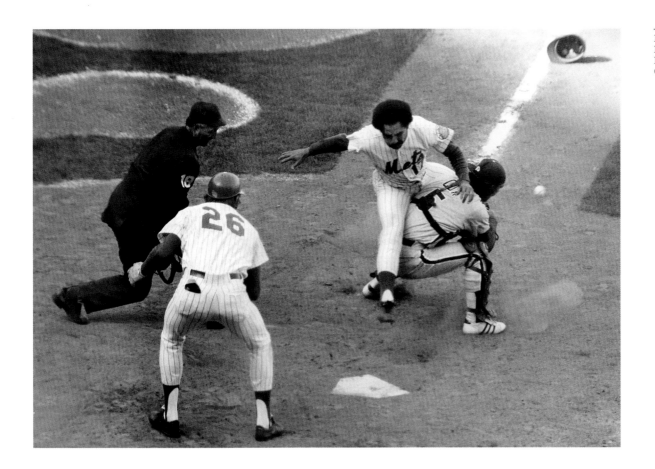

ting cage on his first day to test his surgically repaired right hand.

He declared that the hand "feels just fine. I'm sure it will hurt me when the weather is bad or I'm fatigued, but otherwise, I don't think I'll have trouble."

During the off-season, the Mets had traded two keystones of their 1969 team, sending Tommie Agee to Houston and Gary Gentry to the Braves. The Agee trade was no blockbuster, netting only Rich Chiles and Buddy Harris, but Gentry and reliever Danny Frisella brought back two important cogs for their '73 squad: second baseman Felix Millan, who choked up high on the bat to slap singles, and pitcher George Stone, who would go 12-3.

"I think we got a great chance to win it," Yogi Berra said the day before the season started. "We were all healthy last year when we started and we were in first place until everybody got hurt. Now I've got a healthy bunch and I feel good. I just wish I could play Willie every day. He'll be there Opening Day and I hope we start off good."

They did. Cleon Jones hit two home runs off Phila-

delphia's Steve Carlton, a twenty-seven-game winner the previous year, Seaver threw 7 2/3 shutout innings, and Tug McGraw got the final four outs in a 3–0 win in the April 6 opener at Shea. Yankee owner George Steinbrenner sat near the Met dugout, listening to a portable radio most of the afternoon and frowning, according to Augie Borgi's story in the *News*.

The next day, the Mets beat the Phillies again when Mays ripped a tie-breaking RBI single with two out in the ninth to back Jon Matlack. The Mets were 2-0 for the first time in their twelve-year history.

On April 12, Seaver beat Cardinals' ace Bob Gibson in a game in which the two fired beanballs at one another. After Seaver knocked down Gibson in the sixth, Gibson, according to Dick Young's story in the *News* the next day, yelled, "You got better control than that, Tommy!" Seaver replied, "Remember when you threw under my helmet last year?" Seaver later said he was also retaliating for Gibson throwing at John Milner twice during spring training. These Mets weren't just 4-0; they were also spirited.

But they lost the next night in Philadelphia, 7–1,

1970s

to nineteen-year-old Larry Christensen, and an offensive malaise settled over the team. In late April, they endured a twenty-nine-inning scoreless streak, a bad stretch for any team, but especially for one already so worried about its offense that the pitchers said things like this: "I pitch every game with the attitude I can get beat if I give up a run," Jon Matlack said. "I guess I'd pitch that way for every team except Cincinnati or Pittsburgh. But we'll score runs, I hope."

Added Tom Seaver: "It would be a shame to waste the summer, because we have a team that can win it all if everyone does his job."

A few days later, when the Mets lost one of his starts, 2–1, Seaver noted, "I go into every game thinking shutout, thinking it isn't an urgent necessity, but maybe it is."

Rusty Staub, the man the Mets counted on to be a big hitter, struggled early. On April 23, he was hitting .111. At one point, his parents flew from New Orleans to join the Mets in Houston, and his mother joked to reporters that she had hexed Astros' pitchers.

Berra, desperate for offense, began brainstorming ways to jolt the lineup. After light-hitting infielder Ted Martinez had three hits in a loss in Houston, Berra

toyed with the idea of shifting Martinez to center field to get him in the lineup more. By early May, the Mets had used four different center fielders: Mays, George Theodore, Rich Chiles, and Martinez.

This all coincided with the start of the casualties. On April 19, Cleon Jones suffered a strained right wrist and forearm when he dove for a ball hit by the Cubs' Glenn Beckert.

On April 25, Staub homered twice against the Astros, his first homers of the season, but any happiness was short-lived: Milner pulled his right hamstring stretching for a throw from Harrelson and was out indefinitely. Harry Parker couldn't make a start because of a pulled muscle, and Ed Kranepool was playing with a pulled groin. Milner was put on the disabled list a few days later.

"This crap is starting already," Berra said.

The Milner loss hurt badly—at the time, he was hitting .327 with five homers and thirteen RBI.

Still, on April 29, the Mets were 12-8 and tied for first place. Jerry Koosman started the season 4-0 with a 1.06 ERA and was the National League Player of the Month for April. As May began, Seaver's ERA was 1.13, but he was 2-2.

On May 8 at Shea, the Mets' other ace, Matlack, was struck in the forehead by a line drive hit by Atlanta's Marty Perez a 3-2 pitch. He suffered a hairline fracture of the forehead and was carried off the field on a stretcher.

The play shook both players. "I never want a thing like that to happen again," said Perez, who got a double on the play in a game the Braves won, 10–6. "I almost threw up when I saw him flat on the ground."

"It was one whale of a headache," Matlack said in a 2008 interview. "Actually, on the 2-2 pitch, everyone thought he had swung at a curveball. It was raining lightly. I had nowhere to put him then, so I reared back to throw a fastball. I heard the crack, but I didn't

see the baseball. I picked it up about fifteen feet away from me, got my bare hand up, and it hit the bill of my cap and hit me above the left eye. [Jerry] Grote was there instantly and says, 'Wait for the trainer.' My wife [Dee] is in the stands and she thinks I'm dead. She might have been the first female other than Joan Payson to go into that clubhouse. We got in an ambulance and the ambulance couldn't find its way out of there, so I was directing them. We got to the hospital on a shift change and there were people asking for my autograph.

"I got out of the hospital and went home and there was a film crew waiting there. They were really ticked because there was no sign of damage on me. They wanted to put me in a wheelchair to do an interview. I survived it all and pitched eleven days later against the Pirates [throwing six shutout innings]. I never really thought much about it after that. I believe to this day if I had not lost sight of the ball, I would've caught it or gotten out of the way. I just didn't see it."

Two days later, Jones returned in the Mayor's Trophy game, in which the Mets beat the Yankees,

8–4, doubtless irking a certain new Yankee owner who was fond of transistor radios.

On May 11, though, more bad injury news: Grote was hit by a pitch in Pittsburgh and suffered a broken arm. He wouldn't return until August. On May 12, Felix Millan twisted his left ankle. On May 13, Milner came off the disabled list but didn't immediately return to the lineup. The same day, Willie Mays went on the disabled list with a shoulder injury.

No wonder Dick Young wrote in the pages of the *Daily News* this description of the aching Mets: "Yogi's Volunteers, a thin gray line of red-blooded American boys, held together by Ace bandages and iodine."

To help with the catching while Grote was out, the club purchased Jerry May from Kansas City. It turns out, he was the perfect Met—he came with a long history of injuries and then promptly got hurt himself, a hamstring injury.

Jones returned and played four games, but his wrist was not healthy and he was put on the twenty-one-day DL on June 1. The wrist was placed in a cast, another blow for the Mets, especially since Jones had hit .333 in seven May appearances.

Cleon Jones hurries back to first base as the Yankees' Ron Blomberg attempts to apply the tag during the 1973 Mayor's Trophy Game.

1970s

At the end of May, the Mets had sunk to third place, 5 1/2 games behind the Cubs. McGraw was terrible during the month, recording a 5.85 ERA. Matlack was 0-4 with a 5.28 ERA.

On June 3, George "Stork" Theodore was hit near the left eye by a pitch, shattering his eyeglasses and causing cuts that required six stitches and kept him out for nearly a week. But this being the M*A*S*H Mets, it was hardly the biggest injury news of the day.

Harrelson suffered a jammed left hand when Bill Plummer of the Reds slammed into him trying to break up a double play, and there were reports that Staub would skip the Mets' exhibition against their Triple-A Tidewater club so he could see a specialist about the index and middle fingers of his left hand, which hadn't been the same since he was hit by a pitch on May 11 by Pittsburgh's Ramon Hernandez.

The follow-up news on Harrelson was not good: He would miss at least a month with a broken hand. "I knew it was bad right away because I heard a 'pop' when I hit the ground," Harrelson said.

Foley wrote in the June 6 *Daily News*: "The Mets' chances of taking the NL pennant—or even their division title—pretty much went up in smoke when Bud Harrelson's damaged left hand was encased in a plaster last night." In the same edition, the *News* ran a chart titled: "Mets Medicrew: Tale of Tape," a graphic detailing fifteen injuries the Mets had suffered to that point of the season.

The trip to Tidewater came on the heels of a 3-9 road trip, so the season was spiraling. On June 9, a bright spot: Mays hit home run number 655, his first of the year, on the same day the Mets retired Gil Hodges's number 14 jersey and paid tribute to him as part of Old-Timers' Day.

Hodges's number 14 uniform was presented to his widow, Joan Hodges, in front of a bunch of old Brooklyn Dodgers, including Carl Furillo, Pee Wee Reese, Clem Labine, and Joe Black. Al Jackson, the Met pitcher who played with, against, and for Hodges, said, "You can talk about him all day, but maybe a few words would sum it up: He was a helluva man."

With injuries piling up as fast as outs in the Met lineup, GM Bob Scheffing looked for a hitter, but had no luck. He was booed on Old-Timers' Day because of the Mets' anemic attack.

"There just doesn't seem to be anybody who will take money for a batter," Scheffing said. "I've tried." The Met GM was hurt by baseball's new designated-hitter rule for the American League, which means that older players who can do little except hit already have jobs.

On June 13, the Mets won their first series in more than a month when Seaver beat the Giants and was backed by Millan's first homer of the season. In a quirky coincidence, Millan's last homer had been off Seaver exactly one year earlier, when Millan was on the Braves.

The Mets went on a five-game winning streak, but there was still little to be happy about at Shea, except perhaps for a nice gesture June 16, when the Mets invited two hundred former prisoners of war to a game. The team paid for them to bring their families to New York for three days, including a tilt with the Padres. There was a brief ceremony on the field, a welcoming home of sorts for some who suffered in Vietnam. Joseph Kernan, a naval lieutenant who spent eleven months in a Hanoi prison camp, suited up and joined the Mets' pregame drills.

The Mets held their collective breath June 18 when Seaver was scratched from a start after he hurt his back moving boxes in the wine cellar of his Greenwich, Connecticut, home. Seaver returned six days later and beat the Padres.

By this time, though, injuries and hole-filled bats seemed to have scuttled the season. In the June 27 *News*, Bill Gallo drew a cartoon depicting the Mets "on a silver platter" for the rest of the division, complete with an apple in a drawing of Berra's mouth.

At the end of June, the Mets were 11 1/2 games out of first, mired in last place. On June 30, the Mets beat the Cubs, 2–1, in Chicago to end the month at 11-17. Phil Pepe's story the next day carried this lead: "June, 1973, died Saturday. The Mets did not mourn its passing."

Sure, it had been a bad month for the Mets, but July would be no friend to the struggling team, either. On July 3, the Mets gave up a club record nineteen runs to Montreal; five were knocked in by former Met Ken Singleton.

At about this time, stories started to appear in the papers wondering if Berra would be blamed for the Met misfortunes. One report predicted Berra would be fired, Scheffing would retire, and Yankee executive Lee MacPhail would be brought on as GM.

In one Dick Young column, in the July 7 *News*, the headline read, "Easy to Blame Yogi . . . but Why?" In the piece, Young wrote, "The bombs are bursting around Yogi's beleaguered head. The team has hit bottom. The famed 'Berra Luck,' a legend in baseball for lo these 25 years, has deserted him."

In the same story, M. Donald Grant is quoted as saying, "We have no thought of replacing Yogi. We will not do so, unless forced to do so by public opinion." As Red Foley wrote, that wasn't exactly a vote of confidence.

Meanwhile, Theodore and Don Hahn collided in the outfield on July 7 and the Stork suffered a dislocated right hip, which knocked him out for the rest of the season. That's the same day that Cleon Jones returned. Bud Harrelson was activated one day later and on July 10 made several sensational plays to help Matlack throw a 1–0 shutout.

On July 11, the misguided Fregosi Era ended: The man who was supposed to solve the third-base problems that seem encoded in Met DNA was traded to the Rangers for a player to be named later. More good news: The move made room for Grote, who was ready to return to the lineup.

But whatever was going right for the Mets, they still couldn't seem to solve McGraw's pitching problems. In a rare start on July 17, he was clobbered by the Braves and his ERA ballooned to 6.21.

The Mets went 12-18 in July, and the cellar was seemingly their permanent home. As August started, they were 44-57 and 10 1/2 games out of first.

But no one in the bizarre NL East seemed capable of claiming the division, and the Mets got to midmonth at 53-65 after a 3-6 trip west that left them 7 1/2 games out of first. That same day, Joe Trimble's story in the *Daily News* carried this headline: "Yogi Has Fall-Guy Look." In the piece, Trimble wrote, "The Mets' troubles are physical and possibly managerial."

Soon after, Bud Harrelson became the first Met to make the disabled list twice in the same season.

1970s

Somehow, though, the Mets became contenders while they still wallowed under .500. They swept the Padres in late August to move to 61-70, 5 1/2 games out. On August 23, Trimble called the NL East a "league of lumps" and declared Met pennant hopes still alive "though they seem to defy the laws of mathematics."

On August 24, Trimble's story was headlined "1973: Year of the Mets' Tortoise," and it ran with a Bill Gallo cartoon with the Mets as the tortoise and the rest of the NL East the hare. We all know how that one ended.

The Mets had suddenly become exciting. Or, perhaps more accurately, interesting things were happening to them.

On August 25 they lost to the Giants, 1–0, in a bizarre game that would perhaps foreshadow twelve-year-old Jeffrey Maier's cameo in the 1996 American League playoffs at Yankee Stadium. In the Giants-Mets game, a fifteen-year-old from Scarsdale named Mark Johnson reached out to try to snag a foul ball that Grote was near. While the kid didn't touch the ball and Grote said he didn't get in his way, the pop fell in and, given another chance, Garry Maddox singled through the right side to knock in the only run of the game.

The Mets began a four-game series against the first-place Cardinals on August 30, having climbed into fifth place, 5 1/2 games back. The Cards were 67-65 and held a two-game lead over the Pirates, but their ace, Bob Gibson, had been out since August 8 because of injury.

This was the start of a thirty-one-game stretch in which the Mets played only East Division opponents. They split the first two games to finish August at 18-14 and 62-71 overall. They split the final two games of the series, too.

Meanwhile, McGraw had finally gotten hot. From August 27 to September 15, he had eight saves and two wins in ten appearances, raising his arms and slapping his thigh with his glove in celebration. It had taken him until August 22 to get his first victory.

McGraw had begun the season with such high hopes, talking in April about how he had refined his curveball and how it would give him three nasty pitches. "I feel it can be an out pitch, just like my fastball and my scroogie," McGraw said of his deuce. But much of his season was a wreck, particularly July and August—at one point in those hot, horrible months, McGraw had lost six straight, failed to get a save for six weeks, and watched his ERA soar above 8.00.

"That was a nightmare I wouldn't wish on any relief pitcher, unless it means a pennant for us," McGraw said.

The race was rapidly becoming, as Red Foley put it in the September 11 *News*, "a whacky taffy pull."

From September 4 to 7, the Mets won four straight, including a doubleheader sweep in Montreal on September 7 that brought them to 68-73, four games out of first place. McGraw allowed one run in 5 1/3 innings in relief in the fifteen-inning nightcap win, and Ray Sadecki got the save. McGraw even batted in the fifteenth inning and hit a two-run single.

Seaver lost the next game, but the Mets won the finale in Montreal on a George Stone gem saved by—who else?—McGraw and moved to within three games of first place. Stone, whose grin earned him the nickname "Elmer Fudd," would prove to be an invaluable pitcher down the stretch. For the season, he finished 12-3.

Koosman lost in Philadelphia, but Matlack and Seaver won the last two games of the series there and the Mets, improbably, had drawn within 2 1/2 games of first place. The Mets took two of three from the Cubs at Shea from September 14 to 16, winning the finale on a bold move by Berra.

The manager ordered a squeeze play with Grote at the plate in the eighth inning and it worked, scoring the winning run. What momentum the Mets had,

going into a two-game series in Pittsburgh, which would be followed by a three-game set at Shea.

At this point, the Pirates had a half-game lead over Montreal and were two games up on the Cardinals. The Mets sat 2 1/2 games back, but they were getting their chance, and all the action took place from September 17 to 21.

Seaver lost the opener in Pittsburgh, but the Mets came back to win the next night, 6–5. They were 74-77 and in fourth place, only 2 1/2 games out. That was the last day they spent in fourth place.

On September 19, McGraw pitched three innings of shutout relief and the Mets were tied for second with Montreal and St. Louis, just 1 1/2 games behind.

Fittingly, in a season associated with a miracle finish, there would be a remarkable play down the stretch. On September 20, Duffy Dyer doubled in the tying run with two out in the ninth inning, but the Mets must have known something good was brewing

in the thirteenth inning when the Ball on the Wall miracle happened.

With two out and Richie Zisk on first, Dave Augustine hit a drive to left off Sadecki that hit the top of the wall and came back to Jones, who relayed to Garrett, who threw it to Ron Hodges, who tagged Zisk, ending the inning. Then Hodges delivered a game-winning single with one out in the Mets' thirteenth, slashing the Pittsburgh lead to half a game.

On September 21, in a game for first place, the Mets knocked out Steve Blass in the first inning, scoring four times to back Seaver, who earned his eighteenth win. Milner, occasionally feted by signs at Shea that read "Nailed by the Hammer," later homered, and so did Garrett and Staub. The Mets, who had been in last place only three weeks earlier, on August 30, were now in first place.

It was the first time they were in the top spot since April 29. It was the first time they were at the .500

1970s

mark since May 29. There were eight games left in the regular season.

There was a brief pause in the pennant chase when Willie Mays announced that 1973 was going to be his last year. He'd have plenty more excitement to come, though. September 25 was Willie Mays Night, and there were huge cheers as Mays spoke, telling the crowd it was time for "Willie to say good-bye to America."

Also at about this time, stories began appearing in the papers that Berra, once on the hot seat, would definitely be back in 1974. "I think the decision on Yogi will be favorable when the board meets," M. Donald Grant told Dick Young. "I don't know of any dissenters."

On September 22, Matlack threw a four-hit shutout in a crisp game that took only one hour, fifty-five minutes and the Mets beat the Cardinals, 2–0, raising

their lead to one game. Now that the Mets had gotten into first, they had no intention of being knocked out.

But the Pirates weren't going away, either. The next day, the Mets beat the Cardinals again, but the Pirates swept a doubleheader from the Expos to move to within half a game.

The Mets split a two-game series against Montreal, maintaining their lead, but Seaver came out after getting pounded for five runs in only two innings in an 8–5 loss on September 26, trimming their lead to half a game.

That set up the final series of the season, in Chicago, and the Mets needed two wins to clinch. Two days of heavy rain soaked Wrigley Field, setting up consecutive doubleheaders to end the season. But the Mets gained half a game without doing much other

Fans tear up home plate after the New York Mets clinched the National League pennant at Shea Stadium, October 10, 1973.

1970s

than watching raindrops plink in outfield puddles when the Pirates lost on September 28.

September 30 dawned dreary, too, but the Mets and Cubs played anyway. Matlack lost the opener, 1–0, but the Mets scored three times in the first inning of the nightcap and Jones later homered to help Koosman lower the Mets' magic number to one.

The possibility of a three-way tie among the Mets, Pirates, and Cardinals still existed, but that was erased when Seaver beat Burt Hooton in the opener of the second doubleheader, on October 1. Jones opened the scoring with a homer—his sixth home run in the final ten games, a span during which he knocked in fourteen runs.

But Seaver tired and McGraw, fittingly, came in with the Mets ahead, 6–4, and threw three innings of scoreless relief, notching his twenty-fifth save, icing Seaver's nineteenth win, and clinching the division crown. The Mets's record was a lowly 82-79, the worst ever for a division champ. But they were still division champs. The Cardinals, the only other team in the division to finish at least at .500, were second, 1 1/2 games back, and the Pirates slipped to third, 2 1/2 games out.

Afterward, Berra hugged McGraw, as well he should have. When the Mets clinched, McGraw led a cheer of his own slogan: "One, two, three: You gotta believe!" The Mets shouted it all through the celebration.

Seaver, 0-2 against the Reds during the season, was the pick to open the playoffs, but first he had to test his arm because he had been feeling shoulder stiffness. Seaver threw a few fastballs in the bullpen on a workout day while pitching coach Rube Walker watched, and both men quickly grinned. The *News* ran a drawing of a smiley face, capturing the Met mood.

"Our chances are excellent," Seaver said, "because our pitching is excellent. Pitching is the decisive factor in this playoff. Not *the* pitching, *our* pitching. The way Matlack and Koosman have been throwing

and now that my shoulder feels good, our chances are outstanding."

The best-of-five National League Championship Series opened in Cincinnati on October 6, and late in the game Seaver, who was locked in a pitchers' duel with Jack Billingham, looked prescient. After Bud Harrelson walked with two out in the second inning, Seaver, a pretty fair-hitting pitcher, delivered an RBI double, and he made the 1–0 lead stand up going into the eighth inning, leaving 53,431 Cincinnatians unhappy.

But with one out in the eighth, Pete Rose, who would loom large in this series, struck a game-tying solo homer. The Mets did not score in their half of the ninth, and Seaver remained in the game, but he got only the first out of the ninth inning. Johnny Bench followed with a game-ending home run, and the Reds had a stunning,1–0 series lead.

Game two, the next day, might as well be called the Jon Matlack Game. The Mets' superb lefty threw a two-hit shutout in a 5–0 Met victory that gave them a split in Cincy. Right fielder Andy Kosco, not exactly a household name among the luminaries of the Big Red Machine, had both hits. Matlack had silenced Rose, Bench, Joe Morgan, and the rest of the Reds. Rusty Staub homered in the fourth inning off Don Gullett, and the Mets added four more runs in the ninth.

"I knew what I had watched the day before by Seaver and we had lost, 2–1," Matlack said in a 2008 interview. "I didn't think you could pitch any better than Tommy had pitched that day, and he lost. You couldn't do much better than that and that's the thought I went to bed with. It was a neat feeling to execute the plan I had and be successful.

"Part of it was the game was 1-0 until the eighth. Rusty was great at picking up pitchers' pitches and he told me before the game, 'I got Gullett, I'm going to get him before the day's over.' I said, 'OK.' And he did.

"The final margin looks a lot bigger than it was for the first eight innings. It was tense. They could come from nowhere in an instant with a lot of runs. The Reds and the Lumber Company [the Pirates] were probably the two most prodigious lineups of that era."

The series switched to Shea on October 8, and the Mets stunned the Reds with six runs in the first two innings and nine in the first four en route to a 9–2 victory and a 2–1 series lead. But neither Jerry Koosman's complete game nor Staub's two homers are what's etched in fans' memories about game three. Rather, the fight between tiny Bud Harrelson and brawny Pete Rose at second base is what endures.

The fracas bloomed when Rose slid hard into Harrelson to try to break up a double play in the fifth inning, but its seeds were planted the day before. According to Dick Young's account of the game in the October 9 *News*, after game two, Harrelson had said that Matlack had pitched so well that Cincy hitters were "back on their heels." Someone told Rose, Young wrote, and Rose was angry, saying, "What's Harrelson, some sort of bleeping batting instructor?"

So when the 195-pound Rose collided with Harrelson, he hit the 150-pound shortstop with an elbow. Benches emptied, punches flew. After five minutes

OPPOSITE:
Jerry Koosman.

Cincinnati's Pete Rose sliding into second base in a 1974 game against the Mets.

or so, order was restored, but there was one vivid moment remaining—Reds' reliever Pedro Borbon put on a Mets' cap instead of his Reds' cap. Alerted to his mistake, he took off the Mets cap, "sank his teeth into it and yanked, ripping out a large piece," Young wrote. "You have to be blind with rage or totally color blind not to be able to distinguish a bright red Cincy cap from a bright blue Mets cap."

When the Reds took the field, Met fans said their piece. Or rather offered a piece of their minds by throwing pieces of garbage at Rose and the Reds—apples, beer cans, bottles, and paper. Reds' pitcher Gary Nolan was struck in the face by an object and dropped to one knee. Rose picked up a bottle that had been flung on the field and hurled it into the stands, Young wrote.

Commissioner Bowie Kuhn, who was at the game, and National League president Chub Feeney discussed with the managers and umpires whether there should be discipline, and they decided no one would be ejected.

Finally, the Reds took the field for the bottom of the inning, but during play, Rose, out in left field, was hit in the leg with another flying object and Reds' skipper Sparky Anderson turned to the umpires and said, "I'm pulling my team off the field until you can guarantee their safety."

It was decided the Mets would send a delegation of players toward the stands to placate the raucous fans. Berra, Mays, Seaver, Cleon Jones, and Staub walked toward the left-field corner, and fans cheered. Mays held aloft a peace sign. "Henry Kissinger couldn't have done better," Young wrote.

Ten minutes later, order was restored and the rout was back on. The Mets were only one win away from the World Series.

But the next day, in game four, the Mets and their fans found out how dangerous a riled Red Rose could be. In the twelfth inning of a 1–1 game, he hit a solo homer off Harry Parker, lifting Cincinnati to a 2–1 victory that evened the series at two games apiece.

The *News*'s Phil Pepe wrote in the next day's edition, "If New York didn't like Pete Rose Monday, how do you think it felt about him Tuesday? It's one thing to pick on skinny, little, adorable Bud Harrelson; it's quite another to go tampering with miracles." The *News* also published a cartoon by Bill Gallo titled "The Bull's Revenge," showing Rose as a bull sending a matador with Berra's face flying.

Both teams had gotten terrific pitching. George Stone allowed one run in 6 2/3 innings, and Tug McGraw threw 4 1/3 scoreless innings for New York. Starter Fred Norman allowed one run in five innings for the Reds and Don Gullett threw four scoreless

OPPOSITE: Cincinnati's Pete Rose and the Mets' Bud Harrelson get into a dustup during game three of the 1973 National League playoffs.

ABOVE, LEFT: Cincinnati's Pete Rose pins the Mets' Bud Harrelson to the ground during game three of the 1973 National League playoffs.

ABOVE, RIGHT: Wayne Garrett (11) dives in to help Bud Harrelson's attempt to subdue Pete Rose.

1970s

innings of relief, while Clay Carroll threw two and Borbon one, setting up a sudden-death game five at Shea the next day.

After game four, the Mets said they would start Seaver on three days' rest. Of the Mets' ace, Anderson said, "That man is the best pitcher in baseball." But Billingham had outpitched him in the opener and would try again October 10, when the Mets would play without Staub, who had a bruised right shoulder.

The score was tied, 2–2, going into the bottom of the fifth inning. Doubles by Wayne Garrett and Cleon Jones knocked out Billingham, and after Gullett walked John Milner, pinch hitter Willie Mays knocked in run with a single off Carroll. Don Hahn drove in a run with a grounder, and Harrelson added a single for a 6–2 Met lead.

The light-hitting Mets finished with thirteen hits in their 7–2 victory. Seaver gave up two runs (one earned) in 8 1/3 innings, and McGraw finished up with a scoreless two-thirds, clinching the second pennant in the Mets' twelve-year history.

"Believe! Believe! Believe!" Phil Pepe wrote in the next day's *News*. "The Miracle lives. The Mets are champions of the National League."

The Mets had to wait for the Orioles and A's to settle their AL Championship Series because it went a full five games. They got a preview of the kind of pitching Oakland was capable of in game five, when Catfish Hunter threw a 3–0 shutout at the powerful O's, allowing only five hits, and setting up a fascinating matchup for the seventieth World Series.

The A's, all facial hair and attitude, were braggarts and loudmouths who often seemed just as happy fighting each other—or their irascible owner, Charles O. Finley—as they were when they took on the rest of baseball. But the defending World Champions were also an excellent team, boasting some of the finest talent of the 1970s, from Reggie Jackson and Catfish Hunter to Joe Rudi and Rollie Fingers.

The Mets, considered cannon fodder for the Reds in the playoffs, were huge underdogs in the World Series, too.

On the same day the A's advanced, the Mets got word that Rusty Staub, who had missed game five of the NLCS because of a severely bruised right shoulder, was "very much improved," according to team physician Dr. Peter LaMotte. Staub vowed to play in the World Series, though he admitted he didn't know exactly when. He wasn't able to throw overhand because his shoulder hurt so much. If Staub couldn't play, Berra planned to use Willie Mays in center field and move Don Hahn to right.

Before the World Series even started, Reggie Jackson proved that his play was not the only reason he'd earn the nickname "Mr. October." Jackson was a first-rate provocateur as well as slugger. He made headlines, saying, "Who the heck are the Mets?" He also opined that he'd rather be facing the Reds because "when you beat them, you're beating the best."

"I said what I thought and I'm being criticized," Jackson added. "My teammates think the same way, but they're not putting it on the line the way I do."

He also said, "As far as I'm concerned, the Reds are the best team in that league. They have the players you want to play against in a World Series. I want to play against guys like Rose and Bench and Perez. You beat them, you're beating the best. Against the Reds, you can get up for a game. Except for Seaver and Staub, the Mets don't have a big-name player."

In the October 13 edition of the *News*, Pepe wrote a story headlined, "Mets Out to Make Reggie Eat His Words." In it, an anonymous Met said, "I want to face that Reggie Jackson."

Sparky Anderson, the Reds' manager, thought Jackson's diatribe was loopy. "Mr. Jackson may be sorry he said those things," Anderson said. "He's in for a surprise if he thinks the Mets are easy to beat. We found that out, the hard way."

In game one, with Jon Matlack opposing Oakland's Ken Holtzman, a Met strength failed them in a 2–1 loss, usually the kind of game the Mets won. Felix Millan, whom Pepe described as "so sure-handed he could catch marbles on an oil slick," bungled a ground ball by Bert Campaneris in the third inning that allowed one run to score and set up another.

Just before Campaneris's grounder, Matlack had given up a double to Holtzman. Too bad, for that moment and another later in the Series, there was no designated hitter in the World Series that year.

For the Mets, the worst part of Millan's error is that he was probably the one player on defense they would

OPPOSITE: Tom Seaver delivering a pitch during his record-setting nineteen-strikeout performance on April 22, 1970. He struck out the last ten Padres batters he faced in the Mets' 2–1 win.

ABOVE: Mets hurler Jon Matlack uncorks one of the beauties that befuddled Oakland hitters in game four of the 1973 World Series, a 6–1 Mets victory.

want the ball hit to; even Matlack said so. "He's been tremendous all year," Matlack said. "When the ball was hit to him, I said, 'Great.' I'm glad to see anything go his way. Then I saw it go through, but I'm not going to back off him."

Millan, who had made only nine errors during the season, said, "I just missed the ball. It was an easy out. I was waiting for the hop and it didn't happen. I can't remember ever letting a ball go through my legs like that."

Game two was one of the zaniest in World Series history. It set a record for longest game at four hours, thirteen minutes and veered wildly back and forth with the terrific starters, Jerry Koosman and Vida Blue, stumbling, and the great Willie Mays experiencing humiliation and redemption on the same day.

Jones and Garrett homered for the Mets, but the A's led, 3–2, in the sixth. The Mets scored twice to take the lead, and pinch hitter Jim Beauchamp hit a comebacker to Darold Knowles, who lost his balance while trying to start a 1-2-3 double play and threw the ball past catcher Ray Fosse.

But the Mets couldn't hold a 6–3 lead. With the A's down by two in the ninth, Mays lost Deron Johnson's fly ball in the sun, starting the tying rally.

With two out in the twelfth, Mays got his chance and singled in the tie-breaking run. It was the final hit of his career. The Mets scored three more times on

errors on consecutive grounders by A's second baseman Mike Andrews, which later prompted one of the most bizarre controversies in Series lore. The A's scored one run in the twelfth when Mays lost another fly in the sun to make the final tally 10–7. The Series was even.

But Finley was apoplectic over Andrews's errors. The A's announced afterward that Andrews had been placed on the disabled list and would be replaced by Manny Trillo. The reason? Andrews was having arm trouble—according to the A's, anyway. But Oakland's Sal Bando pointed out that it would be difficult for anyone to believe Andrews's arm was hurting, though the team doctor said so, because Andrews had thrown batting practice before game two.

The A's players were enraged by Andrews's firing by Finley, and Jackson told reporters that Finley's actions could trigger a boycott by the A's against playing the rest of the Series. The A's believed Andrews was being punished for his miscues in game two and wore adhesive tape in the shape of number 17—Andrews's jersey number—on their uniform sleeves.

"I just feel bad for the man," Jackson said. "We all do."

Finley coerced Andrews into signing an affidavit saying he couldn't play, but Baseball Commissioner Bowie Kuhn ordered Andrews reinstated, knowing he wasn't hurt.

1970s

Meanwhile, the Series shifted to Shea for game three, and Garrett homered for the second consecutive game and the Mets built a 2–0 lead against Hunter. Seaver gave up one run in the sixth and another in the eighth, tying the score. Bert Campaneris knocked in the winner in the eleventh, singling off Harry Parker to score Ted Kubiak.

In game four, the Mets knocked out Holtzman in the first inning, thanks in part to Staub's three-run homer. Staub added a two-run single off Blue Moon Odom in the fourth, and Matlack allowed only five hits and one run in eight innings to even the Series at two games apiece.

Koosman, McGraw, and a smidgen of offense were all the Mets needed in game five. Jones doubled and scored on a Milner single, and Hahn hit an RBI triple to give the Mets their only runs, but Koosman threw shutout ball and got help from McGraw, who came in to get out of a bases-loaded snarl in the seventh. McGraw then pitched two more scoreless innings, wrapping up a 2–0 victory that put the Mets one win away from a title.

McGraw went into his normal victory celebration, throwing his arms in the air, slapping his glove against his thigh. Ya gotta believe, indeed.

After the Mets had taken a 3–2 lead in the Series, they seemed to have a clear advantage—Seaver was slated to pitch game six in Oakland, though Berra made what would prove to be a controversial choice. Seaver would be pitching on three days' rest. "There's no big deal," Seaver said. "I've pitched with short rest before."

When someone asked Matlack if he was ready to start a game seven, if there was one, Matlack said, "There's not going to be a seventh game." Seaver, asked how he felt about returning to Oakland, said, "I hope it's only for one day. I've got a golf date Sunday."

Now the Mets were the flip ones, not Reggie Jackson. But perhaps they had reason to be. Their vaunted

pitching had held the A's to thirteen runs and thirty-five hits in the first five games and no home runs.

"The Mets' pitching is the best we've seen this whole season," A's manager Dick Williams said. "We're being dominated by their pitching. We usually hit better than this."

At least one of the A's did hit better in game six, and it was enough to send Oakland to a 3–1 victory—Jackson hit a pair of RBI doubles and scored the A's other run to tie the Series at three games apiece. Seaver, pitching on short rest, had failed, the Mets' had been wrong about game seven, and the World Series would come down to one last tilt, Matlack against Holtzman.

For a guy who did not hit during the season, Holtzman turned out to be a handful for Met pitchers. He hurt the Mets with a double in game one and doubled again in the third inning of the deciding game. Campaneris followed with a home run, the A's first of the Series, and Jackson added another two-run shot, all but finishing the Mets. They did not recover, losing, 5–2. The miracle died, though the Mets had outhit the A's, .253–212, and had a better ERA during the Series, 2.22–2.32.

After the loss, Bud Harrelson said, "It's been a helluva year for a lot of guys. But there's nothing like being a number one. Nothing.

"There's no compensation for finishing second. They're a great ballclub. All the bull they've gone through with Finley and they still go out and play for themselves. But I don't think you can say they're a better team than we are. They just played better and scored more runs."

After what the Mets had improbably accomplished in 1973, the next season predictably began with high expectations; it perhaps came undone because of low run production—a common Met theme throughout the decade—and Tom Seaver's aching pelvis.

The 1974 Mets did not spend a single day in first place, unless you're an eternal optimist who believes every team is in first up until the opener. The Mets would win every "lidlifter," to use a term popular in early 1970s sports sections, of the decade except 1974. Tickets at Shea were only $4.00 for box seats, and the cheap seats, upper-level reserved, could be had for $2.50.

On April 6, the Mets began the season in Philadelphia where the Opening Day hoopla, according to Augie Borgi's story in the *Daily News*, consisted of "Hugo Zacchini, the human cannonball" during the pregame ceremonies and "the world's fattest streaker," who appeared out of the right-field seats just before the ninth. Zacchini was shot out of a 23-foot cannon at second base and went 150 feet into the air, landing on a net at home plate; the streaker was arrested.

Steve Carlton was also on the bill, and the 40,222 on hand figured he and Tom Seaver would be the main event. But the Mets scored three runs in five innings off Carlton and, despite two errors in left by Cleon Jones, held a 4–3 lead going into the bottom of the ninth.

But Mike Schmidt took care of that. This was Schmidt well before he was, well, Mike Schmidt, the perennial home run champion who might be the greatest third baseman of all time. He had ended the 1973 season by going 0 for his final twenty-six. Against Seaver he was 0 for three, but against Tug McGraw, the author of so many memorable relief moments the previous year, he plunged a dagger into Met hearts.

With one out and a runner on first, Schmidt lined a 1-0 McGraw delivery over the left-field fence to give the Phillies a 5–4 victory. "I threw him a good fastball," McGraw said in Borgi's account of the game. "It was inside, where I wanted it. Give the hitter the credit. It's nothing to be alarmed about."

If only McGraw were right about that—1974

turned out to be a poor season for him because of shoulder trouble. He had only three saves and was 6-11 with a 4.16 ERA.

After splitting a two-game set in Philadelphia, the Mets won their home opener on April 10 when Jerry Koosman beat the St. Louis Cardinals, 3–2, on a chilly, windy day. In part because of the nasty weather, only 17,154 showed up at Shea. Koosman did not pitch a complete game, but he probably had more trouble in a pregame bridge game with Jerry Grote and Ed Kranepool than he did with the Cards. Bob Apodaca, a future Met pitching coach, finished the game by getting a double-play grounder.

"I know how to handle the cold," Koosman was quoted as saying in the next day's *Daily News*. "I have a heater for my arm and shoulder between innings. And I like cool weather, but I don't like the way the field looks."

Koosman added, "I would like to correct you writ-ers on one thing about cool weather, though. I didn't pitch in the barn back home [Appleton, Minnesota] because that's one place it's too cold. My brother, Orville, and I tried it only once."

The Mets were 2-1 after their home lidlifter, but they lost their next seven games and ten of eleven, banishing them to the back end of the division. They would not rise above fourth place the rest of the season and ultimately finished fifth, at 71-91, seven-teen games behind the division champ Pirates.

Part of the blame for their tumble certainly goes to their anemic offense. The Mets batted just .235 as a team, second to last in the National League and 20 points below the league average, and hit 96 home runs (eighth in the league). Their 43 steals and .329 slug-ging percentage were both dead last. Players started campaigning for the Mets to add some offense.

John Milner led the team with 20 homers and Rusty Staub hit 19 and had a team-best 78 RBI.

1970s

Seaver's pelvic problem resulted in one of the worst seasons of his wonderful career. He finished 11-11 with a 3.20 ERA. The twenty-nine-year-old righty had one notable achievement, though—he struck out 14 on the next-to-last day of the season, his final start, to reach the 200 mark in strikeouts for the seventh consecutive season. He was the first National League pitcher to do so.

Seaver had shoulder pain during his Cy Young 1973 season, so when he got to spring training in 1974, he decided he would not push himself. He assumed his power would be there during the season, but he hadn't thrown enough to build it up, so he could not throw hard. He began overstriding, causing a chain reaction of pain and muscles shifting out of whack, scaring him. But when doctors discovered that Seaver's pelvic structure was out of balance, it was easy to fix, and that, in part, was how he could enjoy a wonderful finish to the season.

Well, sort of wonderful. This was the Mets, after all. Even though he struck out fourteen and gave up only four hits and two runs, throwing a complete game, Seaver lost to Jim Lonborg and the Phillies because the Mets mustered only one run.

The Mets had a few days to enjoy during a mostly lost season, though. Jon Matlack, who led the National League with seven shutouts and was third in ERA at 2.41, threw a one-hitter on Old-Timers' Day on June 29 to beat the Cardinals, 4–0. Losing pitcher Jack Curtis had the only hit, an opposite-field single in the third inning.

That was a good day to be a Met fan—Ed Charles, one of the stars of the 1969 team, doubled in the winning run in the Old-Timers' game, a hit-and-giggle affair described by Red Foley in the *News* as "a burlesque."

On August 27, Benny Ayala became the first Met and the fortieth big leaguer at the time to hit a home run in his first major league at-bat in a 4–2 victory over Houston. Ayala had arrived at Shea in the afternoon before a night game because the Mets needed someone to sub in left for Cleon Jones, whose left knee was strained.

At the time, Ayala was one of a number of players Met fans placed their fervent hopes on. Would he bloom into the hitting star they so desperately needed? Alas, he hit only two more home runs for the Mets, though he spent parts of ten seasons in the majors, doing tours with Baltimore, St. Louis, and Cleveland.

On September 11, the Cardinals beat the Mets, 4–3, in twenty-five innings, a game that last seven hours and four minutes. The game ended at 3:13 A.M., making it the longest night game in history.

The Mets' hierarchy changed on October 1 when Joe McDonald was named general manager to replace Scheffing. Scheffing had held the job for five years and wanted to return home to Arizona. McDonald had worked his way up through the organization— the Brooklyn native had been hired in 1962 as a statistician for Mets' broadcasters. He had also been Whitey Herzog's secretary when Herzog was running the Mets' minor-league system.

One of the first major moves of McDonald's tenure came on December 3, 1974, when Tug McGraw was traded to the Phillies, a move that depleted the Met bullpen while enhancing a division rival. McGraw, Don Hahn, and Dave Schneck went to Philly for Del Unser, John Stearns, and Mac Scarce, and while Unser and Stearns were useful Mets, losing McGraw hurt.

Not only was his darting screwball important to the Mets throughout his tenure in Flushing, but he also etched a permanent place in Met lore with his "Ya Gotta Believe!" rallying cry that became the theme of the '73 season. McGraw always was a colorful character—he was one of the creators of the comic strip *Scroogie*, about a daffy lefty relief pitcher in the majors, and also uttered some famous hilarious quotes.

Asked once if he preferred natural grass or Astro-turf, McGraw replied, "I don't know. I never smoked Astroturf." He also once said of a new contract, "Ninety percent I'll spend on good times, women, and Irish whiskey. The other 10 percent I'll probably waste."

At the time of the trade, the Mets wondered if

Rusty Staub.

McGraw was sliding. But the shoulder problem that derailed his '74 season turned out to be a cyst, and it was removed after the trade. He went back to being the bullpen stopper who had been so vital for the Mets, and he was so successful in Philadelphia that he's an indelible part of that franchise, too—one of the most famous images of the Phillies' franchise is a snapshot of McGraw leaping into the air after striking out Willie Wilson of the Royals to end the 1980 World Series, the Phillies' first World Championship.

1970s

The Yankees had played at Shea Stadium in 1974 while Yankee Stadium was being remodeled and would be back in 1975. As the season approached, there were some in baseball who wondered if Shea might host a full slate of World Series games because both teams had the look of contenders.

If not, some wondered if the Yankees would overshadow their hosts by being the better team. Yogi Berra wouldn't hear of it, telling Dick Young before the season, "What do I care about the Yankees? They can't beat us. They're in the other league.

"I'll worry about them in October, if we play them."

Before the teams played three games in spring training, both Ed Kranepool and the Yankees' Ron Blomberg talked openly about the chances of a Subway Series. If anything, the Yanks showed they were, at least temporarily, ahead of the Mets, winning two out of three. Doubtless, blustery Yankee owner George Steinbrenner thought it meant something.

Little did the Mets know that a season in which they perhaps held more than their usual amount of spring hope would carry such tumult. During camp, Cleon Jones was arrested for indecent exposure in St. Petersburg when he was found by police in a van with a young woman not his wife.

The charges were eventually dropped, but Jones was fined $2,000 by the Mets. M. Donald Grant, saying he had to "restore the Mets' image," forced Jones to make a public apology in a press conference the legendary sportswriter Red Smith described as "an exercise in medieval torture." *Sports Illustrated*, in its "Scorecard" section, called for Grant to apologize to Jones and baseball fans for concocting the embarrassing press conference.

The Mets hoped that Dave Kingman, the tall, lanky slugger purchased from the Giants for $150,000 on February 28, could provide some sorely needed pop. But Kingman was a big-risk, big-reward kind of player because of his high strikeout totals and poor defense.

The Mets also had a serious question that needed a positive answer if they hoped to have any success during the season—which Tom Seaver would they get? The one who had been perhaps baseball's best pitcher from 1969 to 1973 or the one who was in pain and mediocre for long stretches in 1974, the worst season to date of his career?

Seaver had been successful at the end of the previous season and had a whole off-season for his pelvic problem to fade, so the Mets were optimistic. And on April 8, Opening Day, they could exhale after Seaver beat Philadelphia ace Steve Carlton, 2–1, when Joe Torre drove in the winner in the ninth inning.

Seaver admitted prestart anxiousness, understandable considering what he went through in '74. But Berra called him "the old Seaver," and the ace seemed satisfied, too.

"I felt no pain and I knew I threw good, the way I'm capable of throwing," Seaver said after tossing a five-hitter in which he threw 120 pitches.

But Seaver was peeved after his next start when he was taken out in the seventh inning for a pinch hitter with the runners on second and third and the Mets down, 3–2, to Pittsburgh. The Mets didn't score in that inning, reliever Harry Parker gave up a homer, and the Mets ultimately lost, 5–3.

Seaver groused afterward. "I wasn't outstanding, but I was getting them out," he said. "I just couldn't believe it when he took me out. Well, I can't say anything without being negative about what was an obvious decision to me. I'd be totally negative to the manager, no matter however wrong it looks to me.

"There are times he's working on a hunch and I haven't the slightest idea. The strength of this team, one of the big strengths of this team, lies in the starting pitching."

Seaver's public words about Berra taking him out were not the only complaints about Berra's moves, though many of the others came in private. Even

though Seaver quickly proved he was back to being his old self, the Mets couldn't seem to put much distance between themselves and the .500 mark as the season wore on.

On July 18, there was outright insubordination when Cleon Jones pinch-hit in the seventh inning at Shea against Atlanta and then refused to go in to play defense. He slammed his glove on a dugout wall, threw some towels, and left.

"We're in a state of confusion," GM Joe McDonald said. "We are deciding whether we will be placing him on the suspended list. We thought about welcoming him back tomorrow, about trading his contract to another team, or releasing the player. We haven't decided yet."

Jones was, in effect, suspended, but it took a while for the Mets to figure out their final move with him. Meanwhile, they won a wild, 10–9 game on July 20 against the Astros when Kingman homered twice, driving in six runs. "How many RBI did Kingman get? Seven?" Berra asked. "Six? Is that all?"

The next day, in a 6–2 loss to Houston, Joe Torre tied a major league record by hitting into four double plays. Years later, when Torre was the Yankees' manager, he delighted in jokingly blaming Felix Millan for his dubious record because Millan was the runner erased at second on every double play.

All this time, Jones remained in limbo. But there was a small indication of what might happen on July 22 when the Mets' team picture was taken and Jones was not in it. Jones and his teammates wondered what would happen to him, but the Mets overall kept enjoying baseball. That same day, for instance, Jerry Koosman surprised everyone by stealing a base in a 3–1 victory over the Reds.

He reveled in his only career stolen base in this quote from Red Foley's *Daily News* account the next day: "What's everyone getting so excited about?" Koosman slyly asked after throwing a six-hitter. "It was a play they didn't expect and it worked. It was a delayed steal. And it takes running skill to pull it off. You have to break at the right time. I knew the

Dave Kingman dives back into second base ahead of the tag by San Francisco's Chris Spier.

1970s

Yogi Berra gives
Jerry Grote a pat on
the back after being
fired as manager of
the Mets in 1975.

Reds would never expect me to go and I went. When Wayne [Garrett] took the first pitch, I waited until their catcher was getting set to return to ball to [Reds' pitcher Jack] Billingham. At that point the other infielders are relaxing and that's the time to go."

After splitting two more games with the Reds and then beating the Cubs, the Mets finally announced what they were going to do with Jones: He was released. McDonald sent this teletype to the National League office:

"Having exhausted all avenues in attempting to reconcile this problem, we are offering Cleon Jones his unconditional release. We saw nothing to be gained in going through the arbitration procedure. Regardless of the result, the problem would not be resolved. We have no desire to hurt anyone. The suspension is lifted and Cleon will be paid in full."

Jones was paid for the five games for which he was effectively suspended. Berra wished his former player luck in a story by the *News*'s Augie Borgi on July 27, but he also had some harsh words for him.

"I wish Cleon all the luck in the world. I know he has talent," Berra said. "I think he wasted a lot of his talent and I believe I bent over backward to try to help him. I went overboard." Asked on what, Berra said, "Overlooking things. I know I wasn't going to take any more, that's all. If I was dealing with a white man, I'd do the same thing. It's not a matter of black and white. It's a matter of I wouldn't be able to face any of my players if I took him back. I'm easy to forgive. Like I said, I covered for Jonesy a lot. July 18 was the icing on the cake."

Jones later turned down a contract offer from the Yankees because there was no signing bonus. Jones, only thirty-two when he was released, batted .240 in twenty-one games for that Mets that year. He did not play in the majors again in 1975, and his career was over after only twelve games the next season with the White Sox.

It seemed like Berra had won a battle, but his job's end was coming soon, too.

Some viewed the Mets as a disappointment under

Berra, and his lack of discipline with players sparked some grumbling. The players liked Berra, but may not have respected him as much as a manager should have been respected—odd, considering Berra's relative success as a skipper and his remarkable playing career.

A five-game losing streak from August 3 to 5, which included the Mets getting swept in double-headers by the Pirates and Expos, sealed Berra's fate. The skid dropped the Mets from six games out of first to 9 1/2 games behind.

After the Expos beat the Mets by identical 7–0 scores in an August 5 doubleheader, Berra was fired. The Mets were 56-53 under Berra when they switched to first-base coach Roy McMillan, a brilliant-fielding shortstop as a player who hit only .243 lifetime but made two All-Star teams because of his glove.

"We don't think the team has reached its fullest potential," M. Donald Grant said after Berra was fired. "What is its fullest potential? That's in the papers every day, it's in the percentages. We want higher percentages. This has been a yo-yo season, win five games, lose six games.

"We have been watching this for a long time. The board has had five or six meetings. To us, it became evident a change had to be made. We came close to making it several times, but each time the team would bounce back. On Sunday we were in the thick of it and by Wednesday, in baseball parlance, disaster had struck. To us, this was an indication a change had to be made."

Grant also revealed that there had been talks about firing Berra long before—even in 1973, the year they streaked to the NL pennant with a fantastic finish. The Jones flap, Grant said, did not have anything do to with Berra's ouster, though it couldn't have helped, either.

Berra said he "sort of knew it was coming. I guess you could say the handwriting was on the wall." One of Berra's faults, according to management, was "communication problems," which confused the affable Berra. "Communication problems? I've managed four years and won two pennants," he said, including his stint as Yankee manager in 1964.

"I guess the doubleheader in Pittsburgh did it," Berra added. "I told Mr. Grant they were getting a good man in Roy. I just hope that the players can play well so Roy can keep the job."

On his first day on the job, the forty-six-year-old McMillan said he believed the Mets were not out of the pennant race. They won that night, August 6, beating the Expos and Steve Renko 9–6 at Shea.

The Mets' new manager was in the Hodges-Berra tradition, wrote the *Daily News*'s Larry Fox on Aug. 7—"a stoic with superior abilities at masking his emotions." No less a voice than Bud Harrelson credited McMillan with polishing him into a big league shortstop while a minor league instructor and coach with the Mets. McMillan joined the organization in 1964 as an instructor and he also had managed in the minors. He left to be a coach with the Milwaukee Brewers for three seasons, but returned in 1973 as the first-base coach.

There was no magic in these Mets, however. They were eliminated on September 19, finished 26-27 under McMillan, and were 82-80 for the season, tied for third with the Cardinals and 10 1/2 games behind the Pirates.

Toward the end of the season, with Met playoff hopes dashed, there were two reasons to watch the team. First, the ace was back. Tom Seaver finished 22-9 with a 2.38 ERA and 243 strikeouts to capture his third NL Cy Young Award. On September 24 he came as close to a no-hitter as a Met as he ever would, losing it with two out in the ninth in Chicago on Joe "Tarzan" Wallis's single. It was Seaver's fifth one-hitter.

On September 15, the Mets' next great offensive hope, twenty-three-year-old Mike Vail, tied the league record for a hitting streak by a rookie at twenty-three games, and the milestone ball was sent to the Baseball

Hall of Fame and Museum in Cooperstown, New York. The next night, though, Vail went nothing for seven in an eighteen-inning victory over Montreal, and the streak ended. In the game, his average dropped from .352 to .330.

"I'll just have to start another streak," Vail said.

In thirty-eight games, Vail finished with a .302 average, three homers, and seventeen RBI, and fans were dreaming of him becoming a lineup mainstay and providing the kind of offense the Mets generally lacked.

The Mets certainly thought so. They were comfortable enough with their outfield and offense to add another terrible trade to the Mets' sorry transaction history, swapping Rusty Staub, who set a club record with 105 RBI in 1975, to the Tigers for thirty-five-year-old lefty Mickey Lolich.

The deal was a catastrophe that stung Met fans every time the late 1970s version of the team failed to produce runs. Over the next three seasons, Staub produced 318 RBI, including 121 in 1978, and 61 homers. Lolich, who threw more than 300 innings for Detroit from 1971 to 1974, was a disappointing 8-13 with a 3.22 ERA for the Mets in 1976. Then he retired and unretired, returning for two last seasons with the Padres in 1978 and 1979.

And Vail never lived up to his initial promise, in part because of a foot injury he sustained in the off-season while playing basketball. He played ten years in the big leagues, but he played more than a hundred games only twice—with the Mets in 1977 and the Cubs in 1980. His lifetime batting average was .279. At the trade deadline in 1978, the Indians traded him to the Cubs for Joe Wallis, the man who broke up Seaver's 1975 no-hit bid in the ninth inning.

Ultimately, the Mets decided that McMillan was not their man. On October 3, three days shy of his fifty-third birthday, Tidewater skipper Joe Frazier was introduced as the Mets' new manager. Frazier also had been considered to replace Berra, but Grant said

something that likely would be mocked over today's sports talk radio airwaves: Frazier did not get the job then because Grant did not want to disappoint Tidewater fans—the Tides were leading the International League at the time of Berra's firing.

Frazier was not much of a ballplayer himself, having batted .241 in 217 games for the Indians, Browns, Reds, and Orioles over parts of four seasons in the late 1940s and 1950s. But he had won three straight pennants with Met farm clubs at Memphis, Victoria, and Tidewater. He said of himself, "I'm a fundamentals man. I believe you manage with what you have. You have to manage the young players and hope the older ones take care of themselves.

"I think the Mets have a nucleus here. They have good personnel and we're just going to put it together."

It was only early June of '76, but when your manager says, "I feel like going to the Empire State Building and jumping off," your season might be in trouble. Joking or not, Joe Frazier was quoted saying that in the June 5 *Daily News* just before the Mets started a ten-game western swing. They had lost eleven of their previous thirteen games and were 11 1/2 games out of first, even though they had spent nineteen days in first place already in the season, the last on May 19.

"We're making mistakes major leaguers shouldn't make," added Jerry Koosman. "And we keep repeating our mistakes. We shouldn't do that."

So the fifteenth Mets season was listing already. It would not recover. The Mets finished 86-76, fifteen games behind the division-winning Phillies, who would replace the Pirates as the NL East's power for the next few years.

But there was plenty of Met intrigue to follow during the year. Tom Seaver signed a three-year, $675,000

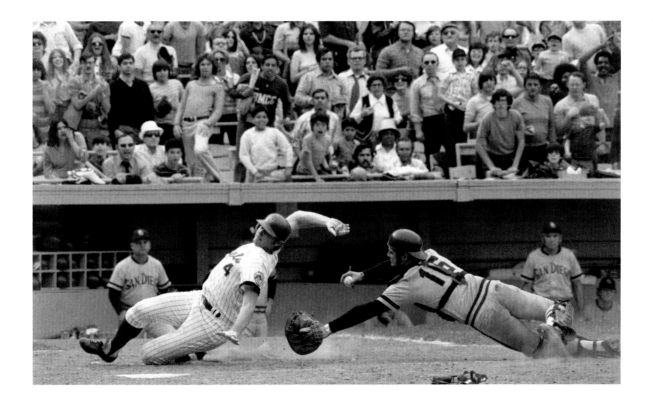

contract just before the season and there was speculation he would be traded. It was the dawn of free agency. Seaver wanted to stay in New York, but there was a lot of money being thrown around for pitchers not nearly as good. This was the start of a staredown between Seaver and M. Donald Grant.

Dodgers' ace Don Sutton had asked for a trade in spring training, and when the Mets visited Los Angeles in June, the normally garrulous Sutton was close-mouthed, telling the *News*'s Augie Borgi, "I'm going to keep my mouth shut. I'd only say something I might regret." Later, reports trickled out that Grant had initiated trade talks to send Seaver to the Dodgers for Sutton.

Jerry Koosman, meanwhile, had perhaps the best season of his career, going 21-10 with a 2.70 ERA. Seaver was 14-11, but struck out 235 batters, the ninth straight year he'd reached the 200-K mark. Skip Lockwood had 19 saves.

Dave Kingman, however, was the Mets' best attraction. He set a then-club record with 37 home runs and also led the team with 86 RBI.

On April 15, Borgi wrote that Kingman hit a 500-foot homer at Wrigley Field, one day after he had crashed what Augie Borgi wrote in the *News* as "a

630-foot shot, the longest in the history of Wrigley Field." While Borgi may have been overcome by sportswriting hyperbole, one thing was certain: Sky King was delivering power.

He hit seven home runs in the Mets' first nine games and was quoted in the April 20 *News* as saying, "This was the first game this season that I felt like a hitter. Believe it or not, I've been struggling."

After Kingman hit two homers in Pittsburgh in April, Pirates' catcher Manny Sanguillen predicted he could hit as many as seventy homers, which would have shattered Hack Wilson's then-NL mark of fifty-six. No less a slugger than Willie Stargell believed Kingman would hit a ball clear out of stadiums. "He's going to be something," Stargell said. "He's already a home run hitter but he's just learned what it's all about. I can say that because he's learned to adjust, learned how to figure out pitchers, learned that the mind must be positive." Met teammate Mickey Lolich wondered if Kingman would be the league's Most Valuable Player.

"All I can tell you about home runs is that they come in bunches," Kingman said. "Most home run hitters hit home runs in bunches. At least I always have. I can't say how many homers I can hit. But I can

1970s

say I'm swinging the way I should, that's what experience is all about. I'm thinking like a hitter at the plate, I'm remembering how they got me out in the past."

Kingman had thirty home runs before the All-Star break and was on pace to threaten Wilson's mark, a strange spot for someone in a Met uniform, considering the team's mostly punchless history. Ultimately, though, there was no great Kingman Home Run Chase—he suffered torn thumb ligaments diving for a fly ball on July 19 and did not return until August 27. After recovering from the injury, he hit only five more homers.

A June 25 game in Chicago brought a wild, 7–4 Met victory that included another Kingman homer, Mike Phillips becoming the third Met to hit for the cycle, and Jon Matlack improving to 9-2. But it also laid bare some hard feelings when Frazier yanked John Milner when Milner did not hustle on a dropped fly ball.

In an incident that reminded reporters of when Gil Hodges walked out to left field and asked Cleon Jones if he were sick and then took him out of the game for not hustling, Frazier sent in Bruce Boisclair to pinch-run for Milner when Milner made first only after Manny Trillo dropped Milner's pop in short right field. Milner angrily threw his helmet when he was removed, Borgi wrote in the June 26 edition of the *Daily News*.

"No, I didn't ask him if he was hurt," Frazier said after the game. "I can tell. If he doesn't run, he must be hurt and we don't want the boy to hurt himself." Milner, who had pulled his right groin a week earlier, refused to answer questions and Matlack was mad too, over Met fielding flubs, and did not go on Jack Brickhouse's local postgame television show.

Phillips, meanwhile, joined Tommie Agee (1970) and Jim Hickman (1963) as the only Mets to have a single, double, triple, and home run in the same game. Phillips was a career utility infielder who played eleven

seasons in the majors though he never hit higher than .268. He had been in a nothing-for-twenty-two slump before doubling in the third inning.

He also, somewhat hilariously, won what the Met players were calling the "snake award" during the game. It was given to a player making a bonehead play in the game, and Phillips got thrown out trying to advance from second to third on a grounder to the shortstop. Torre invented it during an earlier trip to San Diego, buying a fake snake in Tijuana and intending to give it to Lolich. "Now we present it every game," Torre said.

McDonald probably should have gotten one the next month when he sent Del Unser and Wayne Garrett to Montreal for Pepe Mangual and Jim Dwyer, a trade that flopped. There was one glimmer of hope for the '76 Mets, however—a twenty-one-year-old prospect named Lee Mazzilli made his debut on September 7.

For some Met fans, 1977 means only one thing: the "Midnight Massacre" that saw the Mets trade Tom Seaver to the Reds and Dave Kingman to the Padres, a night of infamy in club history that probably led the team to a downward spiral for nearly a decade.

Seaver was "The Franchise," the best Met ever, one of the few reasons to go to games at this point. Even in a year when the "Son of Sam" killer had the city gripped by fear, Seaver's battle with M. Donald Grant that led to the June 15 trade bore its way into New York's consciousness and left legions of fans with a sour feeling about the Mets.

A soap opera in flannel and business suits was carried out on the ball field and the boardrooms. Seaver was one principal and the others, as Bill Madden described them in a 2007 *Daily News* story recounting the drama, were "Grant, the buttoned-down, authoritarian Wall Street stockbroker whose tight-fisted

fiscal policies had contributed mightily to the Mets'
decline and evoked widespread criticism from players and the media; and Dick Young, the *Daily News*'s
acerbic columnist whose siding with Grant in the
dispute evoked conflict-of-interest charges from rival
colleagues and the enmity of Met fans."

Seaver was outspoken during spring training about
his—and, presumably, his teammates'—unhappiness
over the Mets not pursuing any of the new free agents.
Center fielder Gary Matthews would have been a good
fit at Shea, but he signed with the Braves for $1.2 mil-
lion over five years. On February 26, during camp,
Seaver asked a gathering of writers, "How can you
not even try?"

In May, Seaver referred to Grant as "a bleeping maniac" when Grant talked about how much he
wanted to beat the Yankees in the Mayor's Trophy
Game. Seaver apologized the next day, but the two
were at war.

But, as Madden wrote, the seeds of the saga were
planted much earlier, on July 12, 1976, when a new
collective bargaining agreement was reached and
free agency began. Seaver had signed a three-year,
$675,000 contract four months earlier, briefly making
him the highest-paid pitcher. But eleven free-agent
pitchers signed multiyear deals worth $1 million or
more before the 1977 season.

Seaver and Grant had battled over that 1976 contract, and strong feelings still simmered after it was
signed. As Seaver said, "I was made an example of.
I was pictured as the ingrate after nine years with
the club. I was to be punished. And even now, a year
later, I still resent the way they did it."

So a season of change was brewing for the Mets.
But Seaver threw a shutout in the Mets' April 12 home
opener against the Cardinals, the same day Kingman,
who had his own contract issues with the Mets, heard
hoots from some fans.

As the *News*'s Norm Miller wrote, "The boos dom-

Tom Seaver shows
off two of his three
Cy Young awards.

inated the cheers by roughly 60–40." Carl Erhardt, the
Shea signmaker, held signs reading, among others,
"Just Another Greedy Bum," "King Phooey," and "Out-
fielder for Sale Cheap." But other signs supported King-
man, including one in right field that read, "Grant
Dave His Raise."

"I was oblivious to it all," Kingman told Miller
after the game, in which he went nothing for four.

On April 17, Seaver threw his fifth career one-
hitter in a 6–0 shutout of the Cubs. Steve Ontiveros
got the lone hit on a sinking drive to right in the fifth
inning that Ed Kranepool dove for but couldn't get.
"It was a sinking change, low, on a perfect part of the
plate," Seaver said in Jack Lang's story in the April 18
edition of the *News*. "It was not a mistake pitch. He
just reached down and got it. It wasn't a bad pitch."

The Mets, meanwhile, were foundering in Joe Frazier's second year, standing at 15-30 and in sixth place
after forty-five games. On May 31, with the Mets in
a stretch in which they had lost six straight games
and nine of ten, Frazier was fired and replaced by Joe
Torre, who was to become a player-manager. No one
else was considered, GM Joe McDonald said.

1970s

"We think the time had come for a change," McDonald said. "We hope Joe Torre can do the job that will get us back on the track."

The Mets won Torre's first game, beating the Expos, 6–2, so the change at least ended the losing streak. In the June 1 *Daily News* Red Foley wrote, "The Mets clubhouse didn't resemble Times Square on VJ Day, but there was an unmistakable aura of good feeling. While Torre sat in his clubhouse office sipping beer from a mug and puffing a big, black cigar, his players were in the main room smiling and chatting just like the winning clubs do."

Torre, who was hitting .180 when he became the manager, retired as a player eighteen days later. He'd need the extra time to deal with what was coming.

By this time, it was no secret that the Mets would talk to interested clubs about a Seaver trade. In a June 1 column, Young recounted an anecdote in which a competing team wasn't interested.

"Let's talk about Matlack," the club said. "We're not going to trade Matlack," Grant said. "If we trade Matlack, we still have the headache." Then Young wrote, "That's what he has become. Tom Terrific has become Tom Headache."

"He has destroyed his market," Grant told Young. Young also called Seaver "an irreparably destructive force on the Mets" and added, "In his undisciplined rage at the front office, he put down his teammates." Young called Seaver "a pop-off troublemaker" and wrote, "Talent does not give a young man the license to be rude, arrogant, insubordinate.

"In discussing Tom Seaver and his problems, we must never mix up the two Tom Seavers. One is the pitcher, who is tremendous. The other, the person, is less than tremendous."

Rival newspapers began pointing out that Young may not exactly have been impartial when it came to the Mets. His son-in-law, Thornton Geary, had been hired by the Mets a few years earlier as a vice president of communications and, Madden wrote, had put together the Mets' first TV deal with Cablevision. "But as the Young-Seaver war began to rage, he became an unwitting cause célèbre," Madden wrote.

"That was probably the toughest year of my life," Geary told Madden. "There were writers, particularly at the *Post*, who wanted to get Dick and I was a convenient pawn. I admit, I wouldn't have gotten through the door with Grant had it not been for Dick, but I was good at my job."

The defiant Young wrote of the relationship: "My son-in-law does work for the Mets. He has a master's degree and he is probably, if anything, being underpaid. I warned against him taking a job there. I said baseball people in the front office are the most underpaid people in the world."

Meanwhile, the *News*'s beat reporter on the Mets, Jack Lang, was drawn into the contretemps. He had a good relationship with Seaver and, Madden wrote, Young pulled him aside one day to tell him to report the story "as he saw fit. Don't worry about me. You report the news and feel free to take Seaver's side in this thing. Besides, it'll make for good reading if we take different opinions."

On Sunday, June 12, Seaver beat the Astros, 3–1. The back page of the next day's *Daily News* read, "Seaver's Last Met Game?" Before the game, Seaver talked to reporters—something unheard-of today—and admitted, "There is a strong possibility this could be my last game for the Mets. I know they are still talking to other clubs about me. The strong possibility exists that I will be traded. That's all I can say about it."

Added Torre: "I know Tom is very unhappy here."

After the final out, John Stearns hugged him and so did Bud Harrelson. Seaver "quickly walked off the field almost as if to avoid the many handshakes from his teammates," Lang wrote. In the clubhouse,

Seaver, his head down, refused to talk to reporters, which was unusual. "Please leave me alone," he said. "I don't want to talk. I'm sick. Please leave me alone." Lang wrote of a flu bug affecting the team, but he also wrote, "Before the game, when he conceded the possibility of a trade, Tom gave no indication of being ill."

On June 15, the day of the trading deadline, "Seaver vs. Grant" blared from the back page of the *News*. Lang and Young presented differing opinions on what was called "the battle page."

Lang quoted Seaver as saying, "[Grant] put the onus of the trade on me. My unhappiness started with the contract negotiations a year and a half ago. . . . All of a sudden, nine years of performance for the Mets was thrown out the window. . . . They even threatened to trade me if I didn't sign it, so I signed."

Young wrote, "In a way, Tom Seaver is like Walter O'Malley. Both are very good at what they do. Both are very deceptive in what they say. Both are very greedy."

Young also wrote words that would ultimately outrage Seaver and prompt the pitcher to scuttle any peace proceedings, which had started behind the scenes with Grant and the Mets.

Young wrote, "Nolan Ryan is getting more now than Seaver and that galls Tom because Nancy Seaver and Ruth Ryan are very friendly and Tom Seaver long has treated Nolan Ryan like a little brother."

Later that day, a Met fans' worst nightmare happened: Seaver was dealt to the Reds for infielder Doug Flynn, pitcher Pat Zachry, and minor league outfielders Steve Henderson and Dan Norman. In another deal, minutes before the midnight trade deadline, the Mets sent Kingman to the Padres for Bobby Valentine and Paul Siebert. The front page of the *Daily News* read, "Mets Deal Stars: Seaver to Reds; Kingman to S.D."

The Mets released a statement bearing Grant's signature that read, "Last night [Tuesday, June 14], Tom Seaver talked with General Manager Joe McDonald with strong suggestions regarding his remaining with

the Mets. While the owners and directors were considering these suggestions this morning, a message came from Tom Seaver—as was later confirmed—that he had a change of heart. He said, 'Forget what I told Joe McDonald last night. I want out.' Therefore, the board felt an obligation to consider the deal at hand and have decided to accept Cincinnati's offer. It is with sincere regret that we have met Tom Seaver's request and traded him to Cincinnati."

Grant had offered Kingman a $200,000 salary, but Kingman wanted more. Before trading him, they asked him again to sign for that amount, for anywhere from two to six years, Lang wrote. The next day, McDonald said Kingman had asked if the Mets would consider signing him as a free agent after the season.

The pictures in the papers were of sad-looking athletes dressed in the loud, flashy threads of the age. Kingman, in a photo by the *News*'s Dan Farrell, carried an equipment bag while wearing a checked vest that matched his pants.

Seaver and his wife, Nancy, cried the day after the trade. Seaver broke down while cleaning out his locker, according to Norm Miller's story, and at the press conference to discuss his departure. At one point he excused himself from a news conference and went to a clubhouse bathroom to collect his thoughts. His eyes had reddened when he returned.

His voice cracking, Seaver talked about New York fans, saying, "I know they appreciated watching me. . . . If I could regain enough composure to talk sixty seconds, I'd have it made. As far as the fans go, I've given them a great number of thrills and they've been equally returned." Seaver cited a huge ovation he had gotten recently for passing Sandy Koufax in career strikeouts, saying it was "one of the most memorable and warm moments in my life."

At the end, it sounded as if Seaver had hope that he would not be traded. Miller quoted Seaver as saying, "A couple of days ago, I was talking to the club and there was a little discussion about the possibility of a new contract. I understand the club's position about renegotiation. My proposal was to play the next two years under my current contract [three years for $225,000 per season] and talk to them about the three years after that, 1979, 1980, and 1981."

Seaver's contract would be extended by three years for $300,000 the first year and $400,000 the next two, Madden wrote. Seaver called McDonald and told him to break off trade talks with the Reds.

But, Seaver said, any potential agreement was set

ablaze by Young's column and the references to Nancy and the Seavers' relationship with the Ryans. "I don't know how far that got," Seaver said, referring to the contract talks, "because of something that happened the next day. Dick Young's column, when he dragged my wife into it and my family, I called the Mets back and pulled my offer back and said, 'That's it.'"

In fact, Seaver was sitting in the coffee shop of the hotel where the Mets were staying in Atlanta when he heard about Young's column and bolted out of his chair. He stomped back to his room, Madden wrote, and called Mets PR director Arthur Richman and bellowed, "Get me out of here, do you hear me? Get me out of here!" He told Richman to call Mrs. deRoulet's daughter, Whitney, and inform her that the contract deal was off. "And tell Joe McDonald everything I said last night is forgotten."

Thirty years later, Seaver told Madden, "That Young column was the straw that broke the back. Bringing your family into it with no truth whatsoever to what he wrote. I could not abide that. I had to go."

The *News*'s switchboard, Miller reported, lit up with calls the day after the trade with fans outraged at Seaver's departure and Young's role.

Seaver's anger has hardly cooled over the years. He told Madden he has nothing but contempt for Grant, who died in November 1998 at ninety-four.

"There are two things Grant said to me that I'll never forget, but illustrate the kind of person he was and the total 'plantation' mentality he had," Seaver told Madden. "During the labor negotiations, he came up to me in the clubhouse once and said, 'What are you, some sort of Communist?' Another time, and I've never told anyone this, he said to me: 'Who do you think you are, joining the Greenwich Country Club?' It was incomprehensible to him if you didn't understand his feelings about your station in life."

Fan reaction did not favor the trade. In the June 17 *Daily News*, a photo ran of a young woman hold-

A fan displays her displeasure with M. Donald Grant over the trade of Tom Seaver.

ing a sign that read, "Bury Grant. Bring back our Tom." Pete Hamill wrote a column in the *News* that was headlined, "Who's Buried in Grant's Tomb? The Mets and the City." Hamill wrote that his colleague Young "for almost two years has been functioning as a hit man for the Met management and in that role he has helped drive a great ballplayer out of town, helped demoralize younger men and, worst of all, has demeaned his own talents."

A day earlier, Young's "Young Ideas" column carried the headline, "Fans Uptight Over Seaver . . . but for How Long?" He accused Seaver of wanting to be baseball's first player-general manager.

After beating Atlanta on June 15, the Mets were 26-35, fourteen games out of first place, their season going nowhere, their fans mad. All that was left was to see how their new players fared. Henderson had what was probably his best season in a twelve-year career, hitting twelve homers, driving in sixty-five runs, and batting .297 in ninety-nine games and finishing second in the Rookie of the Year balloting to future Hall of Famer Andre Dawson.

Zachry was 7-6 with a 3.76 ERA in nineteen starts for the Mets, and Flynn hit .191 with no homers and fourteen RBI in ninety games. Norman hit .250 in seven games.

Seaver, who was 7-3 with a 3.00 ERA for the Mets at the time of the trade, went 14-3 for the Reds with a 2.34 ERA and finished tied for third in the NL Cy Young vote with Rick Reuschel, bettered only by winner Steve Carlton and Tommy John.

On August 21, Seaver got one of those victories against his old team and his friend Koosman, beating the Mets, 5–1. He got a huge ovation as he came out of the dugout from the 46,265 at Shea. Koosman's eyes welled with tears when Torre came to the mound to take him out of the game in the eighth inning. "It was a very emotional game for him," Torre was quoted as saying in Lang's article the next day.

Seaver, too. "The entire weekend has been very emotional for me, too," Seaver said. "I'm glad the whole thing is over."

The Mets finished 64-98 and in sixth place, thirty-seven games behind the Phillies. It was their first last-place finish since 1967. Other notable moments during the season: On July 13, the blackout that hit the city for two days affected the Mets, Cubs, and 14,626 paying customers at Shea. On August 12, Felix Millan

fought Pirates' catcher Ed Ott at second base, and Ott threw Millan to the ground, breaking the infielder's collarbone. Millan never played in the majors again.

Only 1,066,825 fans came to Shea to the see the Mets, down more than 400,000 from 1976 and starting an attendance plunge there that was understandable considering the direction of the club.

On December 8, the Mets traded another from their stable of pitchers, dealing Jon Matlack to Texas and John Milner to the Pirates in a huge, four-team, eleven-player trade at baseball's winter meetings in which they got Willie Montanez.

Montanez was a twenty-nine-year-old first baseman who hit .287 with twenty homers and sixty-eight RBI for the Braves the year before, and the Mets got Tom Grieve and a player to be named later, who would be Ken Henderson the next spring. That same day, the Mets were close to a trade that would have sent Koosman to the Royals for first baseman John Mayberry and outfielder Joe Zdeb. The Royals were ready to announce it, according to a Phil Pepe story in the *News*, but the Mets then wanted Andy Hassler instead of Zdeb. The Royals said OK, but then the Mets balked again and the deal was off.

"It was my first reality that the game is really a business," Matlack said in a 2008 interview. In the phone call he got from the Mets, Matlack was told there was good news and bad news—the good news is that the Mets had acquired Montanez; the bad news was that Matlack was going to Texas.

"I probably couldn't have told you one player on the Rangers," Matlack added. "Shock, letdown, realization the game really is a business. I had no control over it, so you made the best out of it. That was that."

As for Seaver, he was both happy and sad about the year's events.

"It was both the worst day of my career and the best day as I look back on it now," Seaver told Madden thirty years later. "The team was being run into the

Lee Mazzilli and Joe Torre.

ground by Grant—and really had started to go down after Gil [Hodges] died [in 1972]. If I had stayed, once the whole face of the club had begun to change, would I have won three hundred games? As it was, I got to play with Rose and [Johnny] Bench in Cincinnati, then I got to see the other league and got to play with Pudge [Carlton Fisk] and even got to experience the Red Sox in 1986 and all that Boston energy. It would have been nice to be a Met my whole career, but I'm eternally grateful to have experienced all I did."

The years immediately following the "Midnight Massacre" were so bleak for the Mets that even the club acknowledges that there isn't much they want to remember from that period. The team's 2010 media guide holds a section called "Important Dates in Mets History." There is not one date listed between June 15, 1977—the Seaver trade—and January 24, 1980, the day the Mets were sold to a group headed by Doubleday & Company.

Of course, things happened—mostly losses on the field in games played by some forgettable Mets. Still, there were some decent individual accomplishments: John Stearns stole 25 bases in 1978, breaking a league record for catchers that had stood for almost 80 years. Craig Swan led the NL with a 2.43 ERA, and Nino Espinosa won 11 games.

And Lee Mazzilli, who everyone thought was the Mets' next star, continued his development, leading the team with a .273 average and adding 16 homers and 61 RBI. Montanez hit 17 homers and knocked in 96 runs for a team that scored only 607, eighth in the league.

The Mets finished 66-96, in sixth place again, 24 games behind NL East titlists Philadelphia. Met home attendance dropped further, to 1,007,328, 10th in the 12-team National League.

It was the last season for Met fans to cheer Jerry Koosman, who was traded after a nightmare season in

1970s

which he went 3-15 with a 3.75 ERA, just two years after his only 20-win season.

Another change came, too. On November 8, M. Donald Grant was forced out by the team's board of directors. He had been chairman of the Mets since their inception in 1962 and was directly blamed by fans for the Seaver trade. Also, while the cross-town Yankees and their owner, George Steinbrenner, embraced free agency as a way to improve, Grant did not, and the Mets suffered for it.

In the November 9 edition of the *News*, Mike Lupica wrote, "The Paysons finally caught on to the fact that a once-great franchise, a franchise that produced such memorable summers in this city, had been run into the ground by Grant and his minions. Maybe one of the Paysons got lost on the way to the country in September and caught a weekend series in a grave-yard called Shea Stadium."

A month later, Koosman, one of the few remaining links to the 1969 championship team, was gone, sent to his native Minnesota for right-hander Greg Field and a player to be named later, who eventually was reliever Jesse Orosco.

Joe McDonald said the trade was dictated by two factors, Phil Pepe wrote. "To satisfy a player who has contributed to two pennants and one world championship, a player who has been good for us," McDonald said. He added, "The possibility that Jerry would retire—he indicated he might—and so we wanted to get as much as we could for him."

It was obvious, however, that McDonald wasn't very happy. "The reason I'm not smiling during this announcement is that I still think Jerry has a great arm and, in spite of his record, he can pitch."

For a while, the Koosman deal was supposed to include another trade and another team—Rod Carew was

supposed to go from the Twins to the Giants; Mike Ivie, Larry Herndon, and pitching prospect Phil Nastu were supposed to go to the Twins; and Minnesota was going to flip Nastu to the Mets for Koosman. Orosco worked out better—Nastu appeared in only thirty-four major league games over parts of three seasons for the Giants.

In 1979, the Mets were mostly treading water. How good could the season be if the Mets put their logo on the cover of their official yearbook instead of pictures of their actual players? Even the photogenic Lee Mazzilli couldn't bump the "NY" off the cover.

It was another sixth-place finish at 63-99, thirty-five games behind the World Champion Pirates. The Mets were a woeful 6-32 at home after the All-Star break, which probably played a huge role in their awful attendance—just 788,905 came to see the Mets at Shea, worst in the National League. Shea never saw a crowd that cracked the 30,000 mark.

Lee Mazzilli had perhaps the best season of his career, batting .303 with fifteen homers, a seventy-nine RBI, and thirty-four stolen bases. His only career All-Star appearance was a big night for Met fans. At Seattle's Kingdome, Mazzilli tied the score at 6–6 with an eighth-inning homer off Texas's Jim Kern and drew a walk against the Yankees' Ron Guidry with the bases loaded to force in the eventual winning run in the top of the ninth. He was edged by Dave Parker, who threw out two base runners, for MVP honors.

Ed Kranepool, who began his Met career at seventeen years old in 1962, hung up his spikes at age thirty-four after the 1979 season and was the club's career leader in nearly every offensive category. The last of the 1969 Mets was gone.

After the season, the Mets were put up for sale. More changes were coming, this time for the better.

1980s

DAILY ◉ NEWS

NEW YORK'S PICTURE NEWSPAPER

35¢

Tuesday, October 28, 1986

section

YES!

On January 24, 1980, a group headed by Nelson Doubleday, the president of the world's largest book publishing
firm, bought the team from the Payson family for $21.1
million. Doubleday and his partners, Fred Wilpon and
Saul Katz of Sterling Equities, outbid the investment firm
of Allen and Co. by roughly $2 million. At the time, the
sale price was the most paid for a Major League Baseball
team, Jack Lang wrote in the January 25 *News*.

A statement issued to the news media early on the evening of the sale read, "Nelson Doubleday, president of Doubleday Inc., and a great-great nephew of the man who invented baseball, announced that he had agreed to purchase controlling interest in the New York Mets baseball team. The Doubleday Publishing Co. has been in New York for 80 years."

Doubleday then issued another brief statement via phone that said, "We believe in New York. We believe it is the communications and entertainment center of the world. We also feel the city deserves the greatest team in the world."

That was music to the ears of beleaguered Mets fans, who were unhappy with the state of the team.

Less than a month later, the team announced that ex–Baltimore Orioles' architect Frank Cashen was the Mets' new general manager. At the very least, Cashen made it clear during his introductory press conference that he would be interesting. That, coupled with his résumé of building the great Orioles teams of the previous decade, shot some excitement into the Met fan base, too.

The fifty-three-year-old Cashen, sporting a nasty gash above his left eye sustained playing racquetball, spoke of rekindling "Met magic," according to a February 22 News story by Aaron C. Elson. Cashen declared, "This town is big enough for two baseball teams and I'm not even ready to concede the Bronx.

"We are going to turn this club around," Cashen added that day. "I can't tell you how long it's gonna take to win a pennant, but we're going to win a pennant. I'm not planning any wholesale changes at this time, but I do reserve the right to make any changes that I feel necessary in the future."

So began the task of remaking the Mets, and things did get better immediately, if only slightly. The Mets finished 67-95, in fifth place and twenty-four games behind the Phillies, but they were out of the cellar for the first time since 1976. Attendance also increased

for the first time since 1975, rising to 1,192,073, ninth in the National League.

Second baseman Doug Flynn won a Gold Glove; Mark Bomback, who threw a two-hitter on April 30, led the pitching staff with ten wins in his first full season; and Neil Allen had twenty-two saves. Lee Mazzilli led the team in homers (sixteen) and RBI (seventy-six), and Claudell Washington, grabbed in a trade with the White Sox on June 7, pounds three homers at Dodger Stadium two weeks later.

On June 14, the Mets beats the Giants, 7–6, with a five-run ninth inning capped by Steve Henderson's three-run homer, his first homer in 226 at-bats. The Mets had trailed, 6–0, after five innings and did not have a hit against John Montefusco. The win resonated with fans, who clung to any positive during this era; some called it "the Steve Henderson game."

Henderson and Mazzilli combined on another nifty comeback September 14; Mazzilli drove in five runs and Henderson capped a four-run ninth with a three-run homer off future Hall of Famer Bruce Sutter in a 10–7 win over the Cubs.

The Mets began the season 6-14 but then won 21-14 and were as close as six games out of first place on August 2. But they had a horrendous finish, going 11-38 in their final forty-nine games, including a thirteen-game losing streak from August 31 to September 12. Their longest winning streaks all season were two four-game binges.

GM Frank Cashen watches the action from the dugout during the 1986 pennant race.

Steve Henderson.

1980s

On April 19, the Mets blew a 9–1 lead in Chicago, and their old pal Dave Kingman hit two homers, including a grand slam.

On August 17, the Phillies completed a five-game sweep of the Mets, scoring forty runs and banging out seventy-one hits in the process and essentially crushing any hopes of a postseason at Shea. As Jack Lang wrote in the August 18 edition of the *News*, "Even the usually optimistic Joe Torre referred to it as a 'lost weekend . . . a weekend we want to forget.'" It was the first time since 1964 that the Mets were swept in a five-game set, giving you an idea of where the franchise stood at this point.

On September 29, the smallest crowd in Shea history, 1,787 fans, saw the Mets beat the Pirates, 5–4, on Joel Youngblood's two-run homer in the tenth inning.

The Mets hit only sixty-one home runs, the fewest in the majors, and the *Daily News* had a daily chart comparing their output to Roger Maris's 1961 season, when he hit sixty-one homers all by himself. When the Mets tied Maris, a headline in the *News* read, "The Season's a Success: Mets Tie Maris HR Mark." No Met catcher hit a home run the entire season.

At times, things were bleak enough that what passed for entertainment at Shea was counting how many times pitcher John Pacella's cap flew off his head during his delivery.

But even the late-season bleak times brought hope: Wally Backman, Mookie Wilson, and Hubie Brooks came up in September and were glimmers of something good. The Mets gave Torre a two-year contract after the season, too, figuring he was the man to guide a renaissance.

Ah, what might have been. It's a theme of sorts for the Mets' 1981 season, from their dalliances with big-name players during the winter before it started to the status of a strong-armed prospect named Tim Leary. Ultimately unsatisfying for Met fans, the strike-interrupted 1981 season held such promise, even when the Mets were contending toward the end of the second half but lost eight of their last twelve games.

Over the previous winter, the Mets courted Dave Winfield, the Padres star who was a free agent. They tried to make trades for Fred Lynn and Carney Lansford at the winter meetings in Dallas. But nothing worked.

During the off-season, Joe Torre was so sure Winfield would be a Met, the manager said, "I have a gut feeling he'll come with us." Winfield, however, had made it clear that he wanted to play for a contender.

"You can make us a contender," Torre told the slugger. "We were almost there last summer, the way we played. This isn't San Diego. Our rebuilding program is very close. We're just one or two players away and you can be the one that could help us turn the corner."

Winfield even had a two-hour meeting with Fred Wilpon, according to a Jack Lang story on November 11. But the Mets were not the type of contender Winfield was looking for, though apparently he liked the city fine—he signed with the Yankees.

But the Mets acquired former Cy Young Award winner Randy Jones from San Diego during the winter for John Pacella and Jose Moreno. It wasn't as great as it sounds—the two-time twenty-game winner had four straight losing seasons since winning the award in 1976 and he had been hurt in 1980.

But, Jones said, "I've changed my motion and my mechanics and I'm gradually getting my strength back." Didn't work—he was 1-8 with a 4.85 ERA.

Rusty Staub returned as a free agent and hit .317. The Mets reacquired Dave Kingman from the Cubs for, of all people, Steve Henderson. Sky King, who always had a stormy relationship with the press, promised to talk to reporters this time. Kingman hit twenty-two homers and drove in fifty-nine, leading the club in both categories.

Mookie Wilson and Hubie Brooks were starters, and Neil Allen had seven wins and eighteen saves in just forty-three appearances.

Even Cleon Jones, whose tenure as a Met had ended in controversy six years earlier, was welcomed back as a general minor league hitting instructor in February. Jones told the *News*'s Chuck Slater in the

Dave Kingman blasts his ninth homer of the 1982 season.

February 17 edition, "What's supposed to have happened is an unfortunate situation and I'm still paying for it. I'd like to put it behind me. I'd like to think everyone else will."

Slogans—my, how the Mets love slogans, eh?— promoted the season. One year after famous ad man Jerry Della Femina had coined a campaign for the Mets with the phrase "The Magic Is Back"—often lampooned as "The Tragic Is Back"—the team was declaring "The Magic Is Here."

It certainly seemed that way with Leary, a promising young right-handed pitcher whom the Mets had drafted with the second overall pick in 1979. Dick Young wrote a column headlined "No Irish Malarkey: Leary the Next Seaver." No pressure, Tim.

Torre pleaded with Cashen to let Leary make the big club. Just before spring camp broke, Torre said, "He has enough stuff to pitch in the big leagues. Now it's just a matter of discussing whether he can handle pitching in the big leagues. We will sit down and talk about it—all of us. Frank Cashen, myself, and the coaches. Tim has pitched consistently in all his outings. But we have to decide what's best for Tim

1980s

Leary before, in the long run, what is best for Leary, whether it is now or in June, in the long run will be best for the Mets."

Ultimately, Torre got what he wanted, and Leary made the club. He started April 12 on a damp, forty-seven-degree day in Chicago, one that may have changed the course of his career and perhaps Met fortunes. Leary lasted only two innings—he did not allow a hit or a run and walked one while striking out three—before he came out because his elbow had tightened.

"It was strictly a precautionary move," Torre said afterward. "With a kid like this, you don't take any chances."

It was too late, though. Leary had felt tightness in the same area a week or so earlier at an exhibition game in Jackson, Mississippi. After a diagnosis of a muscle strain, the Mets' original plan was for him to skip one start. But on April 20, he had a throwing session and still felt tenderness, so the Mets put him on the twenty-one-day disabled list.

Leary did not pitch in the majors again until 1983 and pitched in only twenty-three games for the Mets

in his career, though he was later a seventeen-game winner for the Dodgers in 1988, throwing six shut-outs for their World Championship team. The Mets dealt him to Milwaukee on January 18, 1985, as part of a forgettable four-team trade that landed them Frank Wills, who never pitched for them.

Meanwhile, the Mets won only eight of their first thirty games, a worse start than even the all-time losers, the 1962 Mets, who had at least won eleven times in their first thirty. The *News* ran a fan survey wondering whether Torre was to blame for their awful start.

On May 10, the Mets traded Jeff Reardon and Dan Norman to Montreal for Ellis Valentine, a misguided deal that created a jam in their outfield. Immediately after the trade, Joel Youngblood said, "There's got to be anther deal coming. This can't be the end of it. I'm sure they must be planning to make another move. We're up to our ears in outfielders."

The Mets finished the first half in fifth place, 17-34 and fifteen games behind Philadelphia. After the strike was over, they won their second-half opener and were in first place, because Major League Baseball had decided to split the season into two halves, with the division winners from each facing each other in a playoff series to determine who goes to the League Championship Series.

But the Mets stumbled at the end of the season and finished fourth in the second half, 24-28, 5 1/2 games behind Montreal. Overall, the Mets were 41-62, fifth in the NL East.

Torre's coaches did not have contracts for the next season, though he did, and he went to Cashen to discuss it. On October 4, Cashen told them no one, including Torre, had a job for 1982. "I own the dubious distinction of being the first guy to fire Joe Torre," Cashen said in a 2010 interview.

At the time, Torre held the longest tenure of any Met manager. He was replaced by George Bamberger, a Staten Island native, who had spent most of his own playing career in the minors, though he pitched briefly for the New York Giants and Baltimore Orioles. Bamberger had been a tremendous pitching coach for Baltimore when Cashen ran the Orioles, producing eighteen twenty-game winners in his tenure, including four in the 1971 season.

Cashen, recalling how those powerful Orioles teams won with terrific arms, was hoping Bamberger could "prepare the pitching staff for the time when we were going to win."

The fifty-six-year-old Bamberger had managed the Milwaukee Brewers to a third-place finish in 1978 and a second-place finish in 1979, winning ninety-three or more games each year. He had a heart attack in spring training of 1980, but returned in early June after bypass surgery. He resigned in September.

When he took the Met job, he said, "I needed a challenge. But it goes further than that. People forget that when I took over the Brewers in 1977, they were a team that was twenty-eight games under .500—just like this one. So, in that respect, the job ahead doesn't scare me."

"Suddenly, there's a new George in town," read Jack Lang's lead in a story in the February 6, 1982, edition of the *News*. And he didn't mean Bamberger. The Mets were getting close to acquiring Cincinnati slugger George Foster, one of the most feared power hitters in the game. He was almost five years removed from his fifty-two-homer season in 1977, but the thirty-three-year-old Foster figured to be a potent bat in the middle of the Mets' needy lineup.

The Mets sent pitchers Greg Harris and Jim Kern and catcher Alex Trevino to the Reds and then signed Foster to a five-year, $10 million contract, hefty money in those days, but Cashen was eager to show that the Mets were going to compete.

At a February 10 press conference at Shea, Foster delivered a line that was witty at the time but that would come back to haunt him in his first season: "Someone asked me if playing in a ballpark with all those airplanes flying over my head bothered me. I am telling them now to send a warning to the planes not to fly too low over Shea."

It turned out that the planes had little to worry about—Foster didn't send many balls into their flight path. He finished his first season as a Met with just

Opening Day 1982. New Mets manager George Bamberger likes what he sees.

thirteen homers and seventy RBI and was booed as early as May.

The Mets' pursuit of Foster and his disappointing campaign might as well have been a metaphor for the team's season, too—full of hope at the beginning, but ultimately a dud. By the end, no one would believe another thing Foster said at his presser: "I don't believe I have reached my true potential yet. I think I have many big years ahead of me. My goal now is to bring a championship to New York and keep it in the National League."

Spring training was a blur of trade rumors as Cashen tried to find pitching. He knew the Mets' outfield was too crowded, with Lee Mazzilli and Mookie Wilson vying for time in center, Ellis Valentine and Joel Youngblood booked for right, and Foster in left. At one point during camp, Youngblood told reporters, "He [Cashen] said something is going to happen. It has to. We can't go on this way."

While Cashen looked around, he also praised the club the Mets had. "We can win it," he said during spring training. "We could be a contender with an outside shot of winning it."

Mazzilli, the Mets' best player through some fallow times, began feeling lost in the shuffle. There was even talk of trying to turn him into a second baseman. During spring training, Mazzilli told Lang, "All I want is a fair shot. But am I going to get it? The man says I will but I don't know. . . . There's no way I can sit on the bench all year."

Finally, on April 1, Cashen acted. He had tried to pry stud pitcher Dave Steib from the Blue Jays with a multiplayer offer, but it didn't work. So he dealt the twenty-seven-year-old Mazzilli to the Texas Rangers for two minor leaguers who would become familiar Met names: Ron Darling and Walt Terrell.

"With each passing day, Mazzilli was going to get less playing time here and I just felt it would not be fair to him to have him sit on the bench, playing only occasionally," Cashen said. "It would eat him up. So I did the next best thing. I opted for the future and got two pitchers I am sure will eventually pitch for the Mets."

When Mazzilli first got word of the trade, he was so shocked he didn't even ask who he was traded for. When Rangers' GM Eddie Robinson called him a few minutes later and told Mazzilli the details of the swap, Mazzilli said, "I never thought I'd be traded for two minor leaguers."

The next day, Mazzilli bid a tearful good-bye, sunglasses hiding his bloodshot eyes. But not before saying he hoped the trade would one day be enshrined in the Mets' unofficial Hall of Stinkers.

"I don't want this to sound derogatory, but the Mets have made some bad deals in the past. I want this one to be the worst deal they ever made," Mazzilli said. "I never thought it would happen. But it did and when I tried to walk into the clubhouse this afternoon, I couldn't take it. I broke down. It was too much. I said good-bye to a few of the guys, but I couldn't handle it. Just walking into the clubhouse was too much."

Mazzilli even wrote a letter to his teammates that he asked equipment manager Herbie Norman to read to the players the next day.

On April 13, the Mets beat Steve Carlton in their home opener at Shea. Foster was wildly cheered by the crowd of forty-one thousand, and Kingman slugged a vital three-run homer. Another Kingman homer, this one on May 29 with the Mets well behind the Houston Astros, prompted a quirky moment in team lore— after the blast, fans from all corners of the stadium tossed their promotional seat cushions onto the field.

With new manager Bamberger steering them, the Mets got off to a solid start, quicker than in any season since 1976. On June 20, they were 34-30, just three games out of first place. "Bambi's Bandits" were a surprise, all right, but their finish was really shocking.

They went 31-67 the rest of the way, including an awful 5-24 mark in August that included a fifteen-game losing streak from August 15 to 31. Losing Wally Backman for the season after he dislocated his left shoulder in a bike accident didn't help. At 65-97, the Mets finished sixth in the NL East, twenty-seven games out.

At the beginning of August, Bamberger talked about quitting in September if he was unhappy with his performance. However, he stayed on and toward the end of the season agreed to come back in '84, too.

But he had some troubling things to say about the team as it swooned, once remarking, "There are winners on this club and there are losers. Me and my coaches are going to spend the last two months of the season deciding which ones are which. We'll do everything to get rid of the losers."

OPPOSITE:
First baseman Lee Mazzilli is ready for anything hit his way.

ABOVE: Ron Darling.

1980s

thirty-seven homers. Mookie Wilson set a team mark with fifty-eight steals.

Neil Allen saved nineteen games, and Jesse Orosco bloomed into an important bullpen cog. The always-promising pitcher Craig Swan was recovered from rotator cuff surgery and won eleven games with a 3.35 ERA, both tops on the team. On October 1, Terry Leach threw the first extra-inning one-hitter in club history, blanking the Phillies, 1–0, in ten innings.

Attendance was up, too—the 1,320,055 who passed through Shea's turnstiles were the most fans the club had drawn since 1976.

A little more than two months after the season ended, fans had even more reason to be interested in the Mets. As Jack Lang wrote on December 10, "Tom Seaver is coming home."

That's the date the Mets and Reds agreed in principle to a trade, and then Seaver and Cashen hashed out a contract extension for the thirty-eight-year-old ace that would ultimately pay him $700,000 for the '83 season.

At the press conference to reintroduce Seaver to the city that still adored him, Cashen said, "Merry Christmas and in the spirit of giving, I give you Tom Seaver." Flashbulbs popped and television cameras recorded every moment.

The deal sent pitcher Charlie Puleo and minor leaguers Lloyd McClendon and Jason Felice to Cincinnati and came with a warning, from Seaver himself: "You're not going to see the Tom Seaver of 1969 and '70. We change and become different types of pitchers. I have no qualms that I can still pitch. However, I still have to prove that. That's why I didn't feel it was fair to the Mets to guarantee my contract beyond next year. If I can't pitch, why should they have to pay me? If I can't pitch well enough to pick up a paycheck, I don't want to be paid."

Seaver also said his unhappy ending the first time around with the Mets was "all past now. I prefer to

A few days later, on August 4, Joel Youngblood was traded to the Expos. He went one for two in a Met victory in Chicago and then left to join his new club in Philadelphia, where he entered the game in the sixth inning and singled for them, too.

While Foster did not supply as much pop as the Mets had hoped, Kingman tied a club record with

OPPOSITE: Jesse Orosco pitching in relief on Opening Day 1987.

Back in a Met uniform for the first time since 1977, Tom Seaver pitches on Opening Day 1983 at Shea Stadium.

WELCOME HOME TOM

SEAVER

41

1980s

think of those times in terms of Bud Harrelson, Jerry Koosman, Tug McGraw, and the positive things. No, I don't think I'd be back here today if the old regime were still running the Mets, but it would likely have been a mutual thing. I do know I feel very good about this."

Cashen's vision for his emerging Mets was coming together, though slowly. The Mets again finished last in 1983, twenty-two games out. Though they had their best record in seven years, it was the fifth time in that span they finished in the basement, and their 68-94 record was the worst in the National League, only three games better than the '82 downer.

But 1983 was probably the most significant year in the franchise's history since the Mets traded Seaver in 1977. Seaver was back in '83, assuaging a riled fan base, and more help was on the way in the form of the first installment of Cashen's prospect plan.

Six weeks or so after the Mets called up Darryl Strawberry, a tall, twenty-one-year-old outfielder with a whipcord swing, a high leg kick, and raw power that made everyone gape, Cashen made per-

OPPOSITE, LEFT:
Keith Hernandez.

OPPOSITE, RIGHT:
Darryl Strawberry.

Mets manager Frank Howard doesn't look like a man who just lost his job.

haps the greatest trade in franchise history. He sent pitchers Neil Allen and Rick Ownbey to the Cardinals for first baseman Keith Hernandez, a man who would help change the Mets' losing culture.

And then, after the season, Cashen got the manager he wanted installed in the skipper's office when he hired his old second baseman in Baltimore, Davey Johnson.

Seaver was back in his rightful place, on the mound at Shea on Opening Day, April 5. He threw six shut-out innings, allowing only three hits, in a 2–0 victory over the eventual N.L. Champion Phillies.

On May 6, Strawberry made his major league debut, against the Reds at Shea. He had been hitting well at Triple-A Tidewater, and the Mets, already floundering with a 6-15 record, a .222 team batting average, and slow starts from Kingman and Foster, needed a boost.

This was against plan, though. The Mets were concerned about rushing Strawberry, whom they had made the number-one overall pick in the June 1980 draft out of Crenshaw High School in Los Angeles. Strawberry had never even played at the Triple-A level until 1983, but he was hitting .333 there. Still, the Mets wanted him to stay in Triple-A until July to get as many at-bats as he could.

"I was surprised to be called up this soon," Strawberry told reporters the night of his debut. "I was just trying to do my job there. But my big day is coming true; I'm going to play at Shea Stadium."

There were 15,916 at Shea to witness it, and photographers aplenty to take snaps of every one of Strawberry's batting practice swings. He went nothing for four with two walks and three strikeouts in the game and scored on Foster's game-winning homer in the thirteenth inning.

Less than a month later, Bamberger resigned, saying, "I probably suffered enough." The Mets were 16-30 when Frank Howard, a coach, replaced him. They'd go 52-64 the rest of the way—nothing special, but they added Hernandez twelve days after Bamberger quit.

"The trade was one of the easiest trades I made," Cashen said when he was inducted into the Mets' Hall of Fame in 2010. "It was completed in twenty-four hours, the next day. You didn't have to be a genius."

The Mets lost to the Cubs the night of the deal, but the 11,631 at Shea Stadium were happy, anyway. When news of the trade flashed on the scoreboard, fans cheered.

1980s

Hernandez was a master first baseman who had won the National League batting title by hitting .344 in 1979 and shared the MVP award with Pittsburgh's Willie Stargell. But he also had clashed with management in St. Louis, including Whitey Herzog, and generally fallen out of favor there. Hernandez was probably too intelligent and independent for Herzog—the manager was always irked that Hernandez liked to solve crossword puzzles in the clubhouse.

Hernandez said he was disappointed by the trade, though. "'I guess they felt they needed pitching," Hernandez told reporters, referring to the Cardinals. "I'm a little shocked to say the least. I suspected I might be going, but I'm surprised it's to the Mets.

"I knew there would be a day when I would be traded, but I'm disappointed. I loved it here. I have a lot of fond memories of St. Louis. But they feel they made the right move. I talked to Frank Cashen and they're very excited to have me. I feel I can be one of the players to start a winning trend over there."

Cashen was right. Plus, the Mets really didn't miss

Allen and Ownbey. Allen was a serviceable reliever but was done in 1989, and he was never as good elsewhere as he had been with the Mets. Ownbey was 1-6 in twenty-one career games for St. Louis and was out of the majors after 1986.

While the Mets were certainly making strides, they were simply playing out the string of the season. There were some interesting individual achievements, including Strawberry becoming the third Met along with Seaver and Jon Matlack to win the N.L. Rookie of the Year award. Strawberry finished with twenty-six home runs and seventy-four RBI, buoying Met hopes for a consistent power source.

Foster had his best season as a Met, cracking twenty-eight homers and knocking in ninety runs, while Hernandez hit .306 after the trade and won his sixth straight Gold Glove. Rusty Staub tied a major league record with eight consecutive pinch hits and with twenty-four pinch RBI. His twenty-four pinch knocks were one shy of the record.

Jesse Orosco led the staff with thirteen wins and

Manager Davey
Johnson (left) and
Dwight Gooden
share a laugh in the
Mets' clubhouse.

seventeen saves and was N.L. Pitcher of the Month for August. Seaver finished at 9-14 with a respectable 3.55 ERA.

Howard was never going to be a long-term solution as manager, and Cashen had had his eye on Johnson for a while. Johnson had been a winner as a minor league manager, leading the Mets' Double-A Jackson team to a title in 1981 and guiding players such as Ron Darling and Walt Terrell to the championship of all Triple-A baseball during the 1983 season.

The forty-year-old Johnson had been a terrific player during his own twelve-year career. In 1973, he, Darrell Evans, and Hank Aaron became the first trio of teammates to each hit forty or more homers in the same season when they did it for Atlanta. Johnson won three Gold Gloves, made four All-Star teams, and played on two World Championship teams and in the World Series two other times, including making the final out for Baltimore in the 1969 World Series. In

other words, he knew what it took to thrive in Major League Baseball.

"'I felt qualified to manage in the major leagues three years ago," Johnson said at a news conference on October 13 to announce his hiring. "I played for some great managers, like Earl Weaver at Baltimore. There is plenty of young talent in our system and on our roster. I know the whole minor league system better than anyone in the organization."

The mustachioed Johnson was easygoing, but also frank and supremely confident. He kept Howard around as a coach and boldly declared that would not be a threat. Johnson held a math degree from Trinity University and planned to use it—Johnson was one of the first managers to rely on computers and statistics to inform his moves.

With the way Cashen's plan was going, Johnson was going to have some good players to use, too.

Yes, the Mets were ready to jell, thanks in large

1980s

part to Cashen's shrewd moves and the club's burgeoning young talent. But there was a blunder looming that would enrage and embarrass the Mets shortly after 1984 started.

Just over a year after the Mets had reacquired Tom Seaver, righting an old wrong where "The Franchise" had been traded to Cincinnati in 1977, the Mets again lost the best player they ever had. Cashen and the rest of the front office left Seaver unprotected in the free-agent compensation draft, incorrectly assuming—how does that old saying about that word go again?—that no team would take on a thirty-nine-year-old pitcher who was making big bucks.

But on January 20, the Chicago White Sox took Seaver as compensation for losing free agent pitcher Dennis Lamp, who had signed with the Blue Jays. Seaver suggested he might retire instead of report to the White Sox, but that was really only a negotiating ploy—Seaver wanted to discuss his salary and bonuses with Chicago.

The Mets, meanwhile, were stung by their obvious mistake. They were allowed to protect twenty-six players in the compensation pool and chose to safeguard twelve players who had not even made the majors yet. But they were also mad at the White Sox for taking Seaver.

At a news conference, Cashen said the Mets were "grievously and deeply disappointed" that the White Sox had nabbed Seaver. "In retrospect, we made a calculated (and regrettable) gamble, leaving him unprotected in the reentry pool. We were able to protect only twenty-six players in our entire organization and did not feel that a veteran pitcher was a primary need of the White Sox."

Met fans were appalled—some booed Cashen at the New York baseball writers' dinner during the off-season.

So everyone who expected to watch Seaver on Opening Day in Cincinnati had to settle for Mike Torrez instead. But throughout spring training—and even as early as the day he was hired—Davey Johnson had a plan to get another ace into the Met rotation.

In 1982, Johnson had been working with pitchers at the Mets' Class A rookie-league team in Kingsport, Tennessee, and got an eyeful of a seventeen-year-old named Dwight Gooden, whom the Mets had made the fifth pick in the June '82 draft. Johnson thought Gooden was the best pitching prospect he had ever seen, and that included a former teammate on the Orioles named Jim Palmer, a three-time Cy Young Award winner whom Johnson watched soar to stardom in Baltimore.

In Gooden's second pro season, at age eighteen, he went 19-4 with 300 strikeouts in 191 innings at Lynchburg, Virginia, in the Class A Carolina League. Sure, Gooden was young and untested, but Johnson believed he'd be something special, even without more seasoning.

So on the day Cashen told Johnson he was going to be the next Met manager, Johnson started working on the cautious GM, urging him to keep an open mind about Gooden possibly making the team in 1984, though the wunderkind was all of nineteen.

Johnson didn't realize it, but he had an unlikely ally in Cashen. In fact, Cashen was OK with Gooden, Ron Darling, and young catcher John Gibbons having significant roles. Cashen generally would not have taken the risks, but he believed the Mets could be a good team. Not a team that would add a few wins to a low total, but an actual, decent team. Plenty of pieces were in place, from Strawberry to Hernandez to Orosco to Hubie Brooks, though Las Vegas bookmakers saw the Mets as 500-to-1 shots to win it all.

But if they were going to take Gooden north, as the baseball saying goes, the Mets were going to be careful with him. Gooden's spring starts were managed, and they gave him every chance to soak up experience while at the same time gauging his reactions. They brought him to Fort Lauderdale to start against the Yankees so he could work in a packed opposing stadium.

Informed by the Tim Leary debacle in 1981, when

the promising pitcher lasted only two innings at chilly Wrigley Field because of arm trouble that derailed his career, the Mets carefully plotted Gooden's first start in the majors.

They held him out until they went to Houston, where he could pitch in the no-extremes environment of the Astrodome, the eighth wonder of the world, where even the temperature was controlled.

The coddling worked. Gooden made his debut on April 7 against the Astros and allowed one run on three hits in five innings in a 3–2 Met victory. He threw eighty-one pitches, and after the game Astro hitters talked about his live fastball and limitless potential.

The Mets stumbled on Opening Day, and Torrez was knocked out by the Reds in the second inning in an 8–1 loss. But the Mets won their next six games, primed by young pitching—Terrell earned two wins, and Darling, Gooden, and Leary each won once.

Sid Fernandez winds up during a thirteen-strikeout performance in 1985.

1980s

The Mets, with Hernandez as their field general and Strawberry blooming, were swiftly becoming surprise contenders. They were in and out of first until mid-May and got back there in mid-June.

On July 7, they beat the Reds as part of an eight-game winning streak and moved back into first place. They stayed there until August 1. Sid Fernandez, acquired from the Dodgers in the off-season, made his Met debut on July 16, throwing seven strong innings to beat the Astros.

Gooden, meanwhile, took a regular turn in the rotation and held his own. He threw his first career shutout on May 11 in Los Angeles, beating the Dodgers, 2–0. He was 8-5 with a 2.84 ERA in the first half and was picked for the July 10 All-Star game in San Francisco and pitched two scoreless innings, helping the National League to a 3–1 victory. In the fifth inning, Gooden struck out the side, whiffing Lance Parrish, Chet Lemon, and Alvin Davis.

A club record four Mets made the All-Star team, with Hernandez, Strawberry, and Orosco joining Gooden.

The Mets held a 4 1/2-game lead on July 27 after Gooden beat the Cubs at Shea, 2–1. But they dropped their next seven games, including three to Chicago. Then from August 6 to 8, they were swept in a four-game series by the tough Cubs, who bombed Gooden in the opener, and were 4 1/2 out. They got as close as 1 1/2 games out on August 17 but never got closer.

The Mets spent sixty-five days in first place during the season and stayed in the race until September, finishing at 90-72, 6 1/2 games behind the Cubs. It was a remarkable won-lost record, considering they had allowed 24 more runs than they scored during the season (652 runs scored, 676 allowed).

Still, it was the Mets' best season in fifteen years and the start of the best sustained stretch of baseball in club history.

Just because the Mets were playing well didn't mean Cashen stood pat. He kept tweaking the club

and got spirited third baseman Ray Knight from the Astros in a late August deal for Gerald Young, Manny Lee, and Mitch Cook.

There was no pennant for fans to wrap themselves in over the cold winter, but they had plenty to think about to warm them, primarily Gooden. Each one of Gooden's starts morphed into a happening, like Fernando Valenzuela's had been three years earlier, like Stephen Strasburg's would be twenty-six years later in Washington, D.C. His talent was remarkable, and he seemed to get stronger as the year progressed.

On August 6, Gooden was 9-8, but he went 8-1 over his final nine starts, recording double-digit strikeout totals in seven of those games. He threw a one-hitter against the powerful Cubs on September 7. In all, he had fifteen double-digit strikeout games during the season.

1980s

On September 17, Gooden struck out 16 batters for the second consecutive game, but balked home opposing pitching Shane Rawley with the go-ahead run in the eighth inning of a 2–1 loss to the Phillies. With those 16 K's, Doctor K tied a major-league record of 32 strikeouts in consecutive games, matching the mark set by Cleveland's Luis Tiant in 1968 and California's Nolan Ryan in 1974. The NL record had been Sandy Koufax's 31 in 1959.

Gooden also broke Koufax's record of strikeouts over three straight games—Gooden totaled 43, besting Koufax by 2. Gooden's mark is the most over three nine-inning games; Ryan holds the major-league record of 47, but he needed extra innings to do it.

Gooden was the second straight Met to win the N.L. Rookie of the Year award after going 17-9 with a 2.60 ERA and 276 strikeouts. He became the first teenage rookie to lead the majors in strikeouts, set the rookie strikeout record, and averaged an eye-popping 11.39 strikeouts per nine innings.

It made for a fun summer at Shea, and the fans responded—Met attendance was 1,829,482, sixth in the league and the team's highest since 1973. On September 23, the Mets honored three of their own, inducting Bob Murphy, Lindsey Nelson, and Ralph Kiner into the team's Hall of Fame. The trio broadcast Met games together from 1962 to 1978.

Strawberry, featured on the cover of *Sports Illustrated* in April as "The Straw That Stirs the Mets," led the team with 26 home runs and 97 RBI, but did not homer in August. Hernandez hit .311, knocked in 94 runs, and won his seventh straight Gold Glove at first. Hubie Brooks hit .283 and established a club record with a 24-game hitting streak. Orosco set a club record with 31 saves.

Cashen gave fans something else, too, smack in the middle of Christmas shopping season: On December 7 he sent Walt Terrell to the Tigers for Howard Johnson, a talented young infielder.

On December 10 he pulled off a blockbuster trade, acquiring slugging catcher Gary Carter, a perennial All-Star, from the Expos for Brooks, Mike Fitzgerald, Herm Winningham, and Floyd Youmans.

Daily News writers Bill Madden and Jack Lang called the deal part of "a bold contest of one-upsmanship with the crosstown Yankees, who just acquired Rickey Henderson."

"This didn't happen overnight," Cashen said. "Everyone knows of our desire to get another right-handed power hitter. They don't come easy, and they don't come much better than Gary Carter. This is a banner day for the Mets."

The thirty-year-old Carter, nicknamed "Kid," tied Mike Schmidt for the National League RBI crown in 1984 with 106 and finished third in the league with 27 home runs.

"As a five-and-ten man (five years with one club and ten years in the majors), I could have vetoed any deal," Carter said. "I didn't veto it because I was well aware of the nucleus of the Mets. Hopefully, I will be able to help put them over the top and into the World Series."

With the success of 1984 still fresh, plus their off-season moves, the Mets were not going to be surprise contenders in '85, so there was considerable attention on the team before the season. Some of it had nothing to do with Cashen, Carter, or Strawberry, but an eccentric, mystical pitcher no one knew.

He threw an unheard-of 168 miles per hour, and Mets spring training camp was abuzz, though the team tried to keep the whole saga of Sidd (short for Siddhartha) Finch low-key. "I have learned the art of the pitch," Finch told Mets officials, recounting a tale born in the Himalayas. He pitched with one bare foot, the other encased in a hiking boot, and the ball was a blur.

Finch, of course, was a hoax, a hilarious bit of whimsy by *Sports Illustrated* and writer George Plimpton. A story about Finch's feats ran—naturally—in the April 1 issue of *SI* and created a sizzle before readers realized that if you took the first letter from every word in the lead-in of the story, it spelled, "Happy April Fool's Day ah, a fib."

While every major league team could use a pitcher whose fastball reached race car speeds, the Mets, perhaps, already had the next-best thing: Gooden. With a season under his belt, Gooden was preparing to embark on what most believe is the finest individual season ever by a Mets player. Fans hung signs with K's on them in the stands at Shea, chronicling his whiffs.

Gary Carter.

He was on the cover of the April 15 *SI* baseball preview under the heading "Doctor K." He was so good during the season that the magazine put him on the cover again on September 2 as "Dwight the Great."

"Every game was magical," Carter told the *News*'s Wayne Coffey in an interview twenty-five years later. "It was so exciting to go out there and catch a guy who had no-hit stuff every outing."

He was so good there was no way the Mets could not be in the pennant race, and from that, a terrific rivalry developed with the Mets' then-N.L. East counterparts the St. Louis Cardinals. It bloomed in part because both teams were so good in such different

1980s

ways. The Mets had swagger, and they partied just as hard as they played. They had brawny sluggers such as Carter and Strawberry, too.

The Cardinals were putting "Whiteyball" into practice, using Busch Stadium, their cavernous home park, and its artificial surface, to their advantage. Whitey Herzog, the former Met executive who had evolved into one of the most brilliant managers in the game, tailored his teams to rip triples into the Busch gaps while taking them away from opponents with great defense, too. Herzog loved his teams to steal bases and pitch. If they needed a homer, they hoped slugger Jack Clark could do it.

For the next four years, these two teams would dominate the N.L. East. The rivalry got so bitter that twenty-plus years later, feelings still hadn't cooled—Clark did a radio interview in 2009 in which he ripped those Met teams, boasting that he snubbed Mets players at All-Star games, even though they were all playing for that National League at a time when the game held real meaning for players.

So it was perhaps fitting that the two teams started the season against each other at Shea and played two thrilling, extra-inning games. If the first games were any indication, this was going to be a heckuva season, a heckuva pennant race.

Carter, playing in his first game as a Met, had a rough opener, at least at the start. He was hit by two pitches and got nailed by a foul tip, too, on a chilly day. The Cards scored a run on his passed ball, and he even let opposing pitcher Joaquin Andujar steal a base. But that stuff is barely remembered compared to what happened in the tenth inning.

Facing former Met Neil Allen, Carter launched a one-out solo homer, giving the Mets a 6–5 victory. Fans chanted his name and gave him a standing ovation. "What a way to start," Carter said.

Two days later, in the second game of the season, Allen walked Danny Heep with the bases loaded in

High in the grandstand on Opening Day 1985, fans wave their *Daily News* "Doctor K" posters, hoping for a good day from Dwight Gooden.

the eleventh inning, forcing in the winning run. The next day, against the Reds' Mario Soto, Carter hit a fourth-inning homer for the game's only run, and Strawberry hit a walk-off homer in the ninth inning off John Franco on April 13 to lift the Mets to their fourth consecutive nail-biting win.

The Mets won eight of nine to open the season, cementing their contender status and they loitered around or in the top spot for much of the summer despite losing Strawberry for seven weeks when he tore ligaments in his right thumb diving for a ball in right field on May 11. That same day, Sid Fernandez debuted and helped the Mets to their third straight shutout.

On June 11, with the Mets in a stretch where they lost seven of eight games, the Phillies pounded them, 26–7, at Veterans Stadium. Von Hayes, who had been in a six-for-fifty-two slump entering the game and had been benched for the previous two nights, led off with a homer and hit a grand slam later in the first.

Met starter Tom Gorman got only one out, and the Mets trailed, 16–0, after two innings.

In an only-in-Philadelphia moment, Hayes was booed later in the game for making an error.

The Mets' streaky June, including getting swept in St. Louis, meant that they spent only one day tied for first in the entire month.

On July 4 (and 5, really) they won a memorable nineteen-inning game in Atlanta, 16–13, that featured an unlikely home run by light-hitting Braves pitcher Rick Camp in the eighteenth inning off Gorman to prolong the game. The Mets won with five runs in the nineteenth, and Ron Darling, who had thrown a bullpen session earlier in the night, allowed two runs in the Braves' nineteenth but struck out Camp, who hit only because Atlanta was out of players, to hold them off. The game took six hours, ten minutes to finish and was delayed by rain twice.

A fireworks show began after the game—at about 4:00 A.M.—for the few fans who stayed. Some area

residents complained that they thought the neighborhood was under attack.

"It was made magical because of the date, the time of the game, Rick Camp's home run, and Rick striking out at the end," Darling said in a 2010 interview. "It'll go down in history. We always said, as a team, chuckle, chuckle, wink, wink, how is anyone going to beat our club after the bars close? If there's an all-night place, we're going to win."

The Mets swept four games from the Braves, and when Gooden threw a five-hit shutout against the Astros on July 14, the Mets had finished a 10-1 trip to Atlanta, Cincinnati, and Houston.

Then from July 25 to August 13, the Mets won fifteen of seventeen to get back into first. The Cardinals retook the top spot toward the end of the month, and all the baseball world looked away from the pennant

races to the Pittsburgh drug trials, which Hernandez was called to testify in on September 6.

He admitted using cocaine for three years beginning in 1980, but not since he had been dealt to the Mets, and called the drug "the devil on this earth." He was frightened when he woke up one night with a bloody nose and the shakes. He also had lost at least ten pounds.

"I'm sorry if I caused any embarrassment to the Mets or the St. Louis Cardinals and particularly the Met fans," Hernandez told reporters. After testifying, he joined the Mets in Los Angeles, where they won a series against the Dodgers, setting up another important series with St. Louis.

The Cardinals and Mets started a three-game set at Shea on Tuesday, September 10, with identical 82-53 records. The teams were also scheduled to play in St.

1980s

Keith Hernandez snags a line drive during the 1988 National League playoffs.

OPPOSITE: Mets ace Dwight Gooden fires a pitch during the first inning of an Opening Day matchup with the Cardinals in 1985.

Louis from October 1 to 3, and some thought the two series could decide the N.L. East.

It was clear from the first inning of the first game what kind of pennant race this was—the Cardinals took a 1–0 lead on Tommy Herr's homer, and then tempers flared when the Mets batted.

The Mets had already tied the score when Cards' starter Danny Cox intentionally walked Strawberry with two out and one on to face Foster, a much easier task. But Foster lingered outside the batter's box, stalling before stepping in, and Cox hit him with a pitch.

The benches and bullpens cleared, but there were no punches thrown. Afterward, Cox and Foster both feigned innocence. But Howard Johnson followed with a grand slam, and the Mets held on for a 5–4 win and were in first by a one game.

The next night was a pitching duel for the ages—Gooden against St. Louis ace John Tudor, a lefty who had started the season 1-7 and then became unhittable. In almost any season other than Dwight Gooden's 1985, Tudor would have been the N.L. Cy Young Award winner. He had to settle for second place, but he was better than Gooden—by a smidgen—on September 11.

Tudor threw ten scoreless innings in the game, which was won by Cesar Cedeno, who homered off

Orosco in the tenth. Gooden threw nine scoreless innings but got a no decision, the second consecutive start that he had done so. The teams were once again tied.

In the series finale, the Mets took a 6–0 lead after two innings against Andujar, who won twenty-one games in '85. But the Cardinals roared back to tie the score at 6–6. They pounded starter Ed Lynch for five runs, and Willie McGee hit a solo homer off Orosco with one out in the ninth.

But the Mets plated the winner in their half of the inning on a single to left off reliever Ken Dayley that scored Mookie Wilson from third. Hernandez got a curtain call, and the Mets were in first again.

But over the eighteen games in between the titans' late-season series, the Cardinals made it incredibly difficult for the Mets to win the division. While the Mets were 11-7 over that span, the Cardianls won fourteen of their next fifteen games and went 15-3 overall. When the Mets arrived in St. Louis, they were three games out with only six to play.

Tudor faced Darling in the opening game, and it was a flashback to the Tudor-Gooden matchup the previous month. Tudor threw ten scoreless innings; Darling nine. The Mets had tried a squeeze play in the seventh inning, but Darling missed the bunt, and Howard Johnson was caught in a rundown.

In the eleventh, though, Strawberry's awesome raw power captivated the baseball world. He slammed a hanging curveball from Dayley off the scoreboard clock in right field, a blast estimated at 440 feet. The Cardinals got the tying run on second against Orosco when Wilson made an error on a ball hit by Herr. Herr advanced to third on a grounder, but Orosco stranded him there by retiring pinch hitter Ivan DeJesus.

Only two games separated the teams, but the Mets knew they probably had to sweep the series to have much of a chance. They turned to Gooden in the second game, and he beat the Cards and Andujar, 5–2,

ABOVE: Bob Ojeda
working on a shutout
in 1988.

BELOW: Tim Teufel
leaps over an
unidentified
Atlanta player.

1980s

for his twenty-fourth victory. The Cardinals had the bases loaded in the ninth inning, but Gooden got Herr to line to second to end the game after Davey Johnson had visited the mound.

"I thought a tired Gooden was good enough," Johnson said. He was right.

Back in New York, pennant fever was now an epidemic. One more victory would mean the teams were tied for first place. But the Cardinals prevailed, 4–3, in the finale in part because the Mets scored only once in the first inning when they had the bases loaded. Herzog had two relievers warming up and considered taking out Cox, but Cox got out of the jam. It was the Cards' tenth win in eighteen meetings with the Mets.

"We need help from the Cubs that I hoped we wouldn't need," Davey Johnson said afterward.

The end came on the next-to-last day of the season. With the Mets losing to the Expos at Shea, the Cardinals beat the Cubs to clinch the division. The 45,404 at Shea gave the Mets a standing ovation when the St. Louis score became final. The Mets had beaten their primary rival four of six in September, but finished 98-64, three games behind St. Louis. It was the second-most wins in club history at the time.

The present was bitter, but the future bright. Gooden became the youngest pitcher to win the Cy Young Award and the youngest twenty-game winner in modern history, finishing at 24-4 with a 1.53 ERA and 268 strikeouts. He had a fourteen-game winning streak from May 30 to August 25.

Carter led the Mets with 32 home runs and 100 RBI and Hernandez batted .309, won his eighth straight Gold Glove award, and had 24 game-winning RBI. The Mets' home attendance, 2,751,437, shattered the club record and established a mark for New York baseball.

"Next year. Next year," Davey Johnson said. "They've got to get that in their minds. We're just going to figure next year is our year."

Ah, next year. That's what clubs that come up short

always cling to—the Brooklyn Dodgers said "Wait 'til next year" so many times it turned into their mantra. But when it finally does arrive, it is sweet, and it spawns a lifetime of nostalgia.

The Mets' "next year" did indeed arrive in 1986, and with such force that it bowled over the rest of baseball. These Mets were boisterous, boastful, and belligerent, with enough baseball skill to rank with the finest teams in history but all the subtlety of a thunderclap.

They fought with almost everyone, from opposing teams to off-duty police officers in Houston. They guzzled beer, chased girls, slept little, and still won. And then they played one of the most thrilling playoff series ever and a World Series that still amazes all these years later.

In the Mets' twenty-fifth anniversary season, their finest team ever bloomed into a juggernaut. Cashen's plan worked, though his juggernaut was probably a little rougher around the edges than the bow-tied general manager would have liked.

Cashen added several key pieces to the team that had come so close the year before, trading for lefty Bob

Ojeda and infielder Tim Teufel and promoting slugging prospect Kevin Mitchell, who could play anywhere.

Spring training began with high hopes for another spectacular season from Gooden, a breakout year for Strawberry, and a pennant. But the Mets were only .500 in spring training—no big deal, really—but Davey Johnson was irked enough to say publicly he was not pleased with their play.

Gooden, meanwhile, signed a one-year, $1.32 million contract in February, a pile of cash for a twenty-one-year-old star. When he was asked what advice his parents had given him about the money, he replied, "Don't let it change you."

"I won't," Gooden promised.

But it was clear quickly that 1986 was not 1985 for Gooden. He created a minor spring controversy when he sprained his ankle in January but didn't tell the Mets. In mid-April he was involved in what the *News*'s Jim Naughton described as "a drink-throwing fracas at LaGuardia Airport." Under a headline of "I'm Not a Violent Person," the story detailed how Gooden's sister, Betty Jones, had thrown a drink at a

1980s

Hertz agent during a mileage dispute. Gooden admitted swearing at the agent, too.

The Mets tried to teach Gooden a changeup and a two-seam fastball, but they didn't take. Some believed the work ultimately hurt Gooden's pitching.

Still, Gooden beat the Pirates on Opening Day in Pittsburgh, 4–2, in a complete game, even though he gave up a home run to R. J. Reynolds on his third pitch of the season.

The Mets started just 2-3; Howard Johnson described their early play as "listless." But they won their next eleven games. On April 24 in St. Louis, HoJo hit a two-run homer off Todd Worrell in the ninth to tie the score, and the Mets won on Foster's RBI single in the tenth.

Two days later, Wally Backman preserved another win over the Cardinals. St. Louis had the tying and go-ahead runs on base, but Backman made a diving stop on Terry Pendleton's grounder toward the middle and started a game-ending, 4-6-3 double play. The next day, the Mets beat Tudor to complete their first four-game sweep of the Cards since Jimmy Carter was president.

This was huge for the Mets, and not just because

they were 11-3, the best start in club history. "We've had some rough memories here," Davey Johnson said. "It's kind of nice to come in here and play as well as we did. It just kind of proved to St. Louis that we can beat them. I always like to beat them in their ballpark."

"This sets a tone," Hernandez added. "This was a wake-up call. We're beating them the way they beat us last year.

"We're a better team than we were last year. I'm not in a groove yet. Darryl isn't in a groove yet. George isn't in a groove yet. What's going to happen when we catch fire?"

Hernandez believed the Cards were frustrated, even though it was only April. "You can see the look in their faces," Hernandez said. "You can see the way they look as they make a right turn and head back to their dugout. Tudor was frustrated."

The Mets stretched their streak to ten wins on April 29, helped by Strawberry's 420-foot homer against the Braves. Gooden beat the Braves the next day to make it eleven straight wins, matching a club record.

The Braves ended the streak on May 1, slugging

1980s

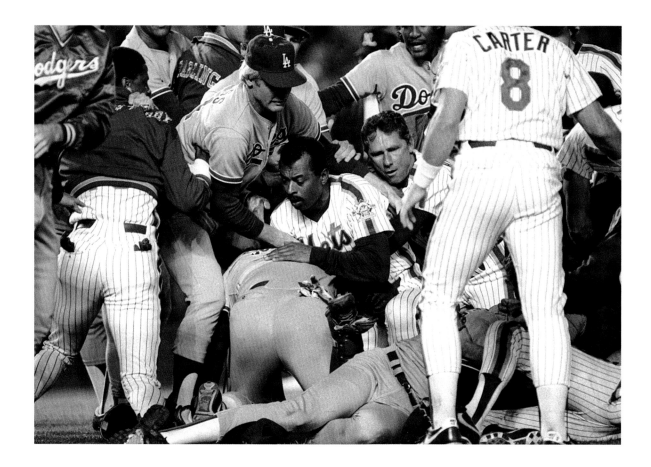

four homers off Rick Aguilera. Small matter—the Mets won their next seven.

Gooden was named Pitcher of the Month for April, going 4-0 with a 1.26 ERA and any warning bells that may have sounded about him seeming like noise pollution. The Mets begin talking about expanding their lead in the division, which was five games before the second streak ended.

"We're really the only team playing well in our division right now," Hernandez said. "Let's take advantage of that, jump on it, open up some space."

Still, all was not perfect. Strawberry was struggling against lefties, and Davey Johnson considered resting him against the league's tougher ones.

Gooden, meanwhile, got pounded by the Giants in a 10–2 loss on May 22 in San Francisco, giving up six earned runs in four-plus innings. In the stands at Candlestick Park hung a sign reading, "He ain't God, man"—a quote from the Giants' Chili Davis.

Gooden had not won in three starts, matching the longest nonwinning streak of his career. His 5-2 record was the worst among Met starters, who were thriving.

"It's strange," Gooden said. "Coming in from the bullpen, you feel great. You throw for a couple innings and you throw good. But it was like after the fourth inning I started losing something. I think the temperature changed during the game. It was nice and sunny at first. I've had worse stuff than today and gotten by."

"It's not going to be the last time he gets hit in his career," Wally Backman said. "But with Doc, they are so few and far between, it's like you can't believe it's happening."

Gooden made it clear everything was OK when he beat the Dodgers, 4-2, at Shea, striking out ten, on May 28. But fans probably remember May 27 even more. That's the day Ray Knight, famously known as a former Golden Gloves boxer, charged the mound after getting hit by L.A.'s Tom Niedenfuer one batter after Foster had hit a grand slam.

Knight, who had replaced Pete Rose as the Reds' third baseman, was coming off consecutive bad years, but he was off to a hot start and emerging as a spiritual leader, too. The Mets admired—and emulated— his pugnacious attitude, and players looked at his

brawl with Niedenfuer and another with the Reds' Eric Davis almost two months later as indications of the fight in the Mets.

On June 6, the Mets fought again, brawling with Pittsburgh after they accused pitcher Rick Rhoden of scuffing the ball.

While the punches flew, the Mets kept winning. On June 15, Ojeda beat the Pirates, improving to 8-2 with a 2.37 ERA. The Mets held a 10 1/2-game lead in the division. "What helps is that we're just scoring runs every day," Ojeda said. "There's no one way to get us out. Very rarely does anybody shut us down."

Still, there was the nagging feeling that something was different about Gooden. He was 5-1 in his first eight starts, but 3-2 over his next six starts, allowing an un-Gooden-like twenty-two earned runs in 43 1/3 innings.

"I'm not happy, but things will straighten out," Gooden said. "I'm not making alibis."

"We're searching for something that's not there," pitching coach Mel Stottlemyre said. "I'm not one of those people who expect him to win 100 percent of his games. Sure he's capable of doing it, but if he doesn't, I'm not going to start looking to see what's wrong. If a certain team happens to beat him on a certain day, I'm like everybody else. I'm surprised because he's won so consistently and he's dominated teams when nobody expected him to."

But an anonymous Met told the *News*'s Jack Lang that there might be a problem with the ace. "I'm worried about him," the Met said. "I haven't seen the consistent pop on his fastball I saw the first two years. Doc is also having trouble getting his curve over and he falls behind on hitters. That's also not the DG I saw the first two years. I have no idea what it is, but I'm worried."

Gooden beat the Cubs on June 29 but he allowed ten hits and four rßuns. Still, he was good enough for Davey Johnson to leave him in with the tying run at the plate in the form of future Hall of Famer Ryne Sandberg. Gooden retired Sandberg on a grounder.

The next day, Ojeda beat the Cardinals to improve to 9-2 with a 2.54 ERA. Folks started to wonder if he was that year's John Tudor.

Speaking of Tudor, the Mets swept his club from June 30 to July 2. The next day, Strawberry tied a game against the Astros with a tenth-inning homer, and then Knight slugged one to win it.

Two days later, the Astros beat the Mets, cutting the Mets' lead to 11 1/2 games, and Davey Johnson quipped, "Shoot, I guess I better panic."

At the All-Star break, the Mets were 59-25 and had a 13 1/2-game division lead. Even Whitey Herzog knew how good they were, selecting Gooden, who was 10-4 with a 2.77 ERA, to start the All-Star game against Roger Clemens and using Hernandez, Carter, and Strawberry as his 3-4-5 hitters in the game. Sid Fernandez also made the team, giving the Mets a club record five selections.

"The Mets are the class of our league," Herzog said. "I would have taken Ray Knight, too, if I could have picked three third basemen.

"I picked Gooden because I think he's the best pitcher in baseball," Herzog added.

Gooden gave up a two-run homer to Lou Whitaker and was the losing pitcher in the game.

Meanwhile, the Mets started the second half with a 13–2 victory over the Astros, but were shut out the next day for the first time all season, by Houston.

Afterward, four of the players were involved in a different kind of fight—a drunken episode at a Houston nightclub called Cooter's that would forever be etched into Met lore.

Darling, Teufel, Aguilera, and Ojeda were out celebrating the birth of Teufel's son when Teufel tried to take an open beer out of the bar. Off-duty cops, working as security guards, tried to stop him, and a fracas ensued in which Darling and Teufel were charged with aggravated assault. Aguilera and Ojeda were charged with hindering arrest. All four spent about eleven hours in a Houston holding cell.

Everything was fair game for teasing in that clubhouse, so teammates draped black paper stripes on the players' lockers "to simulate jail bars," the News's Naughton wrote. Ultimately, Darling and Teufel were sentenced to one year's probation and fined $200, and all charges were dismissed against Aguilera and Ojeda.

The Mets went on to Cincinnati where perhaps their most famous fight of the season was awaiting them. On July 22, Dave Parker dropped Hernandez's

Gary Carter (left) and Darryl Strawberry wait out a rain delay.

1980s

175

and the outfield. The Mets finally won the game, 6–3, on Howard Johnson's three-run homer in the fourteenth inning. McDowell and Orosco delighted in playing the outfield.

Two weeks later: more unrest. The Mets waived Foster on August 6, the same day that newspaper stories appeared in which he was quoted as saying that his reduced role was based on race.

"I'm not saying it's a racial thing, but that seems to be the case in sports these days," Foster was quoted as saying in Naughton's story. "When a ball club can replace a George Foster or a Mookie Wilson with a more popular player. I think they would rather promote a Gary Carter or a Keith Hernandez to the fans. So parents who want to can point to them as role models for their children rather than a Darryl Strawberry, a Dwight Gooden, or a George Foster. The kids don't see color."

"That was maybe the straw that broke the camel's back," Johnson said in the same article.

Foster would never have won a popularity contest in the Met clubhouse, but players such as Knight, a former teammate of his in Cincinnati, and Strawberry were friends with him.

Strawberry blasted the move, saying, "I think they could have handled it better. They didn't show me anything the way they went about it. A guy who had a career like that, he deserves to wait to the end of the year. It hurts for me because we were so close. Maybe some of those things needed to be said. Maybe he felt he wasn't being appreciated. I don't know if it will have an effect on the team. But it might have an effect on certain players on the team. Me, Mookie, Doc, people like that."

Foster was replaced by Lee Mazzilli, who had been signed to a minor league contract less than a week earlier, a move that made Foster suspicious.

There was other trouble, too: Carter went on the disabled list in August with a thumb injury. Davey

fly ball in the ninth inning that would have given the Reds a 3–1 win. But two runs scored on the play, and in the tenth, Knight and Eric Davis fought.

Davis came in as a pinch runner, stole second and third, and slid hard into Knight at third. Insults and shoves followed, and Knight punched Davis in the face. The benches emptied, and wrestling players covered the infield.

Knight, Davis, Mitchell, and Mario Soto were all ejected. The Mets were dismayed to see that Foster had not budged from the bench during the fight.

Rose and Davey Johnson filed separate protests on the game. With the ejections and an earlier ejection for Darryl Strawberry, the Mets had only seven regulars and their pitching staff left, so Davey Johnson alternated Orosco and McDowell between the mound

1980s

ABOVE:
Keith Hernandez and
Darryl Strawberry.

BELOW: Several
members of the Mets
celebrate their 1988
National League East
title after defeating
the Chicago Cubs.

Johnson criticized Sid Fernandez's weight and was constantly on Darling about Darling's bouts of wildness.

None of the tumult affected the Mets' play, though. On August 23, with the Mets up by twenty games, Hernandez described clinching as "a foregone conclusion."

On September 17, the Mets clinched their first division title since 1973 with a 4–2 win over the Cubs at Shea. Fans stormed the field, ripping up grass, bases, anything for a souvenir. Gooden called it "The sweetest game I ever won" in Naughton's account of the game and celebration.

The final out was a grounder off the bat of Chico Walker. "I thought it might be nice to get a strikeout," Gooden said. "But I just wanted a win. I struggled at one point this season and people were saying this was an off-year. This year was awesome for me, better than winning twenty, better than any individual award, Rookie of the Year, Cy Young, better than anything."

Backman fielded the grounder and said, "It was the hardest ground ball ever hit to me and it prob-ably was the easiest ground ball ever hit to me, but I wanted this one. I got down on one knee because there was no way it was going through my legs."

The fans celebrated with gusto; so did the players. "This team was crap for a long time," Hernandez was quoted as saying in Mike Lupica's column. "That's why this one means so much. To be a part of this means an awful lot."

The Mets finished at 108-54, 21 1/2 games up, just the ninth team in modern history to win at least 108 games. They were in first place from April 23 on, and their division-clinching date was the earliest in N.L. East history.

Carter matched Staub's club record of 105 RBI, Hernandez batted .310 and won his 10th Gold Glove, and Strawberry had 27 homers, 93 RBI, and a .507 slugging percentage. While everyone considered Gooden (17-6, 2.84 ERA) the Mets' ace, Ojeda had a better season, going 18-5 with a 2.57 ERA, the best season by a Met lefty since Koosman won 20 games

1980s

in 1976. Fernandez was 16-6 with a 3.52 ERA, and Darling was 15-6 with a 2.81 ERA.

The Astros clinched the West, setting up an N.L. Championship Series between two pitching-rich teams. But, in the words of Whitey Herzog, the Mets had an advantage. Herzog, writing a guest column for the *Daily News*, picked the Mets to win because they had lefties Ojeda and Fernandez, and Houston had only one lefthander, Bob Knepper.

Nationally, the Mets were portrayed as boorish louts. Peter Gammons wrote in *Sports Illustrated*, "By now, we all know how hateable the Mets are."

"They're trying to make us the man with the black hat," Backman told Lupica in a column in the *News*'s October 3 edition. "I thought we were the man in the white hat. We got twenty-four guys who get along, we win, we have fun doing it. That's scummy or something?"

Of course, the Mets had their own brand of confidence. As Knight put it, "If we play the way we are capable of, it's going to be a short series. They are not as good a ball club as we are."

"We're a little pumped up because people have criticized our ball club," Strawberry added. "They called us showboats, called us arrogant. That's just the way we play."

The showboat, arrogant Mets were on their way back to Houston, where an enterprising T-shirt maker was hawking wares with "Houston Police 4, Mets 0" on them, a reminder of the trouble the Mets had already caused there. The Mets had won seven of twelve games against the Astros during the season and were big favorites, but Houston's starting pitching was perhaps as good as even the Mets'.

The opener was a terrific pitching matchup at the Astrodome—Gooden against the former Met Mike Scott, who had revived his career after being taught the split-fingered fastball by Roger Craig. Or was it something else that made Scott so good? There were

whispers that he scuffed the ball, used sandpaper more expertly than a carpenter. There was never enough evidence, though some teams said they found slivers of sandpaper near his mound.

In game one, Gooden was tremendous, but Scott was just a bit better. Glenn Davis hit a solo home run in the second inning for the only run of Houston's 1–0

1980s

179

victory, and Scott tied John Candelaria's NLCS record with fourteen strikeouts.

The Mets had a chance to tie the score in the ninth with one out and Strawberry on second, but Davis dove to rob Wilson of a single. Had the ball reached the outfield, Strawberry would have scored. But Davis fielded the ball and flipped to Scott for the second out. Strawberry moved to third, but Scott struck out Knight to end the game.

With the victory, Scott hadn't just given the Astros a 1-0 lead in the series; he also had delivered a blow to the Mets' seemingly impenetrable psyche. That was something that hadn't happened as they partied, brawled, and romped their way through the National League during the season.

But in game two, the Mets showed the condition wasn't permanent. Bobby Ojeda beat Nolan Ryan in a 5–1 victory. Ojeda threw a complete game and Hernandez had a two-run triple, sending the series to Shea tied.

Game three provided plenty of drama, though it didn't start out that way. The Astros built a 4–0 lead against Darling in the first two innings, including a Bill Doran two-run homer. But the Mets scored four times in the sixth inning against Knepper, highlighted by Strawberry's three-run blast.

The Astros silenced a delirious Shea crowd by scoring an unearned run in the seventh, helped by a Knight error. The Mets had wrested home field advantage from Houston by splitting the first two games, but seemed poised to give it back in their first home game.

In the ninth inning, Backman bunted for a hit against Houston closer Dave Smith. But Hal Lanier, the Astros' manager, argued that Backman had run out of the baseline to avoid Davis's tag. He may have had a case, but ump Dutch Rennert did not agree. One out later, Backman was on second and Lenny Dykstra was at the plate.

Dykstra was awash in confidence, no matter what the competition was. After the Mets drafted him, he demanded to be assigned to a Class A team instead of rookie league, and his brashness made him beloved by the Mets but disliked most everywhere else.

In this instance, Dykstra inserted himself into a city's baseball tradition. He drilled a two-run homer over the right-field fence, lifting the Mets to a 6–5 win.

"Put Lenny Dykstra's name alongside the names of Bobby Thomson and Chris Chambliss on the list of New York's October home run heroes," the *News*'s Phil Pepe wrote afterward.

"Don't get used to this," Dykstra said. "You're not going to see too many game-winning home runs from me."

The Mets needed the victory because "that man" was coming back in game four: Scott. Lanier had set up his pitching so that Scott, who would eventually win the N.L. Cy Young Award because of his 18-10 record, 2.22 ERA, and 306 strikeouts, could start three times. Some believed the Astros had to win only one other game and they'd advance to the World Series.

Scott certainly did his part again, throwing another complete game to beat Fernandez in a 3–1 Houston win. He allowed only three hits and got offensive help from Alan Ashby's two-run homer and a solo shot by Dickie Thon. He was even cleared of scuffing by N.L.

president Chub Feeney, though the Mets were still convinced that Scott's pitches moved so drastically because he was doctoring the ball.

In the final game at Shea, the two teams provided a little foreshadowing in a dramatic twelve-inning contest that started as a pitching duel between two remarkable fastball-curveball pitchers. Gooden allowed one run in ten innings, and Ryan gave up the same in nine innings.

In the twelfth inning, reliever Charlie Kerfeld tried to pick off Backman at first but threw the ball away, putting the pest in scoring position. The Astros intentionally walked Hernandez to pitch to Carter, who was one for twenty-one in the series. Carter delivered an RBI single to center, the second walk-off hit for the Mets in the series and a big dose of relief for the catcher.

OPPOSITE, LEFT: Lenny Dykstra jumps for joy after hitting the game-winning, walk-off two-run homer against the Houston Astros in game three of the 1986 NLCS.

OPPOSITE, RIGHT: Lenny Dykstra is mobbed by his teammates after hitting a two-run homer in the bottom of the ninth inning to give the Mets a 6–5 victory in game three of the NLCS.

A Lenny Dykstra devotee parades through the stands in a wedding dress during game five of the 1986 NLCS.

1980s

So the Mets needed only to split the two games scheduled for the return trip to the Astrodome. In reality, though, they had to win game six—Scott would pitch a game seven, if necessary, and he was clearly already firmly rooted in their heads. Even these swaggering Mets knew they were finished if they had to face Scott again.

So they did what they had to do—mount another October comeback to win. It took only sixteen innings, at that time the longest game in postseason history, and turned out to be one of the most memorable contests in baseball history.

The Astros struck first in a matchup of lefties at the Astrodome, scoring three times against Ojeda in the first inning. Knepper held the Mets scoreless for the first eight innings, and they had only two hits.

Down to their last three outs, the Mets came alive. Dykstra pinch-hit for Aguilera and tripled to lead off. This should have been a signal that Knepper was finished, but he remained in the game.

Mookie Wilson singled Dykstra home, and one out later Hernandez doubled Wilson in. Smith replaced Knepper, but the Mets were rolling. Smith walked Carter and Strawberry, and Knight drove in the tying run with a sac fly. Smith wriggled out of the inning by striking out Heep with the bases loaded, but the Mets were alive.

Roger McDowell came out of the bullpen to throw five scoreless innings, setting up a wild fourteenth inning. Carter singled, Strawberry walked, and one out later, Backman hit an RBI single off Aurelio Lopez to give the Mets a 4–3 lead, their first lead of the game.

Orosco got the first out of the inning, putting the Mets two outs away from the World Series. But Houston's Billy Hatcher launched an epic homer, a drive down the left-field foul line. Hatcher had hit just six homers all year, but this was one that will never be forgotten in Houston.

Members of the Mets stand for the national anthem before a game. From left are Keith Hernandez, Wally Backman, Davey Johnson, Gary Carter, Rafael Santana, Mookie Wilson, an unidentified team member, Bud Harrelson, and Darryl Strawberry.

1980s

1980s

"At that moment," Backman said later, "there were a lot of lumps in a lot of throats."

Still, the Astros did little with the momentum. Two innings later, Strawberry led off the sixteenth with a double off Lopez and scored on Knight's single, and Knight went to second on the throw home. Reliever Jeff Calhoun threw a wild pitch, advancing Knight, and walked Backman before throwing another wild pitch that let Knight score, all before the Astros had gotten an out. Orosco bunted Backman to third and Dykstra singled in another run, giving the Mets a 7–4 lead.

The Astros were hardly done, though. Orosco struck out Craig Reynolds to open the bottom of the sixteenth but walked pinch hitter Davey Lopes and gave up consecutive singles to Doran and Hatcher, bringing the Astros to within two runs. One out later, Glenn Davis singled in another run, and Houston had the tying run at second and the winning run at first for Kevin Bass, an All-Star who would finish seventh in the NL MVP voting after a stellar year.

With the count full, Orosco struck out Bass, clinching the Mets' third trip to the World Series.

"If I had had to watch this game from the stands, I might have had a heart attack," Backman was quoted saying in a Lupica column the next day. "And maybe not just one."

"We had visions of playing all night," Knight said.

Hernandez added what all the Mets—indeed, perhaps all of New York—was thinking: "All I know, and I didn't want to say this yesterday, is that I did not want to face Mike Scott in game seven. I felt today like we were the ones with our backs against the wall."

What more could the baseball world want from these Mets? Maybe they grated on nerves as they grinded away on the season, but they were due real respect now, regardless of what would happen in the World Series against the Boston Red Sox, who had a Gooden-esque pitcher of their own named Roger Clemens. Boston had won their own remarkable playoff series, trailing three games to one and down to their last out when Dave Henderson revived them with a home run off Angels' reliever Donnie Moore. The Sox won game five in extra innings and took the final two games, too.

Before the World Series opener on Saturday, October 18, at Shea, Davey Johnson waffled on whether to start Backman or Teufel at second base. He chose Teufel against lefty Bruce Hurst. Hurst would face Darling, who, though he was born in Hawaii, moved to Worcester, Massachusetts, when he was five years old, and as he put it in a column he wrote for the *News*, "I lived and died—mostly died—with the Red Sox." Carl Yastrzemski was his favorite player, and he always envisioned himself pitching at Fenway for the Red Sox.

Darling was certainly equal to the task of pitching against his powerful boyhood favorites—he allowed one unearned run in seven mostly sharp innings. But Darling's mistakes led to the Teufel mistake that cost the Mets the game. Darling walked Jim Rice to lead off the seventh and then threw a wild pitch, moving Rice to second. One out later, Rich Gedman hit a grounder that went through Teufel's legs, allowing the only run of the game to score.

1980s

Ron Darling tossing
a four-hitter versus
the Cubs in 1987.

OPPOSITE: Michael
Sergio parachutes
onto the field at Shea
Stadium during the
first inning of game
six of the 1986
World Series.

Teufel had provided the offense Johnson hoped for, getting two of the four hits off Hurst, but the Mets couldn't capitalize against the lefty or reliever Calvin Schiraldi, whom they had sent to Boston in the Ojeda deal. Not a good start for the Mets, who had batted only .189 with a meek .264 slugging percentage in the NLCS.

Still, the Mets had Gooden going for them in game two, even if it was against Clemens. But neither did well: Gooden was hammered for six runs (five earned) in five innings, and Clemens came out in the fifth inning, having allowed three runs, five hits, and four walks in 4 1/3 innings. He did not qualify for a victory in Boston's 9–3 triumph, which gave the Sox a commanding 2–0 lead in the Series before they had even played a home game.

"We haven't played good ball," Backman is quoted saying in Naughton's October 21 story. "It's that cut and dried. I have no fear yet. I'm more angry than anything else.

"We won't go quickly," Backman added. "I can promise you that."

The only thing that went quickly in game three at Fenway was the Mets' slump—they scored four times in the first inning, paced by Dykstra's leadoff homer. It was the first of four hits for the lineup igniter and a good way to shut up Boston starter Oil Can Boyd, who had boasted on the Series' off-day that he would "master" the Mets and that Ojeda, a former member of the Red Sox, would be intimidated by the proximity of the Green Monster, Fenway's tall but short—at least in terms of distance from the plate—left-field wall.

"I read it," Dykstra said in Pepe's account of the game in the *News*. "We didn't take too kindly of that. The only one who got mastered was him."

Getting ticked at Boyd was the only off-day workout the Mets had needed, apparently—Davey Johnson had given them a real day off, sensing his weary players could use rest instead of batting practice.

Pitching with the comfortable lead, Ojeda was terrific, allowing one run in seven innings in a 7–1 Mets win that got them back into the Series.

Darling started game four close to his old home,

and the Olde Towne Team couldn't touch him. Darling threw seven shutout innings and Carter launched two home runs over the Green Monster to even the Series with a 6–2 Met win that guaranteed at least one more game at Shea.

"It has worked out this way all year," Stottlemyre told Lupica. "Whenever the team has been down, whoever's turn it's been has come through. There is no stopper on this team. At one time or another, they've all been stoppers."

Gooden started game five for the Mets. This time, surely, it would be different, right? He'd be back to "Dr. K" and lift his team, right?

No. Gooden gave up four runs and nine hits in four innings and Hurst beat the Mets again, putting the Red Sox one victory away from their first title since 1918.

"We're down one game and we have to win two," Ojeda said on the travel day. "But we've won two in a row before."

Maybe not quite like this, though. The Mets had already won one for-the-ages postseason game, and they needed to win another to force a winner-take-all game seven. And it happened.

"After a season during which nearly everything worked, the Mets needed everything to work," Lupica wrote. "They needed to get through the night. They needed a win to get one more shot at champagne themselves."

Maybe everyone at Shea should have realized something crazy might happen that night when a parachutist landed on the field between home and first in the top of the first inning. "So it started with magic or weird science or something," Lupica wrote.

Boston scored once in each of the first two innings, and maybe they felt secure with Clemens pitching. The Mets tied the score in the fifth on an RBI single by Knight and an RBI double by Heep. But Knight's seventh-inning error helped the Red Sox to a 3–2 lead. Carter hit a sac fly in the eighth to tie it, and neither

ABOVE:
Mookie Wilson (1)
is greeted at home
plate by Lee Mazzilli
as Gary Carter (8)
looks on following
Keith Hernandez's
two-run single in
the sixth inning of
game seven of the
1986 World Series.
The Mets went on to
beat the Boston Red
Sox, 8–5.

BELOW: Gary Carter
reacts after Boston's
Marty Barrett struck
out in the ninth inn-
ing of game seven, clinching the 1986 World
Series for the Mets.

OPPOSITE: Gary
Carter and Darryl
Strawberry embrace
after winning the
1986 National
League pennant.

team scored in the ninth to set up an excruciating—for Boston fans—and exhilarating—for New Yorkers—tenth inning.

Henderson, already a proud October hero for the Sox, homered to give Boston the lead, and ALCS MVP Marty Barrett singled in another run. Sixty-eight years of New England angst looked like it was about to end. What could go wrong?

In the eighth inning, with the Red Sox ahead, Lupica wrote, someone had gone into the NBC television booth and told them that Bruce Hurst would be the Series MVP. In the bottom of the tenth, the message board at Shea accidently flashed, "Congratulations, Boston."

Schiraldi retired Backman and Hernandez to start the tenth but then fell apart. Carter singled, and Strawberry would have been next had Davey Johnson not taken him out in an earlier double switch. So Mitchell pinch-hit and singled, too. On an 0-2 pitch, Knight singled, knocking in a run, moving Mitchell to third, and knocking out Schiraldi.

Boston manager John McNamara called on Bob Stanley to pitch to Mookie Wilson, and with the count 2-2, Stanley uncorked a wild pitch. Mitchell scored the tying run, and the Mets were surging.

Stanley seemed to get out of it, though, when Wilson hit a little grounder toward Bill Buckner at first. Buckner was no Hernandez at first, but this should have been easy. Still, Buckner had said before the Series that an Achilles tendon injury would not keep him out of action. He was wearing black, high-top spikes for extra support on his tender ankles.

The grounder slipped through Buckner's legs and bounded into right field, sending a smart bomb of heartbreak through New England. Knight scored the winning run, a giddy grin spreading on his face as he pranced home. McNamara would be forever second-guessed for not using Dave Stapleton as a defensive replacement at first.

On NBC, the great Vin Scully delivered a memorable call: "So the winning run is at second base, with two outs, three and two to Mookie Wilson. Little roller up along first . . . behind the bag! It gets through Buck-ner! Here comes Knight, and the Mets win it!"

Scully paused, letting the bedlam in the ballpark tell the story. He added, "If one picture is worth a thousand words, you have seen about a million words, but more than that, you have seen an absolutely bizarre finish to game six of the 1986 World Series. The Mets are not only alive, they are well, and they will play the Red Sox in game seven tomorrow!"

Well, if Hurst was really going to be the Series MVP, he got another shot thanks to a game seven rainout on Sunday, October 26. That allowed the Red Sox to skip Oil Can Boyd and use the lefty who already had two wins against the Mets. It also gave the Red Sox a chance to relax after their stunning loss. Or did it give them an extra day to think about what had just happened?

Either way, nothing worked for them in game

Jesse Orosco lifts his arms in jubilation after striking out Boston's Marty Barrett for the final out in game seven of the 1986 World Series.

OPPOSITE, ABOVE:
Keith Hernandez and Lee Mazzilli embrace following the Mets' 1986 World Series triumph.

OPPOSITE, BELOW:
Met players celebrate winning the team's second world championship after defeating the Boston Red Sox, 8–5, in game seven of the 1986 World Series.

1980s

ABOVE: Keith
Hernandez (left)
and Gary Carter
hoist the 1986 World
Series trophy at City
Hall after the Mets'
victory parade.

BELOW: Jubilant
Met fans celebrate
during a ticker-tape
parade for the world
champion Mets.

ABOVE, LEFT: Met fans hoping to get a great view of their heroes hang from trees during a ticker-tape parade for the world champion Mets.

ABOVE, RIGHT: Fans sit atop an entrance to City Hall during the 1986 victory parade.

BELOW: President Reagan sizes up his own Met team jacket, presented by Met boss Fred Wilpon (left), at a White House ceremony as several Met players look on.

seven. They built a 3–0 lead against Darling but couldn't hold it, and Fernandez retired seven straight hitters in relief. Hurst shut out the Mets for five innings, but then allowed three runs in the sixth. Schiraldi gave up a homer in the seventh to Knight, the eventual Series MVP, for the Mets' first lead and then allowed two more runs. Even Boston's comeback against McDowell in the eighth fell short—they scored only two runs.

In the bottom of the eighth, Strawberry plunged a dagger into the Sox—a leadoff home run. Orosco even added an RBI single and then slammed the door on the 8–5 victory, striking out Barrett for the final out. The Mets had won their second World Series. The Red Sox remained cursed for eighteen more years.

Pepe's lead the next morning read, "Joy! Jubilation! Delirium! Ecstasy! Champions!" with each word getting its own paragraph. Then, "The Mets are World Champions. Say it again, it sounds so good. The Mets are World Champions!"

Pepe closed with a scene from the bowels of Shea, Carter passing Davey Johnson. "Skipper!" Carter shouted.

"This," said Johnson, "is as good as it gets."

Sadly for the skipper—and the Mets—he was absolutely right. The juggernaut didn't win another World Championship.

In fact, in the winter after the championship, the victorious Mets began to change, in more ways than one.

First, there were personnel moves: The Mets needed an everyday outfielder and, some said, to be rid of Kevin Mitchell, so they sent Mitchell, Stanley Jefferson, Shawn Abner, and two minor leaguers to the Padres for Kevin McReynolds and two other players. Since then, Mitchell said, he believes he was dealt because the Mets thought he was a bad influence on Darryl Strawberry and Dwight Gooden, which Mitchell believes is preposterous.

"In New York, they used me as a scapegoat for them," Mitchell said in a 2009 interview. "I was the

bad seed, they said. But those guys were already in the big leagues and I'm a rookie and I'm telling them what to do? There's no way."

The McReynolds swap wasn't the only deal Cashen made. Just before the end of spring training, the Mets sent three players, including backup catcher Ed Hearn, to the Royals for a young pitcher named David Cone and another player.

Ray Knight, who had brought so much soul to the '86 club, left in a salary dispute with Cashen, signing with the Baltimore Orioles. The Mets were happy to give the third-base job to Howard Johnson full-time.

It had been a winter of celebration, sure, but also of tumult. Dwight Gooden got into trouble in Tampa in a fight with cops after a traffic stop, and Darryl Strawberry had domestic strife, accused by his wife of breaking her nose.

Plus, it seemed like the whole world hated the brash, bragging Mets. Keith Hernandez even said he'd hate the Mets if he were on another team. Many in

the baseball world wanted the supremely confident defending champs to fail.

"They weren't what you necessarily call class winners," Phillies' third baseman Mike Schmidt was quoted as saying in spring training. "They made a lot of enemies. I know a lot of their guys individually and they're great guys. But they flaunted their success last year. The Mets have a Gary Carter personality. Don't get me wrong, I like Gary. But he sets their tone."

Both Johnson and Frank Cashen planned to talk to the team about the off-season difficulties and the target on the Mets' jerseys.

At the same time, the Mets, of course, did nothing to change anyone's opinion. "I expect us to win," Johnson said on the first day of spring training. "If we don't, it'll be my fault." Lenny Dykstra, all of twenty-four, had already penned an autobiography titled *Nails*, his nickname. A media crush showed up on the first day of camp to chronicle the swaggering.

1980s

But there were other, darker shadows flickering around the Mets as they headed into the season. Gooden was in serious trouble. He had missed the victory parade after the World Series, and the Mets were worried about him because of his winter.

On April 1, the news broke that the twenty-two-year-old Gooden had tested positive for cocaine use, stunning the Mets. The next day, he flew to New York to enter a drug rehabilitation clinic—the Smithers Alcoholism and Drug Treatment Center. He would not make a major league start until June 5, missing twelve starts.

In a 2010 interview with the *Daily News*'s Wayne Coffey, Gooden admitted that his drinking soared during the 1986 season. "When he returned to Tampa after the season, the friends he'd smoked pot with had graduated to cocaine," Coffey wrote. "He joined in. He loved the high. He started doing it more often."

"My body started craving it more and more, and that's when it became a big issue for me," Gooden told Coffey. Still, even after rehab, Gooden "never truly felt he had a problem," Coffey wrote. He kept drinking.

At about the same time Gooden was leaving Florida for rehab, Roger McDowell underwent surgery for a hernia, and injuries were another theme for the Mets' season. McDowell was out until May 14.

During the year, the Mets lost Bobby Ojeda to shoulder surgery that would knock him out for four months, and Ron Darling suffered torn ligaments in his right elbow in September. Rick Aguilera and Sid Fernandez missed time, too. The Cone trade immediately became important for the Mets, though he had his own injury problems, too, breaking a finger when he was hit trying to bunt and being out from May 27 to August 13. Gary Carter said later that he had six cortisone shots during the season to keep playing.

But in the April 7 opener at Shea, the Mets enjoyed themselves. They got their World Series rings and saw the championship pennant raised. Cashen threw out the first pitch after all the pomp. Strawberry blasted a three-run homer in the first inning, and Ojeda threw seven strong innings in Gooden's place in a 3–2 victory over Pittsburgh.

Strawberry even said he was dedicating the season to his friend Gooden, and wore Gooden's uniform pants during the game.

With the starting pitching hurting, Cashen reached out to a familiar name: Tom Seaver. The forty-two-year-old Seaver had not pitched since the previous season with the Red Sox, but he was willing to see if he could still do it. He tried a sixteen-day comeback that ultimately failed, though. Seaver, always a perfectionist, was unsatisfied how he was throwing the ball in workouts and tune-ups and retired.

"In my heart," he said and a news conference at Shea, "I feel the time has come for me not to play anymore. I've used up all the competitive pitches in me. I want to thank the New York Mets for giving me the opportunity to find that out."

Meanwhile, Gooden moved through his rehab. The Mets did not expect the old Dr. K when he returned, but when he finally pitched again, on June 5, Gooden beat the Pirates, allowing one run in 6 2/3 innings.

With these Mets, however, commotion was never very far away. Johnson and Strawberry feuded in early June over Strawberry being late to Wrigley Field on consecutive days for a series against the Cubs. Strawberry's reaction to the benching was that he initially said he would not play in the Mets' exhibition against their Triple-A Tidewater team in Virginia.

By July 22, the Mets were ten games out of first, sitting in third place. But after they swept the Cardinals in St. Louis from July 28 to 30, they were only 5 1/2 games behind.

They surged closer to the Cardinals, getting within 1 1/2 games, but St. Louis hurt the Mets in a three-game series at Shea from September 11 to 13, even without slugger Jack Clark, who was sitting with a sprained ankle.

In the opener, the Mets held a 4–1 lead and the Cards were down to their last out, but McDowell blew

OPPOSITE, LEFT:
Dwight Gooden.

OPPOSITE, RIGHT:
1987 *Daily News* front page announcing Dwight Gooden's cocaine problems.

ABOVE: David Cone.

1980s

the lead. Terry Pendleton hit a tying two-run homer. In the tenth, and Jesse Orosco gave up two runs. Darling hurt his thumb in the same game.

The next night, Gooden suffered his quickest knockout—he was gone after giving up six runs in two innings, and the Mets were 3 1/2 games behind with twenty-one to play. On September 13, Cone rescued the Mets—temporarily, anyway—with a strong outing in a sweep-averting win in the finale.

But the Mets could not catch their rivals, and pitching probably was to blame—Met pitchers spent a combined 457 days on the disabled list, and their staff ERA soared from 3.11 in 1986 to 3.84. Orosco lost four games on home runs.

Five pitchers had double figures in wins, anyway: Aguilera (11-3), Darling (12-8), Fernandez (12-8), Gooden (15-8), and Terry Leach (11-1). Leach won his first ten decisions, a club record.

Howard Johnson had a terrific year and so frustrated the Cardinals that Whitey Herzog accused him of using a corked bat. Johnson and Strawberry became the first pair of teammates to have 30 homers and 30 steals in the same season. Strawberry set club records in runs (108), homers (39), and slugging percentage (.583). McReynolds hit a career-high 29 homers.

Davey Johnson had begun grumbling about not getting a contract extension—he had one more year left on his contract—and it seemed like a confrontation between him and Cashen was brewing. At the

end of the season, the Mets got a shock: Davey Johnson announced he would manage the team in 1988, but then step down.

When camp opened for the 1988 season, Johnson's cloudy future as manager was only one of the leftovers from 1987 that the Mets would have to sort through. An interview that Darryl Strawberry gave to *Daily News* columnist Mike Lupica in the April issue of *Esquire* rocked the clubhouse.

In it, Strawberry made several inflammatory statements about the previous season's disappointments, including saying, "Our veterans didn't bring out the leadership they should have. Kid [Gary Carter] for one. He just quit."

Strawberry also questioned Johnson's managerial tactics, saying, "Nobody could figure out some of the stuff he was doing all season." In reference to Keith Hernandez, Strawberry said, "And Mex, I know he was going through a divorce and all, but who knows where his head was half the time last season."

Strawberry, like many athletes who don't like the way their words look in print, claimed his words were twisted. The first line in Lupica's column about the flap: "The first order of business is that Darryl Strawberry said all of it."

On March 9, Johnson held a closed-door meeting and ordered players to stop sniping at each other. It wasn't the only time Strawberry got in trouble in camp: He was fined $100 for being late to an early March workout, harkening back to problems he had with Johnson in 1987.

Despite the uproar, the Mets had high hopes, as usual. Cashen said during camp that it was possible Johnson would return as manager after the season and that he and Johnson would discuss it then. Cashen himself was mulling turning over more baseball responsibilities to Joe McIlvaine after the season.

Gooden groused about taking a $100,000 pay cut after a 15-7 season, but said he was making a new start and not going out anymore. He was happy and relaxed after getting married in the off-season. He was still undergoing drug testing.

Kevin Elster was set at shortstop after the Mets traded Rafael Santana to the Yankees during the winter, and Tim Teufel was given the second-base job by Johnson following Wally Backman's rough 1987, in which his average fell 70 points to .250 and he got only three hits in thirty-five at-bats right-handed.

Lenny Dykstra made a spring splash when he showed up at camp musclebound—he was twenty pounds heavier after a winter of what he said was lifting weights. Johnson was unsure if Dykstra had done the right thing—he did not want the pesky hitter to obsess over home runs.

The Mets got off to a fast start, clobbering the Expos on Opening Day in Montreal by smashing six home runs, including two each by Strawberry and Kevin McReynolds. Strawberry's second home run hit a bank of lights that sat beyond right field, 160 feet above the ground. It was the first time a fair ball had been hit there in Olympic Stadium.

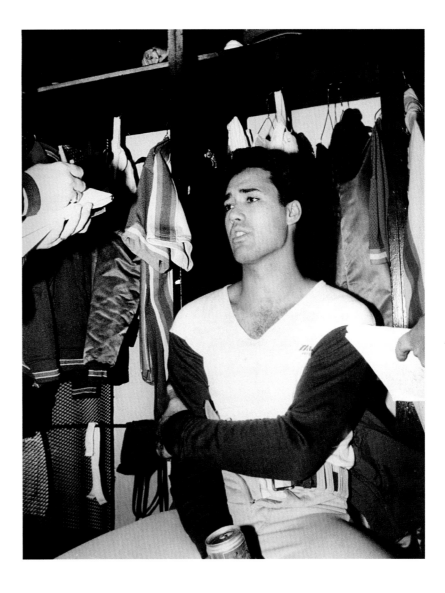

Ron Darling answering questions in the clubhouse following a game.

On May 25, the Mets were already five games out in front, at 31-12. On July 19, their lead over the Pirates had slipped to 1 1/2 games. But the Mets pushed the lead into double-digits in September and, on September 22, Ron Darling threw a six-hitter to beat the Phillies, 3–1, and clinch the Mets' fourth N.L. East crown. The Mets finished 100-60 and won the NL East by fifteen games. It was the fourth division title in club history and the second in three years.

The team drew a record 3,047,724 fans to Shea as Davey Johnson became the first manager in N.L. history to win 90 or more games in each of his first five seasons.

Strawberry tied his own club record of 39 homers, leading the National League. In the process, he set the Mets' club record for career homers: 186. Kevin

Phillie players try to
jinx the Mets' David
Cone with the latest
styles in headgear.

McReynolds had a career-high 99 RBI and stole 21 bases without being thrown out.

But pitching, as usual, was key. The Mets led the N.L. in ERA (2.91) and strikeouts (1,100), and all five starters won in double figures, including big years by Gooden, who was 18-9 with a 3.19 ERA despite suffering a sore shoulder in August, and Darling (17-9, 3.25). Even the relievers thrived: Randy Myers stepped in for the traded Jesse Orosco and saved 26 games, and Roger McDowell had 16 saves.

But their ace was twenty-five-year-old David Cone, who blew away everyone's biggest hopes by going 20-3, his .870 winning percentage the sixth-highest for a pitcher with twenty wins. Cone had guts, which he proved on May 22 when he didn't back down to Pedro Guerrero, who was angry after Cone hit him in the shoulder and flung his bat toward the mound. Cone said it was an important moment in his fledgling career. Fans aped the *Saturday Night Live* skit "The Coneheads" by wearing Coneheads at Shea.

There were signs that things weren't the same around the team, too, though. Gregg Jefferies, the team's best prospect, came up and provided a September spark. Carter caught more than a hundred games for the twelfth straight year, but had only eleven homers and forty-six RBI and went nearly three months without homering. Hernandez suffered a torn hamstring and then reinjured it after one inning when he tried to come back. He missed sixty-seven games and batted .276, his lowest average in ten years. Howard Johnson's numbers dipped as he played through torn cartilage in his shoulder.

And on September 21, with the playoffs in sight and the Mets arranging their rotation, they suffered the worst injury of them all when an electric hedge clipper nearly severed the upper part of Bob Ojeda's left middle finger while he was trimming the honeysuckle bushes at his Port Washington home. With his career in jeopardy, Ojeda had five hours of microsurgery at Roosevelt Hospital in Manhattan, and doctors expressed optimism he could throw again the next spring. After he got out of the hospital, Ojeda vowed to pitch again.

1980s

The Mets roared into the N.L. Championship Series against the banged-up Dodgers, winning twenty-nine of their last thirty-six games. They were heavy favorites after going 10-1 against the Dodgers during the regular season, outscoring them, 49–18. In the Mets' lone loss to Los Angeles, a 4–3 decision on June 1, they had the tying run at second base when the game ended.

In addition, they had Gooden, and he was awesome against the Dodgers, carrying an 8-1 career record and a 1.22 ERA against them, including a 4-0 mark and 0.34 ERA at Dodger Stadium, where the series opened on October 4. In two wins against the Dodgers during the '88 season, Gooden had thrown two complete games, allowing one run total.

Gooden's opponent, though, was the best pitcher in the world at that moment: Orel Hershiser. Hershiser was 23-8 with eight shutouts and a 2.26 ERA during the season and would eventually win the N.L. Cy Young Award.

Going into his start against the Mets, he had thrown an all-time record of fifty-nine consecutive scoreless innings. He had not given up a run since the Expos scored twice off him August 30 in Montreal.

In game one, Hershiser pitched his streak all the way up to sixty-seven straight shutout innings. But Gooden pitched well, too, and the Mets had the last word in the ninth inning, something they had done repeatedly during the regular season when they won nineteen games in their final at-bat.

Hershiser was just two outs away from yet another shutout, leading, 2–0, when the Mets started scoring. Jefferies led off the inning with a single and moved to second on a ground ball. Strawberry followed with a double, trimming the Dodger lead to one run, but perhaps more importantly, knocking out Hershiser. It was the first run Hershiser had given up in thirty-five days.

Closer Jay Howell entered and walked McReynolds

and then struck out Howard Johnson. He got ahead of Carter, nothing and two, but Carter correctly guessed that a breaking ball was coming and looped it into short center field. John Shelby dove but couldn't snare it.

Strawberry scored easily, and McReynolds bowled over Dodger catcher Mike Scioscia to score the go-ahead run. The Mets held in the ninth to take a 3–2 thriller in game one.

But it turned out that this series' drama was only just beginning. Cone, who once had aspired to be a sportswriter, had agreed to collaborate on a series of ghostwritten columns on the series for the *Daily News*, along with beat writer Bob Klapisch. The next

Gregg Jefferies struggles to catch a pop fly on a sunny day.

1980s

day, with Cone scheduled to start game two, the *News* carried an incendiary column that enflamed the Dodgers so much they tacked it to their clubhouse bulletin board.

"Orel was lucky for eight innings," the column said. It added, "I'll tell you a secret: As soon as we got Orel out of the game, we knew we'd beat the Dodgers. We saw Howell throwing curveball after curveball and we were thinking: This is the Dodgers' idea of a stopper? Seeing Howell and his curveball reminded us of a high school pitcher."

The Dodgers clobbered Cone in game two, knocking him out after two innings by building a 5–0 lead in a game L.A. went on to win, 6–3, to tie the series. After the cross-country flight to New York, where the series was slated to resume on October 7, Cone decided to spike his column, writing a farewell piece in the *News* headlined, "A Forlorn Correspondent."

He told reporters his cracks about the Dodgers were intended as humor and that he would apologize to Howell, Hershiser, and the Dodgers. He added that the Mets did not force him to put the cover on his typewriter. "Short, but exciting," is how he summed up his newspaper career.

Game three was rained out on October 7, so the Dodgers made a daring move and tapped Hershiser to start again on only three days' rest against Ron Darling, who had been 14-1 with a 2.29 ERA at Shea during the season.

In wet, rainy conditions, the Mets made another rally, overcoming a 4–3 deficit by scoring five times in the eighth inning in an 8–4 victory. The Dodgers had taken the lead when Randy Myers walked Mike Sharperson with the bases loaded, forcing in the go-ahead run.

Howell came in to protect the lead and got to a full count on McReynolds when Davey Johnson came out of the dugout to ask plate umpire Joe West to check Howell's glove.

West and Harry Wendelstedt, the crew's senior ump, went to the mound and inspected the glove and tossed Howell out of the game for having pine tar on it. The umpires took the glove and presented it to N.L. president A. Bartlett Giamatti, who later suspended Howell for two days in the series.

Davey Johnson credited one of his coaches, Bill Robinson, with tipping him off about the glove, but a *Daily News* story also credited the Mets' Double-A manager, Tucker Ashford, for picking it up while watching Howell on television pitching in game one.

The Mets quickly took the lead. Wally Backman doubled in the tying run, Wilson singled in a run to put them ahead, Hernandez walked with the bases loaded, and Strawberry singled in two more.

Pitcher/scribe Cone, of all people, pitched a scoreless ninth and the Mets were ahead, 2–1, in the series.

The Dodgers took game four, Mets-style. A two-run homer by Strawberry and a solo shot by McReynolds off old Cardinal nemesis John Tudor in the fourth inning gave the Mets a 3–2 lead, and they had increased it to 4–2 going into the ninth.

Since the first inning, when he gave up a two-out, two-run single to Shelby, Gooden had been cruising, allowing only one hit. But Gooden walked Shelby to start the ninth, and Scioscia tied the score with a two-run homer. In the twelfth inning, hobbled Dodger slugger Kirk Gibson lifted L.A. with a homer off McDowell, and the series was tied.

The next day, the Mets lost again, their flair for rallying falling short. Sid Fernandez got tagged for six runs in four-plus innings in the 7–4 loss, putting the Mets on the brink of elimination.

Lenny Dykstra hit a three-run homer in the fifth inning, halving the Dodgers' lead, and the Mets scored once more in the eighth. But with the tying runs on base later in the inning, Kevin McReynolds hit a grounder that took a high hop and hit Jefferies' spikes. Jefferies was automatically out for being struck by a batted ball, and the Mets' threat was over. An inning later, so was the game.

Now it was up to Cone, who ached to win since his journalism had so fired up the Dodgers before game two. He was up to the challenge, allowing one run in a five-hit complete game that went 5–1 Mets, tying the series. McReynolds had four hits, including a homer, and knocked in three runs.

The game's crucial at-bat may have come in the first inning after Cone walked the first two Dodgers, throwing eight balls in his first nine pitches. The Mets were holding a 1–0 lead, but Gibson was at the plate. Despite a strained hamstring, Gibson had smashed homers in each of the previous two games and was the Dodgers' biggest threat.

But Gibson was hurting—he had to test himself in the batting cage before the game before he could be sure he'd play. Against Cone in the first, he tried to bunt and popped it up, buoying the struggling pitcher. Cone caught it and got out of the inning and the Mets went on to force a game seven.

Dodgers' manager Tommy Lasorda had been talking about how his team was a "team of destiny," and Lasorda's bunch quickly took control of game seven. Darling did not get an out in the second inning and was charged with six runs (four earned) in one-plus innings in a nightmare start. Errors by Jefferies and Backman helped the Dodgers score five times in the second.

Facing a 6–0 deficit so fast with Hershiser on the mound, the Mets had no chance, and that was the final score. The Mets, convinced all season they'd be going on to the World Series, were stunned that the Dodgers would face the Oakland Athletics a few days later in a Series that should have been theirs.

Hershiser, who threw a five-hit shutout, was named the series MVP. He won game seven and saved game four and recorded an ERA of 1.09.

A week after the Dodgers had shocked Oakland, too, the Mets resolved their differences with their

1980s

But the fine-tuning turned into a huge season of transition. Some things were still the same—surprise! There was spring training unrest, and Johnson again talked of the Mets being the team to beat. But there was change, too.

The previous December, the Mets had traded one of their tough, scrappy igniters, Wally Backman, to Minnesota for three minor league pitchers and had spent chunks of the off-season talking to the Braves about trading for Dale Murphy and the Mariners about Mark Langston, though neither deal happened. Gregg Jefferies was an emerging hitter, but where was there room for him on the field? Second base seemed the logical spot.

Changes were afoot, but the big story in camp was more Darryl Strawberry unrest. Strawberry had two years left on his contract, but he wanted an extension and talked repeatedly about leaving as a free agent in 1991, when his current deal expired. Before the playoff series against the Dodgers, he "casually" mentioned that he might one day want to play in his hometown of Los Angeles.

Dwight Gooden, meanwhile, signed a three-year, $6.7-million contract during the winter, making him the highest-paid Met in history at the time. He said the security relaxed him.

Strawberry, though, was tense, in part because he was only the sixth-highest-paid Met. On March 1, he threatened to leave camp if progress wasn't made on an extension. The next day, his angst bubbled over into perhaps the most notorious team photo session in sports history.

When Keith Hernandez was asked by reporters about Strawberry's demands the previous day, he said, "A deal's a deal. I think he's getting bad advice. I think it's his agent's fault." When the team gathered for the picture, Strawberry asked Hernandez why he had said those things.

"I'm tired of your baby stuff," Hernandez answered.

manager. Davey Johnson would indeed be back in 1989—in fact, he signed a three-year contract with an option for a fourth year. Cashen kept citing Johnson's record of 488 wins in five years, one world championship. And Johnson was hungry for more.

"We don't have a lot to do," he said. "Just some fine-tuning."

"I've been tired of you for years," Strawberry shot back. Then he took at swing at Hernandez, a man he had called a mentor, but one he also believed at various times was behind anonymous remarks in the papers about him. Hernandez later said he was grazed on the cheek by a backhand. That was the only punch, the combatants were separated, and amazingly, the picture was taken.

Later, the two met with Met psychiatrist Dr. Alan Lans and shook hands. But Strawberry also walked out of camp because of his contract, though he said he'd be back at some undetermined point.

Strawberry stayed away on March 3, but said he'd return the next day. He added he'd give the Mets two good years and leave as a free agent when his contract was up. There'd be no more contract talks.

Strawberry returned the next day and made a grand entrance. He was booed when he came onto the field after he was introduced by the PA announcer, but made it a memorable moment by grabbing Hernandez around the neck, hugging him, and planting a kiss on his cheek. Later, Strawberry homered. All this took place in front of the Dodgers, the team that had conquered the Mets the previous fall, in the Mets' exhibition home opener.

The Mets, meanwhile, still had plenty of talent, but Gary Carter and Hernandez were both thirty-five and entering the final years of their contracts, too. Howard Johnson was coming back from off-season shoulder surgery and then endured a winter of hearing his name in trade rumors.

The Mets won their opener at Shea against the Cardinals, but Gooden wasn't super sharp in the 8–4 decision, allowing four runs (three earned) in seven innings. On April 16, they lost to the Cardinals and fell to 3-7 and already were five games out of first place, And Johnson, already irked by lackluster play in spring training, blasted the team and told them to stop playing golf on the road.

"Maybe less relaxing time, no golf and cards on the road until we start doing the job we're capable of doing," Johnson told reporters. "When we play like this, there's no place for golf."

In May, one week apart, Carter went on the disabled list with a knee injury that needed surgery and missed more than two months, and Hernandez broke a kneecap in a collision with L.A.'s Dave Anderson and missed almost two months.

The Mets were hovering around first place in mid-June when the transitions continued. Frank Cashen and Joe McIlvaine sent Roger McDowell and Lenny Dykstra to Philadelphia for Juan Samuel. The Mets envisioned Samuel as their center fielder and leadoff hitter, though Samuel had only recently converted from second base to center and had not mastered the position.

Davey Johnson said Samuel, who had speed and some power, reminded him of Bobby Bonds. But he was wistful, too, at losing two sparkplugs and symbols of Met success in McDowell and Dykstra.

On July 2, Gooden tore a muscle in his right shoul-

OPPOSITE:
Gregg Jefferies in the Mets' dugout.

ABOVE: Juan Samuel.

1980s

der and missed more than two months. Still, the Mets hung in the race. On July 25, they were in a virtual tie for first with the Cubs, and the front office was still tinkering.

The Mets fell into a seven-game losing streak leading up to the July 31 trade deadline and, about one minute before the deadline, pulled off a desperate blockbuster, sending five players, including Rick Aguilera, David West, and Kevin Tapani, to Minnesota for the 1988 A.L. Cy Young Award winner, Frank Viola. Viola, a New Yorker who went to St. John's, was, at the time, "one of the best left-handed pitchers in baseball," Davey Johnson said.

The Mets also shipped Mookie Wilson to Toronto for pitcher Jeff Musselman. They had started the year with two center fielders, Wilson and Dykstra, and had shed both. All the trades and moves had left Strawberry, only twenty-seven, as the man with the longest tenure on the team. There were only ten players left from the 1986 champs.

From August 1 to August 21, the Mets went 16-5 to move within 1 1/2 games of first again. But then they lapsed into uneven play. They lost their next

five, won three straight, then lost four in a row to fall 4 1/2 games back. They never got closer than 2 1/2 out the rest of the way and finished at 87-75, holding off the Cardinals' charge for second place by winning their last four games. Both teams were staring up at the Cubs.

The last few weeks of the season saw typical Mets ups and downs—on September 13, Gooden returned and proved he was healthy by throwing three scoreless innings of relief.

A week later, Strawberry and McReynolds angered Johnson by going into the clubhouse and starting to get undressed during the ninth inning of a loss to the Cubs. The Mets were taking their last at-bats at the time. There were reports that Johnson and Strawberry had a shouting match during a team meeting. Both players were benched and fined.

On September 27, the Mets' final home game of the season featured a wild scene moments after Philadelphia's Roger McDowell had retired Jefferies on a grounder to end the game. Jefferies charged the mound, tackling his former teammate. McDowell and Jefferies did not like each other when McDowell was

a Met. McDowell apparently was tough on Jefferies, who was perceived by some Mets as Johnson's pet.

And late in September, Johnson's future all of a sudden didn't seem so secure anymore. Team brass didn't like the team's attitude in a disappointing season and there was a perception that Johnson did not get as much as he should have from the Mets' talent. Johnson was so convinced that he was going to be fired he cleaned out his office at Shea and did not renew the lease on the house he lived in on Long Island.

While Johnson hung in limbo, the Mets quickly resolved whether two of their 1980s cornerstones would be back: Hernandez and Carter were both told after the season that they would not be offered new contracts. It was truly the end of an era: Two old pros who had helped the Mets grow up were gone.

Their Met careers sputtered to an end after they returned from injury. Carter, who finished with a .183 average and two homers in fifty games, later signed with the Giants. Hernandez batted .233 with four homers in seventy-five games and signed a two-year deal with the Indians in December.

Throughout the season, the Met hierarchy had wanted to make changes. That was one goal the Mets reached: change. The decade ended, however, with most Mets and their fans feeling like they had not won enough championships with the remarkable talent they had assembled.

Keith Hernandez waves to fans following his final Shea Stadium appearance as a Met.

1980s

MET MEMORIES

FRANK CASHEN

*On February 21, 1980, Frank Cashen signed a five-year
contract to be the Mets' general manager, and the organization was never the same. The Mets were a punch
line in the late 1970s, from the Seaver fiasco to the scads
of forgettable players patrolling Shea. Cashen, who had
run the powerful Orioles' teams of the late 1960s and
early 1970s after careers in sportswriting, racetracks,
and a brewery, helped guide them through the catacombs
of futility to the years of mid-1980s success, including
the 1986 World Series title.*

I ran two ball clubs in my career, the Mets and the
Orioles, and the Orioles, when I took them over, were
a pretty darn good ball club. There wasn't much to do.
When I agreed to take over the Mets, they had finished last or next to last for a while. They had drawn
eight hundred thousand or so, and their farm system
was in tatters. It was a massive job, and I sometimes
wonder how I got talked into taking it. I had a good
job with the commissioner's office at the time—Bowie
[Kuhn] let me run the baseball part of the business.

Nelson Doubleday, who had just bought the ball
club, was majority owner, and was looking forward
to hiring a GM, and someone told them about me. In
the ten years I was with the Orioles, we were in four
World Series [1966, 1969–1971], and in '73 and '74
we won the AL East but lost to the A's in the playoffs.

When I went with the Mets, I said I think I had the
best experience I ever had in baseball and the worst
experience in baseball with them. In '69 I had the O's,
and the Mets beat us. That was the low point in my
baseball career. I thought we had a super team and we
did, we were in the World Series the next two years.
The high point of my career was '86 because we had
built that thing up and it was the high point. The sad
part was the team was put together to win for a couple
more years and we didn't. Some of the younger players we had got interested more in some off-the-field
activities, and the team was never as good as I thought
it should have been. I own the dubious distinction
of being the first guy to fire Joe Torre—he was Met
manager when I got there.

In April of 1980, the only thing I could do was
get ready for the draft. We picked Darryl [Strawberry]
number one and then took Billy Beane and John Gibbons also. Of all the young ballplayers I've ever seen,
the guy who had more talent than anybody was
Darryl Strawberry.

I believed you built a club from within and it was
just as important they learn to win in the minors
because if you get them to the majors and they've
never won, that's not the time to start teaching them.
If you ask guys like Gooden and Strawberry, they
never played on a losing club going through the
minor leagues. That takes time to teach. Doubleday
asked me how long it would be and I said four or five
years. In four years, we had turned the thing around
and I knew we were going to win.

DUGOUTS WILL BE CLEARED
OF ALL NON-UNIFORMED
PERSONNEL 1/2 HR. PRIOR
TO GAME TIME

We had a few more moves to make—we got Keith [Hernandez] I knew we were one ballplayer away, and I went to my friend John McHale and asked about trading for Gary Carter. We talked and talked and then I knew we were full then.

The most controversial trade I made was Lee Mazzilli. I knew I couldn't win unless I got pitching, so I traded him [to Texas] for Ron Darling and Walt Terrell, who we later traded for Howard Johnson. I knew those two pitchers, plus Bobby Ojeda, would help. I had seen Ojeda pitch at Pawtucket when our Triple-A club was there playing the Red Sox Triple-A team. I had fond memories of him and eventually traded for him. Then we traded for Sid [Fernandez].

I fired Joe Torre and I said, "If I'm going to start winning, I need to get my own people in here." I got George Bamberger in who had been an outstanding pitching coach for me in Baltimore and I made him the manager. But the reason I got him was I knew if he was the manager he'd prepare the pitching staff for the time when we were going to win. When the time came after that, when we were ready to win, I got Davey Johnson, who had played for me in Baltimore and I had traded him in a terrible trade.

Davey is a very talented guy. He came in to Earl Weaver and he had all these computer printouts, why we should be doing certain things. Weaver swept it all into the wastebasket. But Davey was intelligent, and ballplayers could believe him because he was very sincere. He was a math major in college and he knew about computers and things long before I ever did, I'll tell you that. To this day [in 2010], he's the best manager not working right now in the majors, along with Bobby Valentine.

One of the interesting things about running that ball club was going against George Steinbrenner and the Yankees. We did so very successfully. We drew three million people before the Yankees ever did, and that was not to George's liking, I'll tell you that. We had Strawberry and Gooden. He [Steinbrenner] was a supreme egotist.

Manager Davey Johnson (left) and pitching coach Mel Stottlemyre look glum during a 6–0 defeat in Philadelphia, September 15, 1986.

1980s

HUBIE BROOKS

Hubie Brooks was the Mets' first-round draft pick (third overall) in 1978 and one of their most promising youngsters as the 1980s dawned. He made his debut on September 4, part of a group of players who would help turn around sagging Met fortunes.

I enjoyed my career. The best thing that happened to me was to start my career where I did and when I did. I really enjoyed it. It was a great thing to do for a living. It was good for me that I started where I did—when I first came up to the Mets, the team wasn't winning a lot of games. The talent was in somewhat of a change, and then some of the better players got there and then you had to learn how to play when there weren't people at the ballpark. Then to see it start to change in '83 and '84, that was so exciting to see. They hadn't won in so long, but then crowds started coming.

They got the prospects coming up and that was good. The change, I don't think it would've been as fast if it hadn't been for Mr. Wilpon and Mr. Doubleday. They were really committed to improving it. When they came on, a lot of things started to change. You could see the whole organization get better.

Joe Torre was my first manager and he really gave me a chance and I really appreciated that. At the time, that's what he did.

One of my favorite memories—and you're going to laugh when I say this—is when I got drafted by the Mets [as the third overall pick in the 1978 draft]. They flew me to New York and I got to meet people. My first interview, I got to meet Lindsey Nelson. He was there at Shea. I think about that so much. People say, "The guy with the different-colored jackets!" When I went back to my hotel, I thought about it, how I couldn't believe that was Lindsey Nelson. We'd see him from the coast. That is really a fond memory. I was a young

kid seeing him, and he was there and he talked to me. It dawned on me where I was playing.

Later, Davey came in. And there was nothing like the young Doc Gooden. He was something to see. That young man was something else. The big thing was when the team made the deal for Keith Hernandez [in 1983].

I never won one [a World Series]. It would've been nice to have won one. But that's how the game is. That trade [Brooks and three other players were sent to Montreal for All-Star catcher Gary Carter] had to be made for them to get what they wanted. I've never felt bad about that. Something had to go and it was me, but that's they way it goes. I never took it personal. At least the Mets thought well enough of me to give me my first opportunity to play, they were my original team. And that was OK. To have that opportunity, I can never say nothing bad about that. And I came back again.

The organization was good to me when I was there. The people were good to me. I thought Doubleday and Wilpon were good folks, good people. There was never a time I regretted being there. I never had a thought like I didn't like being there, being a part of the city.

JAY HORWITZ

Jay Horwitz, the Mets' director of media relations, has worked for the club since 1980, and saw firsthand the phenomenon that was Dwight Gooden when "Dr. K" first hit the big leagues in 1984. Gooden, only a teenager, required some special attention because of all the attention he attracted.

I called Steve Brener—he was the PR guy with the Dodgers—and I asked him what they did with Fernando Valenzuela [in 1981] and they had a policy that he would only speak after his start. Nothing before. Dwight was just eighteen, nineteen, and we just tried to protect him as much as we could. He had 300 strikeouts the year before at [Class A] Lynchburg, and at the time he came up, we weren't very good. Darryl [Strawberry] had come up the year before and we were still getting better. We didn't want to make Gooden out to be the savior or anything, so we came up with a policy. We wanted to protect him and limit the access to him. The problem was, he got better and better and things got good and more and more people wanted to speak to him. We had to stay firm with that policy through the whole first year. We changed it the next year when we opened it up a little bit where we scheduled stuff, one or two a week, stuff we could control, to not let it get out of hand.

Every time he pitched, you expected a no-hitter or fifteen strikeouts. He had the presence on the mound. He just got the fans excited. Those two years, in my time here, those are the two most dominant back-to-back years that any pitcher ever had. He had all those strikeouts, the wins, the Cy Young, won the triple crown of pitching in '85. It was just two magical years. The people came to see him. I think we averaged like eight thousand to ten thousand more fans per game on the days he pitched. It was a great combination with him and Darryl together,

and we had that run in the '80s where we were first or second every year.

I wouldn't say Dwight was shy. He came from Florida and wasn't that used to the big city. The problem was, with Darryl and Dwight that was really unfair to them, is that they were perceived as being the saviors and even though we protected them, we probably did too much with them. I learned from my mistakes with Darryl, we did everybody, everything. He was the black Jesus. We cut it down with Dwight. We probably just really used him too much, even though we cut back. If the team had been better, it wouldn't have been as bad but because we weren't good, so much was expected from them and it was a big, tough burden on two young kids to bear. In this market—it wasn't Kansas City or Pittsburgh, it was New York. We were bad from the late 1970s to '84, and this was the second coming and so much was asked of them. It was tough on them to have that burden on their shoulders.

Met players mob Ron Darling after New York beat Philadelphia, 3–1, to clinch their second National League East title in three years, September 23, 1988.

1980s

1990s

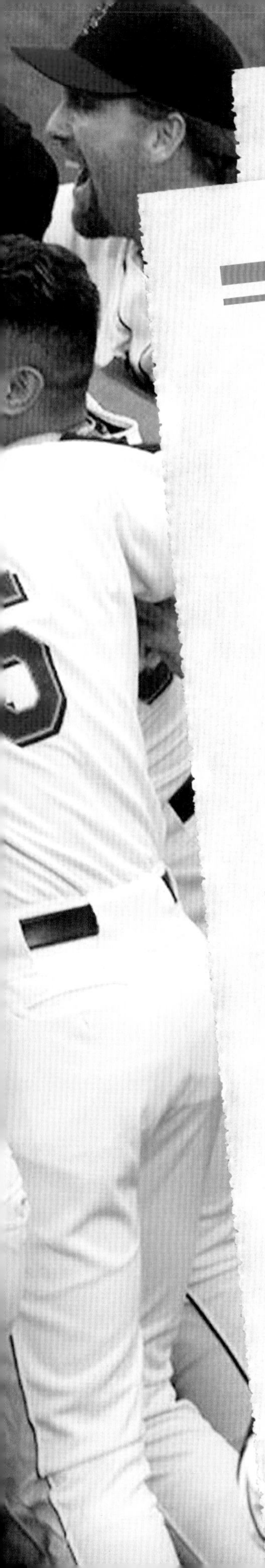

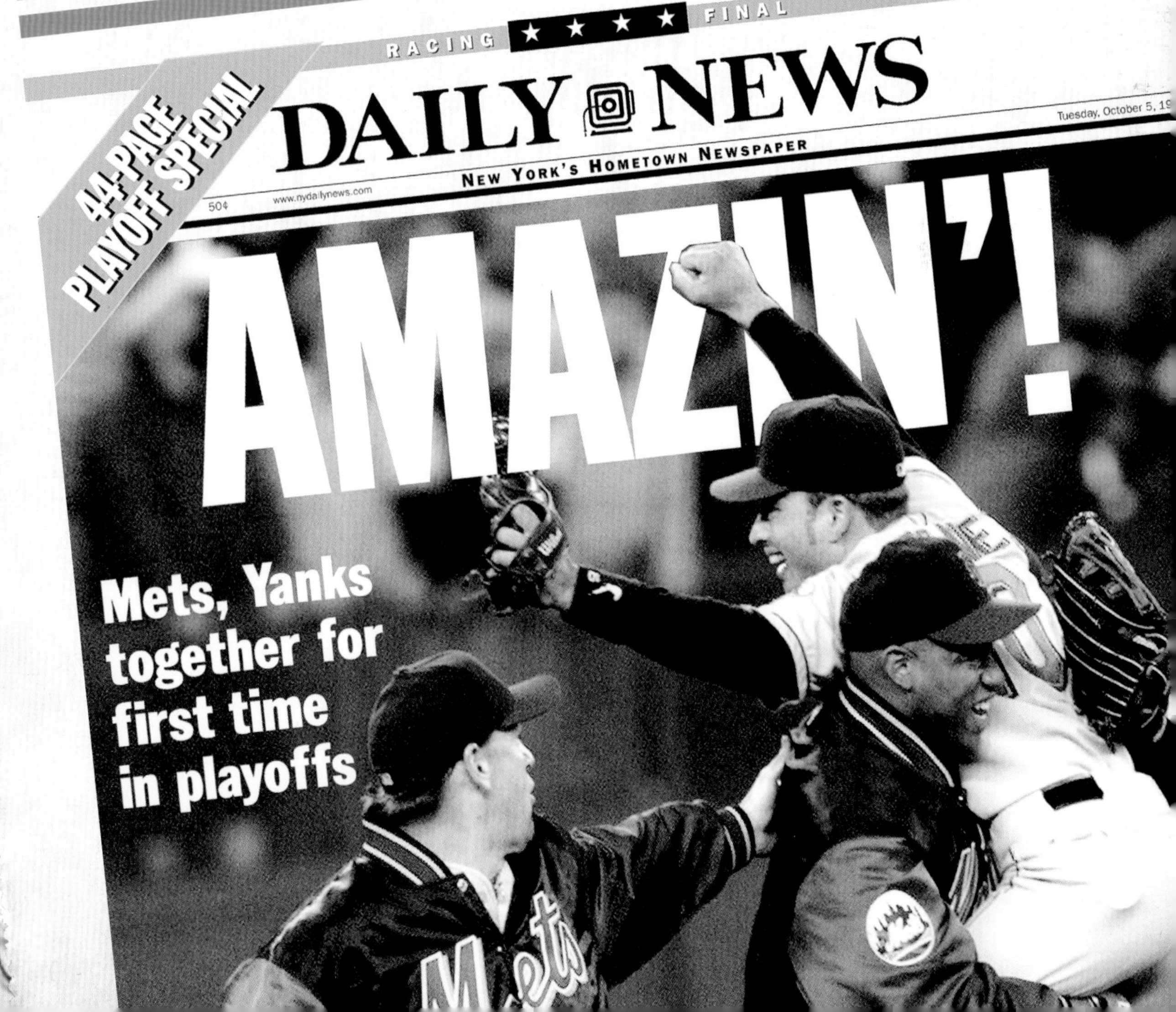

RACING ★ ★ ★ ★ FINAL

DAILY NEWS

NEW YORK'S HOMETOWN NEWSPAPER

Tuesday, October 5, 19

50¢ www.nydailynews.com

44-PAGE PLAYOFF SPECIAL

AMAZIN'!

Mets, Yanks together for first time in playoffs

It is difficult to know which feat is more elusive in sports: Winning a championship, or remaining on top after experiencing that first season of success. Years of planning, work, and luck are needed to take a franchise from losing to winning, and in most cases those events never result in a title. It is an exceedingly rare feat to win it all in one's respective sport. Though they have enjoyed other periods of excellence and contention, the Mets built two winners in their history.

OPPOSITE: The Mets celebrate their victory over the Red Sox in the 1986 World Series.

Frank Cashen and Davey Johnson.

In the 1960s, longtime Cardinal general manager Bing Devine took a brief furlough from St. Louis to run the Mets, and helped assemble the unlikely 1969 miracle team. That team, however, was never a juggernaut. Rather, they were a group of solid players combined with below-average talents enjoying a career year. They soared to a title because of a group of talented young pitchers, including Tom Seaver, Jerry Koosman, Gary Gentry, Nolan Ryan, and Tug McGraw—and just barely enough offense.

It was no surprise that those Mets did not dominate the early-1970s after that miracle year. The reason they did not remain on top was simple: They were a good but not a great team.

The theme was different with Frank Cashen's Mets of the 1980s, who should have achieved far more than they did. After winning the World Series in 1986, drug use by star players and the discarding of key clubhouse characters created fundamental problems with the organization, and all but assured the team of several years in the wilderness.

That became the dominant trope of the 1990s. It was a very dark decade for the franchise, although one partially redeemed by a thrilling, if ultimately unsuccessful, finish. It began with the final thrusts of Cashen's,

Davey Johnson's, and Darryl Strawberry's respective eras, as those three icons saw their Met careers fizzle.

The void created by that prematurely dead near-dynasty proved difficult to fill, and led first to a poorly assembled and extremely expensive disaster that inspired an unflattering book titled *The Worst Team That Money Could Buy*. As that early-to-mid-1990s team amounted to nothing but scandal and playoff misses, the Mets slowly rebuilt, and took on an entirely different personality by the end of the decade.

Far removed from the Johnson, Strawberry, Gooden, and Keith Hernandez era, they would make a spirited run at the World Series in 1999, a prelude to actually reaching it in the first year of the new decade. By then, players named Piazza, Leiter, Ventura, and Ordóñez would help fans forget the blandness of many recent seasons. Long before that, though, as the 1990s began, many of those classic 1980s Mets were still in place—though something essential had changed.

After missing the playoffs in 1989, the Mets did make several changes before the 1990 season began. Catcher Gary Carter, a strong personality on

1990s

the team and a future Hall of Famer, was released in November 1989. First baseman Keith Hernandez, the undisputed leader of in the 1980s, signed as a free agent with the Cleveland Indians that same month, after the Mets had signaled they felt Hernandez could no longer contribute.

In December, the team shipped reliever Randy Myers to Cincinnati for fellow reliever John Franco, a native New Yorker who would remain with the Mets through the 1990s and beyond.

Cashen, who had always sparred with Johnson over discipline, considered firing the manager after a disappointing 1989. Johnson, the general manager had long felt, was too lax with the players, and not supportive enough when the front office tried to impose rules. Now that the Mets had failed to make the playoffs in two of the three seasons that followed 1986's World Series championship, Cashen could justify dismissing the manager.

He opted to needle him instead. During the off-season, Cashen fired two of Johnson's favorite lieutenants, hitting coach Bill Robinson and third-base coach Sam Perlozzo.

With the manager disgruntled after the team dismissed his friends, the Mets' most prominent player found himself in more legal trouble. Darryl Strawberry's first marriage had long been explosive, and on January 26, 1990, the tensions led to legal trouble.

On that night, Lisa Strawberry returned to the couple's California home at about three o'clock in the morning, causing a confrontation with her drunk and angry husband. During that dispute, Darryl struck Lisa across the face with his hand, leading her to beat him with a metal rod.

The argument escalated to the point where Strawberry retrieved a pistol and pointed it at his wife. Lisa's mother then entered, called the police, and had Darryl arrested and charged with possession of a unlicensed handgun. It was an unfortunate way for the

outfielder to begin his campaign for a new contract and extend his Mets career.

Strawberry saw that alcohol was at the root of his unstable personal life and increasingly inconsistent professional performance. He'd batted just .225 in 1989, and while he hit twenty-five home runs, he drove in just seventy-seven runs, production well below his capabilities.

In an attempt to save his career from sinking prematurely, Strawberry checked himself into the rehab facility the Smithers Institute on February 3, 1990. As the major leagues endured a spring training lockout while ownership and the Players' Association quibbled over arbitration eligibility, Strawberry worked his way through a twenty-eight-day stay at Smithers.

Meanwhile, in Port St. Lucie, unrest and trouble with the team were clear. Davey Johnson was speaking to reporters in remarkably blunt fashion, criticizing current and former players while attempting to explain the disappointments of 1989.

Gregg Jefferies, Johnson said, "acted like it was the end of the world every time he made an out."

The young phenom had become a controversial figure for the Mets, a heralded up-and-comer whom many veterans felt lacked the fiery attitude that characterized the 1986 Mets. Johnson said he nearly benched Jefferies the previous summer, claiming "I was willing to get fired over it."

The manager conceded that while the Mets could still win, they would not dominate as they had a few years earlier. "We don't have the man-to-man advantage we used to," he said.

Johnson also, surprisingly, cited Carter and Hernandez as negative influences in the clubhouse during their final season with the team, and criticized them for failing to handle their declines with grace. On several occasions in 1989, Carter and Johnson were overheard screaming at one another, with the door closed in the manager's office. The catcher, nicknamed "Camera" for his love of attention, did not enjoy playing a part-time role.

"I don't know how you break down a selfish player," Johnson said. "You can say, 'You're being selfish,' but he'll just say bleep you, 'I'm making $2 million, you're a bleep.'"

Johnson also was harsh in his review of Hernandez's final year in New York. "Some of the leadership in the clubhouse was not good," the skipper said the following spring training.

"Keith was a bad example at times. His intensity was an inspiration to the team. But when he was hurt, he had no intensity level at all. Him sitting in the clubhouse [during games] was an example of that. Keith was so great for the Mets for years, but Mex wasn't the leader at the end of his career, like certain great players. I'm talking about Don Baylor or Frank Robinson or Andre Dawson."

A few days later, Hernandez sniffed, "I have no comment, no comment at all. I'm not [with the Mets] anymore, so I have nothing to say."

It was one thing to rip two departed players, but

Gregg Jefferies looks to turn a double play after forcing Cincinnati's Paul O'Neill at second base.

Johnson also elaborated on his criticism of Jefferies, who not only remained with the club, but was still seen as an important part of its future. "What really ticked me off was when Gregg would walk back real slow after making an out. It bothered me, and I'm sure it bothered the players.

"But you know what? Once I said that to him, he stopped. I think there was a lot of petty jealousy toward him. The resentment was overdone."

With those comments, Johnson managed to simultaneously slap Jefferies and the players who did not like him. He sounded more like a man burning bridges than building them.

A more positive development came on March 1, when Strawberry completed his stay at rehab—though he flew immediately to California to undergo police questioning about the gun incident with his wife (Lisa Strawberry would soon drop the charges).

Four days later, with the lockout still freezing baseball activities, Strawberry reported to Port St. Lucie and declared that he would not ask for a contract extension during spring training. He would instead focus on "being happy with my family, and being a better player for the New York Mets."

1990s

Still, the contract issue loomed as a potential problem. Strawberry had been a true superstar for the Mets in the 1980s, and retained the talent to remain a top player. But his personal life and disappointing performance in 1989 raised legitimate questions, and the Mets faced a decision during or at the latest after the season of whether to gamble on more years of Strawberry.

As the team planned for its future, Gooden presented yet another question. Because of the lockout—which finally ended on March 18, after thirty-two days—Opening Day was in doubt in 1990. The Mets knew in March, though, that if it did take place, Gooden would not be able to pitch because of a lingering shoulder issue that cut his year short in 1989.

With the labor dispute shortening spring training, Gooden simply would not have enough exhibition practice to get that shoulder ready. That ensured another shortened season, and made the two brightest stars of early in the previous decade the team's biggest mysteries heading into the current one. As it turned out, both players were effectively finished as impact

players with the Mets, but no one realized or wanted to admit it during the easy optimism of March 1990.

In that context, Strawberry tried to convince himself and others that all would be better. He tattooed "Lisa" on his left arm. He wore a gold crucifix around his neck, signifying an effort to refocus on family and religion. He arrived at the team's spring training complex before most of his teammates after the lockout.

"I'm not a controversial player anymore," he said, and while the effort was clearly earnest, it had not yet proven sustainable. It had not yet been tested by the realities of his marriage, potential conflict with the Mets over his contract status, or life on the road.

Heading into that season, more potential conflict within the team centered around Jefferies, who had been incredibly unpopular the year before. "I really hate it when a guy tells you, 'Great job, great play,' and then you walk away and he's telling another [teammate], 'Can you believe that baby?' That's bad for any team," said Jefferies.

Players thought that management viewed Jefferies as the new Strawberry, a potential superstar. Teammates correctly felt that this symbolized much of the problems with the current Mets versus the team of a few years before. While Strawberry had many issues, he loved stepping up to big moments, and he was generally popular among his teammates, even those he occasionally infuriated.

Jefferies, although he ultimately enjoyed a respectable career with other teams, was miscast as the Mets' next leader, and players knew it by 1990. "He's the new Darryl, the new cornerstone of the franchise," said Ron Darling. "Obviously, we have to be a little more sensitive, because Gregg is a more sensitive guy. But I'll admit, he wasn't imagining things. It got ugly in here, as ugly as it could get."

More ugliness came toward the end of spring training, when Johnson informed Bob Ojeda that he would begin the season in the bullpen, rather than the starting rotation. Ojeda immediately demanded a trade.

"I've been getting the bleep end of the stick for three years now," he said. "I'm Dirty Harry."

A few days later, Mackey Sasser complained that Johnson had told him nothing about the catching situation, and he was unsure whether he or Barry Lyons would be the starter (Lyons would win the job out of spring training). "No one has told me a thing," Sasser said. "All I know is what I read in the paper."

Potential trouble and discontent percolated everywhere as the Mets prepared to open the season April 1 at home against Pittsburgh. Johnson's hold on the locker room was waning, if it had not disappeared entirely, and with his coaches already dismissed, the manager's job security remained an open question.

From the visitors' locker room a Shea Stadium—a most unfamiliar place for him—new Pirate and 1980s Met stalwart Wally Backman offered his take on why the team had lost its 1986 mojo.

"The '86 team was a great team, and in my opinion, there were a lot of changes real fast," the second baseman said. "The expected lots of guys to take over

instantly, and it's not that easy. Take Gregg Jefferies, for instance. He is going to be a good hitter. But they put a lot of pressure on him last year, and he couldn't handle it. You see great teams taken apart all the time, but not usually as rapidly as they did after 1986."

Still, Opening Day allowed the Mets to begin the decade with optimism, though the feeling would ultimately prove false. Frank Viola and John Franco, two relative newcomers who had grown up Met fans, combined to shut out the Pirates, 3–0.

Frank Viola.

David Cone working
on a one-hitter against
the Cardinals on
September 21, 1991.

"We're both just so thrilled to be back here with this team . . . the team we both grew up rooting for," gushed Viola, the Long Island native who had come to the Mets from Minnesota in a trade-deadline move the previous summer. Viola would be the Mets' best starter that April, going 7-0 that month, with an 0.87 earned-run average.

But the team did not begin well, and Johnson found himself facing an increasingly uncertain future with the team. The end of that month featured a memorable moment in Met ineptitude, one that would come to illustrate the slide from winning baseball.

David Cone was one of the team's best pitchers. Acquired from Kansas City after the 1986 championship, he enjoyed several productive seasons with the team before going on to win championships with Toronto and the Yankees, and pitch a perfect game in the Bronx in 1999.

But his gaffe on April 31 would live on in blooper reels for years to come. The Mets trailed the Braves 2–1 with two out in the fourth inning in Atlanta, with Dale Murphy on second base and Ernie Whitt on first. Mark Lemke sent a bouncer, which Jefferies fielded, into the hole between first and second base.

First baseman Mike Marshall was not close enough to the base to cover it, so Cone dashed to first and received the toss from Jefferies. First base umpire Charlie Williams ruled Lemke safe, claiming that Cone's foot had not touched the base. Cone disagreed—vehemently—and stood at the bag, screaming at Williams. One problem:

The play was not dead, and while Cone argued, Murphy scored from second, and Whitt ran home all the way from first.

As this horror show unfolded, Howard Johnson and Mackey Sasser tried to get Cone's attention and remind him that no one had called time. Johnson, who had left the dugout to argue, stopped near third base, regarding Cone with hands on his hips, stunned. Though replays proved Cone correct about the call at first, his handling of the situation seemed to indicate that the Mets were focused on all the wrong things. It was not the only lapse that Johnson had noticed. Before that very game, Johnson told reporters that "we've got some guys not paying attention to certain aspects of the game."

The manager even spoke with Kevin Elster about "getting rid of some of the blank stares in the infield."

As the month progressed, discontent grew. Tim Teufel, who had re-signed with the team as a free agent in the off-season, expressed frustration with sporadic playing time, despite production when he did play. "I'm more of a convenience to the manager than anything else," Teufel said on May 14. "And it does bother me, because we would all like to be rewarded for the contributions that we make."

Teufel was far from the only dissatisfied Met. Strawberry, who had emerged from rehab hoping to be renewed as a player and person, and ink a long-term contract extension that would keep him a Met for life, was slumping terribly. As the Mets traveled west for a mid-May road trip, the right fielder was lost in a five-for-forty slump, batting .226 on the season.

Johnson had even moved Strawberry from fourth to fifth in the batting order, though the manager restored the slugger to his customary spot after a few games.

By May 20—a very early date for a player to make this type of comment—Frank Viola said "we seem to be going through the motions," and an anonymous

Met coach told the *Daily News* that "Davey really seems to be feeling the heat right now."

Several other moves disrupted the already discontented team. When catcher Barry Lyons went on the disabled list, Mackey Sasser assumed that the job would be his, but the Mets recalled prospect Todd Hundley from the minor leagues instead and said he would receive most of the playing time.

"It really pisses me off," Sasser said. "I feel like I should be playing. I had a good year last year, and I deserve the chance . . . it's a great chance for Todd, but to me it's a slap in the face. That's like the Mets telling me they have no plans for me anymore. I don't know what the hell to think."

At about the same time, Ron Darling, after allowing seventeen hits and fifteen runs in his previous thirteen innings, was sent to the bullpen. Bob Ojeda replaced him in the rotation. Darling was unhappy, but more reserved than Sasser.

"Obviously, this team has enough problems without hearing my gripe," Darling said. "I'll go to the bullpen and keep my mouth shut."

Other players even extended their gripes to the

A distressed Davey Johnson contemplates his next move.

1990s

New manager Bud Harrelson enters his new office at Shea Stadium, June 1, 1990.

umpires. "We're getting robbed more than most teams by the umpires. This is no coincidence," Kevin Elster said.

With Davey Johnson's situation appearing direr by the day, Howard Johnson called a players-only meeting on May 20, saying that "it doesn't seem like enough guys care . . . at this rate, Davey has no chance."

Davey Johnson spoke harshly of his team. "When we're behind, or when we're in a low-scoring slow game, we have the quietest bench in the world," he said. "Our attitude is all wrong, and that's what disappoints me. There are a lot of guys who are unhappy."

Asked if the manager should yell and rip into the club, HoJo said, "I'm sure it wouldn't hurt."

For his part, the manager seemed resigned and bitter, saying after the Mets lost 3–1 to San Diego following that meeting, "It's the same old story."

But it wasn't; it was worse. On the same day as the unpleasant meeting and the flat loss, Gooden suffered a freak injury when Sasser accidentally broke the pitcher's toe. Before the game, Gooden stood in the locker room, autographing baseballs, when a seated Sasser moved his chair onto the pitcher's foot. It was that kind of spring for the Mets, though Gooden did make and win his next start.

The Mets who played every day were also concerned that those on the bench war not pulling for them. "Give us something to cheer about, and we will," said Teufel.

By May 23, Johnson saw that his tenure with the Mets might be ending. "If we don't play up to expectations, then Frank has no choice," he said, once again sounding angry with his players. "You don't fire the players. That's just baseball. Sometimes things happen for the best. But I'll tell you what, after I'm gone, people will start to appreciate me after I've left."

The Mets were 19-19 when Johnson made those comments, sounding so resigned to losing his job. That was after an 87-75 finish in 1989, which followed five consecutive seasons of ninety wins or more.

Though his firing seemed inevitable on May 23, Johnson carried a .654 winning percentage as Mets skipper into that day. The issue, however, was not his past; that was indisputably successful. Johnson's problem was the present and the future. He appeared to have lost the team, and his ability to steer them in a winning direction.

The drama finally reached its conclusion on May 29, when the Mets fired Johnson and replaced him with Buddy Harrelson. It began when traveling secretary Bob O'Hara called Johnson at about 11:00 A.M. that day, telling Johnson to call team vice president Al Harazin. Johnson, stubborn and antiauthoritarian to the end, instead phoned Frank Cashen's secretary.

"If he is going to fire me, put him on the phone," Johnson said. "Let him tell me himself."

Cashen was not in his office, though. He was in Harazin's suite at the team hotel in Cincinnati, waiting for Johnson.

The manager delayed taking the elevator to the eighth floor, and tried to believe that a better conversation awaited him. He called a few friends in baseball, and heard a rumor that the Mets were working on a trade for Boston outfielder Mike Greenwell. Maybe, he thought, they want my advice on that.

But he knew what the meeting would be about. Johnson put on a jacket and tie, went to Harazin's suite, and learned that his highly successful Mets career had ended. What would he do next?

"I'm going to my backyard, get me a little sun," Johnson said the following day in a telephone conversation with the *Daily News*'s Bob Klapisch. "I've got my swimming trunks on, and I'm going to have a nice, long chat with my daughter. I'll be out by the pool."

Harrelson was a valued member of the 1969 championship team, but he faced a difficult task in trying to reorient the disgruntled group in 1990. His early moves showed how he would be different from the permissive Johnson, and more aligned with the conservative Cashen. The new skipper immediately instituted a curfew on the road, banned card-playing in the clubhouse, and limited morning golf outings.

"Frank has wanted to do these things for a long time," said Johnson, whose legacy, though defined by years of success and a championship, also included the downfalls of several players because of alcohol and drugs.

Though players grumbled about the new rules, Harrelson apparently helped the Mets refocus for the rest of the season, which ended better than it began. Perhaps it was simply the talent that remained on the roster. Pitchers Viola, Gooden, Cone, Sid Fernandez, Darling, Ojeda, and John Franco, along with Strawberry, Howard Johnson, Kevin McReynolds, and Dave Magadan, were strong, and stopped playing beneath their abilities.

Whatever the reason, the Mets did not look like a franchise in decline for the rest of the year. The team stormed through June, and reached first place after a June 29 win over the Reds, in which Strawberry homered. But the superstar's contract situation would soon become a negative distraction for the team, especially after Oakland A's slugger Jose Canseco inked a five-year, $23.5 million extension in late June.

Strawberry felt he was as important to the team, and wanted his new deal to reflect that. And while his numbers in 1989 did not argue for that, his performance in 1990 so far did. At the midseason point, he

Darryl Strawberry receives congratulations from teammates after smashing a homer.

try's biggest market. He also failed to limit the excessive behavior and say no to the temptations of that same market. His rise was fast and spectacular, his fall grim—and by 1990, he appeared to be stabilizing.

But just as the team's apparent stabilization that year turned out to be a mirage, a mere respite from the long-term struggle about to set in, the majority of Strawberry's troubles were ahead of him. After that year, in which the Mets finished 91-71, just four games behind division-winning Pittsburgh, the right fielder signed with the Los Angeles Dodgers for a contract in line with his demands and numbers.

Strawberry had finished 1990 with thirty-seven home runs, 108 runs batted in, and a .277 batting average. Still, the Mets made clear they wanted to forge on without him, so he signed a five-year, $22.25 million deal with the Dodgers. He would never again experience personal success like he had found with the Mets.

The slugger's tenure in L.A. began well enough, as he hit twenty-nine home runs and drove in ninety-nine runs. Strawberry was still only twenty-nine years old, still full of ability. Then, very abruptly, the Mets' predictions of decline came true. Strawberry hit just five home runs per season in 1992 and 1993. The Dodgers released him in May 1994, and the San Francisco Giants gave him a chance he was unable to take advantage of, as he hit just four home runs with his new team.

On-field performance turned out to be the least of Strawberry's issues. At the beginning of the 1995 season, he was suspended for a year for cocaine use, and his career seemed effectively over. Strawberry, however, has always seemed capable of Lazarus-like reemergences, and in the following season he began a partially redemptive second act.

Still looking to play in 1996, Strawberry signed on with the St. Paul Saints of the independent Northern League. The attempt to showcase his abilities worked,

was not only hitting big home runs for the Mets but also was among the top ten in the National League in batting average.

Still, the Mets saw trouble, and did not want to re-sign him. By mid-July the Mets cut off negotiations, suddenly making a divorce seem likely. No longer the future of the franchise, Strawberry would soon be joining Keith Hernandez and Gary Carter as Met castaways.

It was a dramatic fall for the man who had once represented limitless possibilities to a forlorn organization. The National League's Rookie of the Year in 1983, and a perennial star since then, Strawberry— along with Gooden—embodied everything positive and negative about those 1980s Mets.

As any New York player who hopes to thrive must, he embraced the attention and glamour of the coun-

and the New York Yankees noticed. They signed him on July 4, 1996, and he joined onetime Mets teammates Gooden and Cone in the Bronx.

The Yankees were in the first year of the Joe Torre–Derek Jeter dynasty, and did not need Strawberry and Gooden to star as they had a decade earlier in Flushing. The environment proved perfect, and both became unlikely contributors to their second World Series–winning team.

Gooden pitched his first and only no-hitter that year, and Strawberry thrived in a part-time role. He starred in the American League Championship Series, hitting three home runs and batting .417 against the Baltimore Orioles. It seemed like a happy ending for the outfielder, but several dark periods were ahead.

On October 1, 1998, Strawberry received a shocking diagnosis: He had colon cancer, and would need surgery. There was still more bad news soon after, when doctors found that the disease had spread into his lymph nodes. The news came during a resurgent season, as Strawberry hit twenty-four home runs, his most since 1991.

But the cancer news, and the personal turmoil it would trigger, effectively ended his time as a player. The trauma of treatment proved too difficult for a man trying to recover from various addictions, and on April 3, 1999, Strawberry was arrested in Tampa, Florida, for solicitation of a prostitute and cocaine possession. Baseball once again suspended him, this time for 140 days.

On September 11, 2000, Strawberry fell asleep while driving under the influence of painkillers and rear-ended another car. His probation was changed to house arrest. His life became even more dire a month after that, when he sneaked out of a rehabilitation facility to use drugs once again. On November 3, he told a judge that he no longer wanted to live, and had stopped participating in his chemotherapy treatment.

Strawberry's life seemed as bleak as it could pos-

sibly be, but as it turned out, he would drift still lower. In 2001 and 2002, he landed in legal trouble again for violating terms of his probation and fleeing rehab. Then, miraculously, the cloud began to lift, and Strawberry slowly climbed out of the darkness and into another personal resurgence. By the end of the decade, he married for the third time, became a devout Christian, and became an analyst on the Mets' television network SNY. He has gone years without legal or health problems.

Drugs spoiled some of the potential that Strawberry brought to the Mets in 1983, but they did not ruin his life or prevent him from becoming a Mets icon. As with Gooden, the question *What might have been?* surrounds him, but the mercurial right fielder nonetheless left a lasting impression.

The Dodgers' Darryl Strawberry sticks his tongue out at disapproving Met fans.

1990s

Manager Jeff Torborg watches his team from the Mets' dugout.

With Strawberry and Davey Johnson, two of the strongest ties to 1986, gone from the Mets, the team's decline resumed in earnest. After the second-place finish in 1990, the Mets tumbled toward the bottom of the standings in 1991, finishing 77-85, at 20 1/2 game behind Pittsburgh, who again won the National League East. Harrelson was fired in September, replaced temporarily by third-base coach Mike Cubbage.

The failure that season, the bleakest in years for a franchise that had become accustomed to winning, helped to create the 1992–1993 squad. The desperate attempt by the Mets to buy their way back into quick contention led to *The Worst Team That Money Could Buy*, the title of a classic book about of the '92 debacle written by then–*Daily News* beat writer Bob Klapisch and *New York Post* beat writer John Harper, who would later join the *News* as a columnist. Their title would perfectly describe the early-1990s-era team.

It began when co-owner Fred Wilpon told general manager Al Harazin, the former Frank Cashen lieutenant who succeeded the retiring executive, to hire Jeff Torborg as his next manager. Part of Torborg's appeal was his conservative nature, which helped him appeal to the Mets and snag him a four-year, $1.9 million contract, one of the richest deals for a manager at that time.

Where Johnson was lax with his players, allowing bad behavior to flourish and establishing a rebellious, antimanagement persona of his own, Torborg was strict. He had done well as manager of the Chicago White Sox, helping to lift downtrodden teams into respectability, but he was a mismatch in New York from the beginning. One of his first moves was to ban alcohol on team airplane rides, a move that shocked and angered the carousing Mets.

The strict manager was perhaps destined to clash with the headstrong veterans brought in by the front office. They signed first baseman Eddie Murray away from the Los Angeles Dodgers and outfielder Bobby Bonilla from the Pittsburgh Pirates for a combined cost of about $40 million. Former St. Louis Cardinal Vince Coleman had signed the year before. All told, the Mets' payroll at the beginning of the 1992 season was $44.5 million, the highest in baseball.

The Mets made another significant move in the winter before the 1992 season by finally giving up on Gregg Jefferies, trading him, Kevin McReynolds, and Keith Miller to the Kansas City Royals for ace pitcher Bret Saberhagen. It was suddenly a very different roster, and one with impressive talent. The only remaining Mets from 1986 were Dwight Gooden and Howard Johnson, and the team felt ready to embark on a new era of success.

The plan began to unravel almost immediately. The first taste of drama came courtesy of old friend Darryl Strawberry, who had penned a memoir. On February 21, an excerpt leaked that accused Gooden of using cocaine during the 1986 season. Though the pitcher had been suspended the following year for doing so, this new revelation suggested that the ace's—and perhaps the entire team's—off-field issues were deeper than anyone knew.

That waft of scandal, which occupied tabloid headlines for a few days before fading, proved a mere prelude to the controversy that would erupt on March 11. The 1992 Mets were deeply flawed no matter what, but a case could be made that they never recovered from what transpired that day, when the St. Lucie Police Department released a statement saying that three Mets had been accused of rape.

The names and details were not immediately clear, but soon emerged. The alleged rape had taken place a year earlier, in spring training of 1991. The day after the initial accusations became public, multiple outlets reported that the alleged event had occurred in Gooden's home. The next day, the *Miami Herald* reported that Coleman and outfielder Daryl Boston were the others involved.

As the New York papers sent crime reporters to Florida to work the story, more details emerged, and the situation became a public relations nightmare for the team. The woman claimed to have seen the players

1990s

meeting and finally end the boycott. The pitcher read a brief statement to reporters, and the team began a season already cloaked in distasteful story lines.

Some of the drama related to actual baseball issues. Torborg had implemented several puzzling decisions during spring training, including telling Howard Johnson that he would be playing center field, despite spending nearly all his career as an infielder. Johnson was a sensitive man, suddenly placed in a high-pressure situation, and the early results of his change were mixed. Gooden, in addition to dealing with the scandals that followed him that spring, also was trying to recover from off-season shoulder surgery, making his health and reliability major questions for the rotation.

The new players would be tested by the unique pressures presented by playing in New York, and most seemed to lack the personalities to handle that challenge. Bonilla had been quiet and surly with the media, and Coleman and Murray were worse. Despite the exorbitant payroll, new manager, and general manager, these Mets looked shaky as the season began.

The poorly constructed roster had begun to take shape after the 1990 season. Strawberry had been inconsistent both personally and professionally, but the Mets encountered great difficulty trying to replace his offensive production. In the same off-season that team brass decided to let Strawberry sign with the Dodgers, Cashen made the ill-advised call of bringing in Coleman.

The speedy but one-dimensional outfielder had made his reputation in the 1980s as a St. Louis Cardinal, chopping infield hits high off the artificial turf in Busch Stadium. His skills were limited and specific to his former stadium, but Cashen inked Coleman to a four-year deal.

That turned out to be Cashen's final major decision as GM. The man who built and helped dismantle the Mets' quasi-dynasty in the 1980s retired from that job

in a Port St. Lucie bar, talked with them, and offered Gooden a ride back to his house. She claimed to have gone inside to use the bathroom, at which point the players assaulted her.

Though charges were never filed, the case created unbearable tension and negativity during spring training. As players became increasingly unhappy about seeing details of their sex lives in the newspaper, John Franco called a meeting and proposed a boycott of the media. It was decided: The Mets would no longer speak to reporters. The bad vibes lasted all month, and the boycott began to garner a great deal of attention.

The players were prepared to take it into the regular season, but Commissioner Fay Vincent, GM Al Harazin, and members of the Players' Association flew to Baltimore on April 2, where the Mets were to open the Orioles' gorgeous new stadium with an exhibition game. The higher-ups convinced David Cone to call a

1990s

at the end of the 1990 season. Harazin, a lawyer who had never played the game at any level, was promoted to replace his old boss.

Harazin's first major move was to lure Bonilla to New York in a $29 million deal. The Pittsburgh Pirates outfielder had been second banana to Barry Bonds in a small media market and had fared well. But he lacked the dynamic talent of a Bonds or a Strawberry, and turned out to be ill equipped to handle a major role on a major stage.

This became immediately evident when Bonilla supported extending the media boycott into the 1992 regular season. When reporters approached Bonilla before and after the boycott, the outfielder would often say, "I just want to be one of the guys." The comment showed a lack of understanding that a high-paid free agent in New York would be a lightning rod for attention.

On April 6, Opening Night in St. Louis, Bonilla hit two home runs, including a game-winner in the tenth inning. Teammates surrounded him at home, and David Cone said afterward, "We haven't had a leader like Bobby since Keith Hernandez."

As Harper and Klapisch pointed out in their book, "That was a stunning endorsement of a man who had played a total of ten innings as a Met. But that's how desperate this team was for somebody to believe in again. After losing Straw, after seeing Davey Johnson and Buddy Harrelson both fired, the renegades and all the rest needed someone to say, 'Climb on my back, boys.'"

Bonilla made it clear after his game-winning performance that he would not be that guy. The press, used to Strawberry's self-assured and entertaining press conferences after heroic acts on the field, approached Bonilla expecting more of the same. "I'm not here to be Darryl Strawberry," Bonilla said. "I'm not here to hit forty home runs. All I did was get good wood on the ball."

ABOVE: Cub catcher Joe Girardi tries to stop Met Bobby Bonilla from charging the mound.

BELOW: Bobby Bonilla shares a laugh with New York City mayor David Dinkins.

ABOVE: Met catcher
Todd Hundley tags
out the Pirates' Gary
Redus at the plate.

BELOW: Willie Ran-
dolph completes a
double play despite
an attempt by the
Braves' John Smoltz
to break it up.

And so began the 1992 season, marked by dour players and a cranky vibe. The players resented the press, one another, and a manager they saw as an overly stern authoritarian. While Bonilla and Coleman were cranky, Eddie Murray was totally noncommunicative.

The team never recovered from a poor start and finished 72-90. Among the memorable on-field disasters was a losing streak posted by pitcher Anthony Young, who from May 6, 1992, to July 24, 1993, lost twenty-seven consecutive games in which he had a decision. That was, and remains, a major league record for futility.

In the spring of 1993, Harper and Klapisch published *The Worst Team That Money Could Buy*, exposing the team's dysfunction, both on the field and off. The trouble continued into the following season, and was made worse by the tell-all book.

Before the second home game of the season, Bonilla confronted and threatened Klapisch in the clubhouse at Shea Stadium, cursing him and threatening physical violence. Clubhouse manager Charlie Samuels and PR man Jay Horwitz had to hurry over and step between the two.

It was hardly the last ugly moment before the

1990s

Worst Team That Money Could Buy finally broke up. The Mets started 13-25 in 1993, and replaced Torborg with Dallas Green on May 19. The change did not help; the team went 59-103 in 1993, good for last place in the National League East.

The Mets' on-field problems in 1993 were not their ugliest. Far more distasteful than Bonilla's behavior was that of Vince Coleman, who—months after injuring Gooden's arm by recklessly swinging a golf club in the locker room—hurled firecrackers at fans outside Dodger Stadium, injuring several people, including an eleven-year-old boy and a two-year-old girl.

Coleman was charged with endangerment and sentenced to community service. Angry owner Fred Wilpon condemned Coleman's actions, saying at a press conference, "I can tell you, he will not play here again—as a Met."

Wilpon followed through, suspending Coleman for the rest of that season, and trading him to Kansas City that winter. That was the low point of Met behavior in the early 1990s, but it was not the only incident in 1993. Also that summer, Bret Saberhagen sprayed bleach into a group of reporters, continually lied about doing so, then finally admitted it.

It seemed that the franchise could sink no further, but its issues became still deeper in 1994. Gooden suffered a broken toe at the outset of the season and went on the disabled list. During this period of inactivity, he returned to a vice that had derailed his success in the previous decade: cocaine.

Gooden realized that Major League Baseball drug testers, a part of his life because of his flawed past, had not followed him into the minor leagues. So on June 2, 1994, Gooden snorted cocaine. He rejoined the Mets three days later in Cincinnati, where he was once again tested. It was a nightmare scenario for a team missing every popular player from its glory years but Gooden.

1990s

In late June, baseball suspended Gooden for sixty days. The pitcher went home to Florida and continued drinking and using cocaine, regularly failing drug tests. The league sent Gooden to the Betty Ford Clinic, where he detoxed and prepared for reinstatement in August.

But the onetime icon, Strawberry's charismatic partner in reviving the Mets and thrilling fans in New York during the 1980s, seemed destined to never again pitch for the team.

Fourteen days before he was set to return, the Players' Association decided to strike on August 12, 1994. Instead of moving on from a regrettable period and resuming his athletic career, Gooden had nothing to do but remain in Florida and sink deeper into addiction. He continued to drink and use drugs. After he failed another test, the pitcher finally exhausted the Mets' patience; the team released once of the brightest stars in its history.

MLB was no more forgiving, electing to suspend Gooden for the entire 1995 season. Feeling that his life had gone from promising to irredeemably bleak, Gooden became suicidal. He received a letter on

November 5 from commissioner Bud Selig, saying that he had been suspended.

Gooden retrieved a gun from his dresser and pointed it at his head, ready to end his life, when his wife entered the room. She and Gooden's mother were able to convince Gooden to hand over the pistol.

Over the next several years, Gooden was able to find partial redemption as a player and person, though his health remained cloudier than Strawberry's. The Yankee and former Met pitching coach Mel Stottlemyre brought Gooden aboard in 1996, and the pitcher contributed an emotional no-hitter on May of that year against the Seattle Mariners.

New Yorkers who had long followed Gooden's career cheered the event, but that triumph did not demonstrate a full return to form. Gooden ended the 1996 season 11-7, with a 5.01 ERA, and did not appear in the Yankees' playoff run, which resulted in their first World Series title since 1978.

Gooden won nine games the following season but continued to exhibit troubling personal behavior. When the Yankees were in Dallas for a series against the Texas Rangers, Gooden argued with a cabdriver who was taking him home from a strip club. Such incidents tainted the redemptive aspect of Gooden's second-chance tenure with the Yankees.

New York cut ties with the pitcher after that season, and he signed with Cleveland in 1998. Over the next three seasons, he passed through Tampa Bay, Houston, and once again the Bronx. A sympathetic George Steinbrenner brought Gooden back to the Yankees in 2000, by which time the pitcher had lost his power fastball but was old and wise enough to find some success as a soft-throwing reliever.

Gooden was 4-2 that year, with a 3.36 earned run average. He did not pitch in the World Series, as the Yankees defeated the Mets in five games.

After he was released by the Yanks in spring training of 2001, Gooden retired, leaving regret and speculation on greatness largely squandered. Though he won 192 games in an impressive career, Gooden earned more than half of those victories before turning twenty-five.

His life in the decade after retirement has remained a struggle between progress and relapse. Gooden maintained relationships wit the Yankees and the Mets, and helped to negotiate his nephew Gary Sheffield's contract with the Yanks in 2004.

Though he did not visit Shea Stadium for nearly eight years following the 2000 Subway Series, Gooden returned for the ceremony that followed the final game played there, on September 28, 2008. He appeared at Citi Field in 2010 to accept induction into the team's Hall of Fame.

But a series of arrests and self-inflicted misfortunes undercut those positive highlights. In 2002, Gooden was arrested for driving under the influence of alcohol in Tampa, and also charged with having an open container in his car. Just eleven months later, he was again arrested for DUI, this time with a suspended license stemming from the first incident.

In the middle part of the decade, Gooden's son Dwight Jr. began experiencing legal and personal issues. He was arrested in 2004 for crack-cocaine possession, and in 2005 for violating probation by having marijuana and bullets in his car.

His father continued to model similar behavior, driving away from a police office who had pulled him over in 2005, and going to jail in 2006 after showing up to a probation meeting high on cocaine.

After four quiet years, Gooden again captured headlines on March 24, 2010, when he was arrested in Franklin Lakes, New Jersey, after leaving the scene of an accident. He was later found to be intoxicated, and was charged with being under the influence of a controlled dangerous substance; driving under the influence of a controlled dangerous substance; endangering the welfare of a child; driving while intoxicated, with a child passenger; leaving the scene of an accident; reckless driving; failure to keep right; and failure to change his address on his driver's license. His five-year-old son Dylan was in the car at the time of the accident.

By the mid-1990s, the Mets had sunk so deep into disreputable baseball and behavior, they were almost entirely unrecognizable from the team that had enjoyed spectacular but aborted success a decade earlier. The excesses and attitudes that defined the 1986 champions had led to a brisk downfall, and was extended by the front office's poor personnel moves. As deftly as Cashen had built the club into winners, he was incredibly clumsy in attempting to assemble another championship team.

His successor, Al Harazin, fared even worse, and he was fired after the 1993 season. Former Met scouting director Joe McIlvaine, who had left in 1991 to become the San Diego Padres' GM, returned to New York to try to rescue the team.

That project was deep and took several years. The first attempt to deliver the Mets from last place fizzled, though it began with much promise and a marketable slogan, "Generation K."

It is always dangerous to affix young pitchers with too much hope, because what they do is so fragile. But the Mets, desperate for anything that suggested a better future, did just that in 1995 with top prospects Paul Wilson, Bill Pulsipher, and Jason Isringhausen.

The title was a play on Generation X, the popular term created by author Douglas Coupland to describe young people of the early 1990s. It was a trendy phrase, conjuring youth, grunge music and fashion, and commercial viability, so the Mets co-opted it to sell themselves and their fans on a trio of promising arms.

The movement began when the Mets made Pulsipher their second-round draft choice in 1991, out of Fairfax High School in Clifton, Virginia. Before turning twenty, Pulsipher posted sub-3.00 ERAs at three minor league levels; he arrived in the major leagues in 1995 with more than two hundred minor league innings already in his arm.

He was 5-7 that year with the Mets, and missed the end of the season with ominous elbow pain. As it turned out, Pulsipher's best and most promising professional baseball was already behind him.

By the conclusion of spring training in 1996, Pulsipher was still experiencing elbow pain. He underwent an MRI, which revealed torn ligaments and led to that most dreaded of recommendations for a young pitcher: Tommy John surgery, meaning a full reconstruction of his elbow.

Though that procedure knocks pitchers out of action for about a year, many are still able to return and resume successful careers. Pulsipher's elbow, though, was not his only problem; he also suffered from severe depression.

In 1997, after being diagnosed and given the antidepressant drug Prozac, Pulsipher again experienced

success in the minor leagues. He finally returned to the Mets in the spring of 1998 but did not fare well, and was dealt to Milwaukee before the July 31 trade deadline.

Pulsipher hung on with several teams until 2005, but won just thirteen games in the major leagues. He was one of many promising young pitchers whose health does not allow them to fulfill their potential, and one of many Met hopes that went unfulfilled.

The other two members of Generation K found more success in the major leagues than Pulsipher did but could never help the Mets. Isringhausen arrived in Flushing after Pulsipher and made an immediate impact in the major leagues. Recalled from the minor leagues in July 1995, he went 9-2 for the rest of that season, joining Pulsipher as exciting pitchers heading into the 1996 season.

As with Pulsipher, though, the injuries commenced at that most inopportune time. Isringhausen began to break down during his first full season in the major leagues in 1996, missing time with rib cage issues, a torn labrum, and other maladies. He, too, underwent reconstructive elbow surgery; his came in 1998.

That essentially ended Isringhausen's Met career.

The team traded him to Oakland in July 1999, casting aside a player about to enjoy years of success in the bullpen. First as A's closer and then functioning in the same role for the St. Louis Cardinals, Isringhausen enjoyed a long and productive career—just not for the team that had hoped it would lead them out of half a decade of losing, at the top of their starting rotation.

Wilson was the final, and perhaps most promising, member of Generation K. Throwing a hard fastball and slider, he debuted in 1996 but went 5-12. That was it; Wilson never again pitched for the Mets, and did not appear in a major league game until 2000, for the Tampa Bay Devil Rays.

Wilson built a respectable career as a back-of-the-rotation starter for Tampa Bay and Cincinnati; he retired in 2005.

With Generation K, the Mets' first concerted effort to recover from the Bonilla-Coleman-Murray era, having quickly failed, ownership sought another direction. On August 26, 1996, the Mets

1990s

Manager Bobby Valentine shags flies during spring training.

As a young player, he impressed coach and future Dodger manager Tommy Lasorda. As Lasorda recalled in his memoir *The Artful Dodger*, Valentine approached Lasorda and said he wanted to grow hair on his chest. Lasorda advised him to eat the fat off of steaks. The tale may be apocryphal, but in Lasorda's telling, Valentine mustered the focus and determination to actually grow chest hair. From there, the Los Angeles icon knew Valentine would find success somehow.

It was not as a professional athlete, however, that Valentine made his name. He won minor league Most Valuable Player Awards in 1969 and 1970, and made his major league debut in 1969, at age nineteen.

Valentine could never duplicate his success in the major leagues. After serving as a decently useful utility player for the Dodgers, the team traded him to the California Angels in 1972. There, he suffered an injury that would effectively ruin his already floundering career.

On May 17, 1973, Valentine crashed into an unpadded outfield wall while chasing a home run; he shattered his leg and missed the rest of that season, and the leg never properly healed. By 1975 Valentine was a middling utility player, and the Angels traded him to the San Diego Padres.

It was that club that facilitated Valentine's initial marriage with the Mets, by trading him to New York, with minor league pitcher Paul Siebert, for Dave Kingman on June 15, 1977—the same day the Mets sent Tom Seaver to the Cincinnati Reds for Pat Zachry, Doug Flynn, and Steve Henderson.

During his brief time with the Mets, which ended when he signed with Seattle and retired in 1979 at age twenty-nine, Valentine formed several important relationships. He impressed the team with his hyper-awareness of the game and obvious energy and intelligence. Valentine also met teammate Tom Grieve, who would later launch Valentine's managerial career.

Knowing he wanted to remain in the game and ultimately manage, Valentine took a job as a minor

moved toward their next brief phase of winning by firing Dallas Green and hiring Bobby Valentine to manage the team.

The Stamford, Connecticut–born Valentine would prove to be one of the most outsized characters to ever manage the Mets—and just the fourth skipper to take them to a World Series. He had once been a standout athlete in Stamford, one of the most impressive the state of Connecticut had ever produced.

Though colleges also recruited him as a basketball player, Valentine attended the University of Southern California as a baseball player, and was drafted fifth overall by the Los Angeles Dodgers in 1968.

league infield instructor for the Padres; in 1981, the Mets brought him on to do the same job. He made a quick assent to the big league coaching staff, hired by manager George Bamberger in 1982 to be the Mets' third-base coach. At thirty-two he was uncommonly young for that job.

Valentine lasted in that position until 1985, when Grieve, as general manager of the Texas Rangers, hired him to manage in Arlington. Brought in to replace Doug Rader thirty-two games into that season, Valentine finished with a losing record. The Rangers were 62-99 in 1985—and, in an unexpected recovery led by Valentine, went 87-75 the following year, good for second place in the American League West.

That ended up being Valentine's best year in Texas, where he was controversial for the same traits that later defined him as Met manager. Known as brash, outspoken, and aggressive, Valentine had a way of aggravating—and being aggravated with—the press, his opponents, and often his own players.

After he was fired in 1992, Valentine could not find another major league job. He went to Japan for the first of two stints there, and in 1995 led the downtrodden Chiba Lotte Marines to an unlikely second-place finish—then was fired for personal disagreements with that team's general manager.

The Mets brought him back to manage their Triple-A team in Norfolk, Virginia. After Valentine guided the Norfolk Tides to an 82-59 record, Fred Wilpon tapped him to replace the fired Dallas Green that August. An era of fun, drama, and recovery from the doldrums had begun.

I t is rarely one architect who builds a winning team. Most successful eras for ball clubs happen due to contributions from managers and executives long gone before they can enjoy the success.

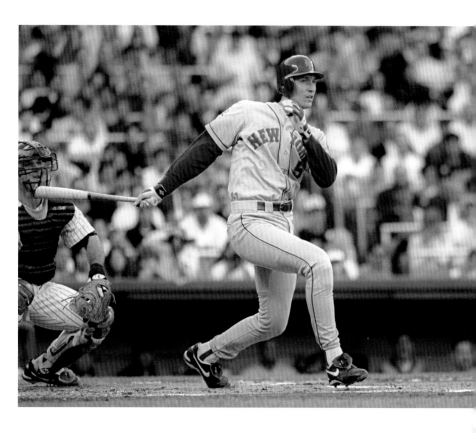

John Olerud bats against the Yankees in a 1997 interleague game.

A rewind from 1999 and 2000 Met teams, both of which provided their fans with exciting playoff baseball and the latter of which reached the World Series, share a number of architects in the late 1990s. Sinking the team in the first half of the decade had required a group effort, and rescuing would as well.

Valentine brought a high-energy and modern style. His garrulous personality and fun-loving style, though they would grow old by 2002, provided the players with a relief from the Dallas Green days, when that veteran manager was seen by some as aloof and unsupportive. Valentine stressed preparation, and arrived at spring training in 1997 with binders full of computer printouts.

The darker, or at least more grating, side of Bobby V. also emerged quickly. The Mets finished 1996 with a 71-91 record, parking them in fourth place in the National League East, and Valentine used the newspapers during the offseason to publicly agitate for major trades. McIlvaine was not thrilled, but nevertheless made one in December, sending minor league pitcher Robert Person to Toronto for first baseman John Olerud.

Olerud joined an infield that would soon become

ABOVE, LEFT: The Mets' Rey Ordóñez turns a double play as Pittsburgh Pirate pitcher Kris Benson is out at second base.

ABOVE, RIGHT: Edgardo Alfonzo connects for a double in game one of the 1999 NLCS against the Atlanta Braves.

BELOW: Rey Ordóñez makes a spectacular diving grab of a line drive, robbing the Yankees' Chad Curtis of a base hit.

1990s

one of the best of its era. Edgardo Alfronzo, signed as an amateur free agent from Venezuela way back in 1991, when Frank Cashen was still general manager, debuted in 1995. Though he was still seeking an ideal position and developing as a hitter, "Fonzie"—later the Mets' second baseman and a top offensive contributor to the 2000 World Series team—had shown promise by the time Valentine arrived.

Shortstop Rey Ordóñez also was in place. Signed in 1994 after defecting from Cuba, Ordóñez immediately developed a reputation as a top defender. After Ordóñez made a dazzling relay throw home in his major league debut on Opening Day in 1996 against St. Louis, Cardinal defensive wizard Ozzie Smith labeled him "the second coming of me."

While he would never be a strong hitter, Ordóñez continued to develop into an adequate offensive player and superlative shortstop. The Mets, meanwhile, moved forward in 1997, posting a winning record of 88-74 and finishing third.

Midway through that season, the team's progress led ownership to assess the state of the organization and conclude that changes were necessary before the Mets could become true contenders. On June 17, Fred Wilpon and Nelson Doubleday announced in a press conference that McIlvaine was being demoted from general manager to the head of minor league development, a position the team thought he was better suited to.

McIlvaine's reputation had always been as an executive who enjoyed visiting the team's minor league outposts and who believed in building from within. Though he would later prove successful in assembling the first pieces of an N.L. championship team, McIlavine's reputation as a development-oriented GM was not helped by the failures of Pulsipher, Wilson, and Isringhausen to create a dominant young rotation.

In ownership's view, the Mets were closer than they had been in years to becoming legitimate contenders, and needed a few big moves, via trades and/

or free agency. They did not believe that McIlvaine was the person to execute those moves.

Rather than hire an experienced GM, though, the Mets promoted from within. Wilpon and Doubleday tapped thirty-four-year-old assistant GM Steve Phillips to succeed McIlvaine as general manager, naming a brash front office prodigy who would match Valentine in ego and outsized personality.

A former minor league player for the Mets who decided to forgo college after being drafted but later earned a psychology degree from the University of Michigan in his spare time, Phillips joined the front office in 1990.

He would clash with Valentine but outlast the manager, who was fired in 2002. Phillips continued into the 2003 season, before the team sunk yet again into the lower reaches of the standings. He then landed a high-profile job as a studio analyst on ESPN's *Baseball Tonight*, which he lost in 2009 after a twenty-two-year-old production assistant went public about their office affair.

The married Phillips later underwent treatment for sex addiction, an outcome foreshadowed early in his Mets tenure when he took a leave of absence from the team in 1998 to deal with sexual harassment allegations. Rosa Rodriguez, a team employee based in Port

Manager Bobby Valentine appears uninterested in what owner Fred Wilpon is saying.

1990s

hitter in Marlins history on May 11, 1996. Nearly as appealing as his talent, Leiter had grown up a Met fan in Toms River, New Jersey.

The next season, the Mets would finally find themselves in playoff contention, helped by their most significant trade yet. The Marlins were still in fire-sale mode in May, when they dealt Gary Sheffield and four others (including, by the way, Bobby Bonilla) to the Dodgers for All-Star catcher Mike Piazza. The expectation around baseball was that Florida would use Piazza to restock their farm system by flipping him to a contending club.

A frenzied week ensued as the Mets pursued the catcher while publicly bluffing. "Everyone says, 'Well, if you can add one of the best offensive players in the game, why don't you add him?'" Steve Phillips told reporters on May 19. "Well, it's not that easy. It's not Rotisserie baseball, where you can sell you player for $5 and buy another player for $7 and put your team together."

On the same day, Valentine dismissed the idea of trading for Piazza a "fantasy." For one thing, the Mets had a catcher in Todd Hundley, who met with Phillips on May 20 and received assurances that the team would not pursue Piazza. Though Hundley was on the disabled list recovering from reconstructive elbow surgery, he expected to resume his role as a key part of the Met offense when he returned.

Despite Phillips's promises to Hundley, the GM two days later completed one of the most significant trades in franchise history. He nabbed Piazza for three minor leaguers who would not be missed: outfielder Preston Wilson and pitchers Ed Yarnall and Geoff Goetz.

Hundley said, "It was too much like, 'Don't worry it won't happen. 'I was thinking, 'How could it not happen? How can you not go after this guy?'"

Hundley, who had set a single-season Mets record for home runs, and broken former Dodger Roy Cam-

St. Lucie, accused Phillips of harassment after allegedly having a relationship with the GM.

Despite those issues, though, Phillips capably bolstered the Mets' core of talent with high-profile acquisitions, just as he was assigned to do. First, the team secured Valentine, inking him to a $2.1 million deal that extended his contract through the 2000 season.

Next, on February 6, 1998, the team traded for a pitcher who would lead the rotation for several seasons. The Mets had finished third in 1997, behind the second-place Florida Marlins, who won the wild card and went on to take the World Series in seven games over the Cleveland Indians. After that triumph, Marlin owner Wayne Huizenga decided he no longer wanted to win on the field while operating at a loss, and he dismantled most of his $53 million roster.

The Mets were poised to take advantage, and targeted Al Leiter, the pitcher who had started game seven against Cleveland and allowed two runs in seven innings of what would ultimately become an eleven-inning win. Leiter had also tossed the first no-

panella's mark for a catcher with forty-one in 1996 (and who in 2007 was named by the Mitchell Report as a beneficiary of performance-enhancing drugs), would soon become another trading chip that helped the team reach its next World Series: After a brief attempt to return from surgery as an outfielder, Hundley found himself traded in December 1998 to the Los Angeles Dodgers in a three-team deal that brought Baltimore reliever Armando Benitez to New York. Though famously inconsistent and mercurial, Benitez would eventually push John Franco into a setup role, creating a formidable late-inning combination.

When the Mets announced the trade for Piazza, they signaled a willingness to spend money on star players. Piazza's impending free agency had scared the Dodgers and Marlins into dealing him, as the catcher was widely expected to see one of the richest contracts in history.

"I don't want to negotiate in your columns," Fred Wilpon told reporters that day. "But we know what the ranges of these things are, and Steve is going to make those choices."

The co-owner added that if the team had been scared off by Piazza's expected asking price, "we would not be here now." (Indeed, the team would

later sign him to a seven-year, $91 million contract in the off-season.)

The New York media raved about the move. "It's like the Mets were back in the baseball business yesterday, for the first time in a long time," wrote *Daily News* columnist Mike Lupica. "Once, the Mets had the stars, and the star team around here. The young Dwight Gooden. The young Darryl Strawberry. Keith Hernandez and Gary Carter. Backman and Dykstra and Ron Darling. The Mets of 1986 were the Yankees of 1998. They were the team to watch, to talk about, to follow from one back page to another. Now they get Piazza, a baseball star as big as any the Yankees have."

The headline for that column? METS DELIVER: FINALLY GETTING UP AND FIGHTING BACK.

The Piazza era began well, with the new Met debuting in front of 32,908 fans at Shea Stadium on May 23, driving in a run with a fifth-inning double and catching an Al Leiter shutout against Milwaukee.

Player and city immediately liked one another. "I

ABOVE, LEFT: Met pitcher Al Leiter sports his new uniform at Shea Stadium.

ABOVE, RIGHT: Mike Piazza reacts to his game-winning homer off San Diego's Trevor Hoffman.

1990s

feel like a movie star, a rock star," Piazza said. "I'm amazed at the reception."

Fans were not the only ones to welcome Piazza. Franco, a team leader and the longest-tenured Met, gave him the uniform number 31, which both players had worn throughout their careers. Franco switched to number 45, previously the property of bullpen coach Randy Niemann; the players compensated Niemann with a set of golf clubs. The Mets also placed Piazza's locker next to Franco's, a subtle attempt to integrate him into the team, and prevent him from fleeing at the end of the season.

The reloaded Mets ended up making a push for the wild-card spot before making it clear they were still a year away from being a legitimate playoff team. They actually had the lead in the race for that final playoff spot in late September, but stopped hitting at the most inopportune time.

A late-season three-game sweep at the hands of the Montreal Expos sunk them into a tie with the Cubs, and they responded by suffering a sweep in a doubleheader against Atlanta.

In the last game of the season, with the Mets still clinging to a chance of making the playoffs, Valentine wanted midseason acquisition Hideo Nomo to start. Nomo declined the assignment, saying other players were more deserving. So Valentine started Armando Reynoso, who was shelled and knocked out by the second inning. Nomo pitched four shutout innings in relief, but the Mets lost, 7–2, and finished one game behind the Cubs for the wild card.

Closer to playing October baseball than they had been since the 1988 National League Championship Series loss to the Dodgers, the Mets decided to double down in the off-season. In addition to re-signing Piazza, they brought back the free agent pitchers Leiter and Dennis Cook.

To merely retain a roster that missed the playoffs would not be enough. The Mets decided it was time to spend on more veterans, and brought in future Hall of Famer Rickey Henderson, the greatest leadoff hitter of all time. They also signed sought-after Japanese pitcher Masato Yoshii, and brought back Bonilla (the latter, and highly curious, move was the only one that did not prove wise).

Most significantly for a franchise that had always struggled to find productive third basemen, Phillips pursued and landed Robin Ventura, a free agent formerly of the Chicago White Sox. Though Chicago had judged its five-time Gold-Glover to be declining, the Mets disagreed—and were proven correct when Ventura hit .301 with thirty-two home runs and 120 runs batted in during the first season of a four-year contract.

All that spending led the public to assume, for the first time in nearly a decade, that the Mets would be one of the best teams in baseball. When expectations go unmet, there are consequences, and everyone was surprised when on June 5, 1999, the Mets were 27-28, and on an eight game losing streak.

Valentine suddenly faced rumors about his job security, but the front office instead opted to honor a long and generally pointless baseball tradition by firing a group of coaches instead. On June 6, Phillips axed Valentine's favorite members of the staff, Bob Apodaca, Randy Niemann, and Tom Robson. The latter was a particularly close friend of Valentine's, who had worked with him both in the United States and Japan.

Those moves further strained an already chilly relationship between Valentine and Phillips, though the two would continue to coexist. Several days later, on June 10, Valentine executed his most memorably puckish move. After being ejected from a game against Toronto, Valentine returned to the dugout in the twelfth inning wearing glasses and a fake mustache. An unamused league office would fine Valentine for the stunt, but it would only serve to further solidify his image of a spotlight-loving figure perfect for New York and to elevate the profile of a Met team that had toiled anonymously for most of the decade.

By midsummer, the Mets were consistently playing to their potential, at one point in July winning twelve of fifteen games. Before the July 31 trade deadline, they moved to bolster their rotation by acquiring lefthander Kenny Rogers.

By September, the Mets held a slim lead over Atlanta in the National League East, and a wild card lead over the Cincinnati Reds that grew as large as four games. But just when the team's first playoff berth in eleven years seemed secure, they once again began a September collapse.

They lost eight of nine between September 21 and 30, sank underneath the Braves and Reds, and trailed the latter for the wild card by two games with three to play. Virtually eliminated, the Mets stumbled into the final weekend of the season, and a series against the Pitts-

burgh Pirates. Miraculously for a team that seemed irredeemably lost just days before, they swept the Pirates, while the Reds dropped two of three to Milwaukee.

The result of that wild weekend was a tie for the wild card, and a one-game playoff in Cincinnati. Leiter started and pitched a two-hit shutout, leading the Mets to a 5–0 win and a spot in the division series against the Arizona Diamondbacks.

1990s

Bobby Valentine
contemplates
his answer to a
reporter's question.

over the Yankees in 2001. Third baseman Matt Williams, outfielder Steve Finley, and ace Randy Johnson proved formidable, especially the latter, a six-foot, ten-inch effectively wild intimidator.

Johnson started game one, in what seemed like a mismatch against Mets starter Masato Yoshii. But Edgardo Alfonzo made an early statement, knocking a solo home run in the first inning. John Olerud added a two-run shot in the third, and the teams arrived at the ninth inning tied 4–4, with Johnson still in the game.

The ace would go on to win several important postseason games in his career, but on this day, he loaded the bases to end his outing. Alfonzo then hit a grand slam off reliever Bobby Chouinard, giving his team an 8–4 lead. Armando Benitez followed by pitching a perfect bottom of the ninth against the shellshocked D-Backs.

Then, after defeating Johnson, the team came out flat in game two against Todd Stottlemyre, losing 7–1 and losing Piazza for the remainder of the series with a sore thumb.

Unsure how potent their offense would be without the man who contributed forty home runs and 124 RBI during the regular season, the Mets returned to Shea Stadium with the series tied at one win apiece. In game three, one of the key acquisitions of the previous off-season provided the necessary spark, as Rickey Henderson had three hits and a stolen base, steering the Mets toward a 9–2 victory.

Leiter took the ball in game four, with a chance to end the series and help the Mets advance to the National League Championship Series. Once again, a solo homer by Alfonzo represented the game's first run, though this one came off Arizona starter Brian Anderson in the fourth inning.

The Mets held a 2–1 lead going into the eighth inning, but Jay Bell's two-run double in that frame gave the Diamondbacks a sudden advantage and made a fifth and deciding game appear likely. The '99 Mets, though, had a habit of creating late dramatics; they

But the franchise has never seemed capable of experiencing uncomplicated success. As they prepared for that first playoff series in what they hoped would be a long October, the Mets were dismayed and distracted by a *Sports Illustrated* article by S. L. Price in which the manager had offered blunt and sometimes harsh assessments of his players.

"You're not dealing with real professionals in the clubhouse," Valentine told the magazine. "You're not dealing with real intelligent guys, for the most part."

The article left virtually every member of the organization—players, owners, Phillips—incensed that their manager would air such grievances in public. Valentine did not apologize, and the organization was left to reaffirm what they already knew about its manager: You took the bad with the good.

Everyone was glad to return their focus to baseball, and a Diamondbacks team loaded with veterans, and building toward an eventual World Series win

would win, and ultimately lose, in the strangest and most dynamic ways.

This one began to get wild in the bottom of the eighth, when Roger Cedeno tied the game with a pinch-hit sacrifice fly, a run that ultimately sent the game into extra innings. After Franco pitched a scoreless tenth, backup catcher Todd Pratt (another Met later named in the Mitchell Report as a steroid user) created an unforgettable niche for himself in Met lore.

Playing only because of the injury to Piazza, Pratt launched a fly ball deep to center field off pitcher Matt Mantei. Steve Finley tracked the ball, leaped at the wall, and upon landing looked into his glove to see if he had caught it.

He had not, and Pratt had won the series with a walk-off home run. The Mets were ready to advance to the National League Championship Series, where they would meet a far more established juggernaut, the Atlanta Braves.

While the Mets had flailed and floundered through the 1990s, Atlanta had become the superpower of the National League. Proving that success in baseball is cyclical, and rarely can one franchise remain on top forever, the Braves had been dismal and anonymous for most of the 1980s, while the Mets became a perennial contender.

By 1991, though, general manager John Schuerholz and manager Bobby Cox had taken over and begun to build a perennial winner. Led by an all-time rotation of Tom Glavine, Greg Maddux, and John Smoltz, the Braves represented the N.L. in the World Series in 1991, 1992, 1995 (their only championship), and 1996. Arriving at Turner Field that October, the Mets hoped to prevent them from earning another visit.

The recent history between the two teams suggested a challenge for New York. During that late-September losing streak that had very nearly ended in a total collapse, the Mets had lost five of six to the Braves, leading to rhetoric that would intensify what was already a natural division rivalry.

"Now all the Mets fans can go home and put on their Yankees stuff," Braves third baseman Chipper Jones said in September when the Mets seemed dead.

Reliever John Rocker—who that month would find himself under intense scrutiny when a *Sports Illustrated* profile by Jeff Pearlman aired racist comments, including some that disparaged New Yorkers riding the number 7 train to Shea Stadium—took this swipe: "How many times do we have to beat them before their fans will shut up?"

At the beginning of the NLCS, Valentine alluded to those comments and said, "They better be ready to play some ghosts, because we were dead and buried two weeks ago."

Unfortunately for Valentine and the Mets, the team appeared immediately lifeless in the best-of-seven series. They dropped the first two games in Atlanta, 4–2 and 4–3, as Yoshii and Kenny Rogers fell to Atlanta starters Maddux and Kevin Millwood.

A 2–0 deficit in a postseason series was difficult, but a 3–0 hole was basically insurmountable. Going back to Shea for game three, the Mets hoped to avoid falling into that abyss.

Leiter started against Tom Glavine, and both lefthanders dominated. One very early moment ulti-

mately decided the tense game: In the top of the first inning, Leiter walked Gerald Williams. Bret Boone then hit a comebacker to the pitcher, who threw it wide of Olerud; Boone was safe at first, and Williams scampered to third.

Minutes later, Boone took off for second in an attempted steal, and Piazza threw the ball into center field. Williams scored an unearned run, but it was still very early in the game, and the Mets had nine innings to recover.

Glavine, however, did not allow them to do so. He pitched seven scoreless innings, followed by Mike Remlinger in the eighth and Rocker in the ninth, and the Braves won, 1–0.

At that time, no baseball team had recovered from a 3–0 deficit to win a playoff series (half a decade later, the 2004 Boston Red Sox broke precedent by storming back from a 3–0 hole in the American League Championship Series to defeat the Yankees). The Mets could well have collectively shrugged, rolled over, and decided to enter the 2000 season ready to build on the progress of 1999.

Instead, they did the opposite. They revived a boring series, and very nearly came back to win it. The campaign commenced in game four, with the Mets an inning away from elimination.

Atlanta led 2–1 in the eighth inning when Rocker trotted in from the bullpen to some of the most vicious boos and taunts ever heard in a New York stadium. The fireballing reliever had insulted the people of New York and quickly became a reviled figure. Though he had successfully shut down the Mets in game three, on this night Rocker surrendered a two-out, two-run single to Olerud in the eighth.

The Braves had been four outs from sweeping the series, and now had to return for another day at Shea. Game five, which began at about 4:00 P.M. and stretched long into the evening, proved one of the most memorable in team history.

John Olerud at bat in
the eleventh inning
against the Atlanta
Braves in game five of
the National League
Championship Series
at Shea Stadium,
October 17, 1999.

The Maddux-Yoshii matchup was, of course, favorable to Atlanta, but Olerud hit a two-run homer in the first with Henderson on base. The Mets held that lead into the fourth, when doubles by Boone and Jones, and a single by Brian Jordan, tied the game at two.

Managing with his season in the balance, Valentine lifted Yoshii for veteran Orel Hershiser, the second of a postseason-record nine pitchers New York would ultimately use in the game. With rain falling—not quite enough for a delay, but steadily—the game wound into extra innings. The Braves squandered seemingly endless chances to end the series, and eventually stranded nineteen base runners in the game, another playoff record at the time.

They finally broke through in the top of the fifteenth, when Keith Lockhart hit a run-scoring triple off of rookie reliever Octavio Dotel, giving his team a 3–2 lead. With Rocker already burned (he pitched 1

1/3 scoreless innings in the thirteenth and fourteenth as jeers and debris rained from stands; while leaving, Rocker returned the taunts, pretending to boo while as he walked off the field), Bobby Cox sent his own rookie reliever, Kevin McGlinchy, to close out the series.

Shawon Dunston began the Mets' fifteenth-inning rally with a single, which Matt Franco followed by drawing a walk. After Alfonzo successfully executed a sacrifice bunt, McGlinchy issued an intentional walk to Olerud to load the bases, and an unintentional one to Pratt to tie the game.

That brought up Robin Ventura, part of the reason why the Mets had fared so poorly in the series. One of the Mets' most productive hitters all season, Ventura had just one hit in his past eighteen at-bats.

At 9:47 P.M., nearly six hours after Yoshii had thrown the game's first pitch and with rain still pounding the field, Ventura sent a 2-1 fastball from

1990s

McGlinchy over the right-field wall. It would have been a grand slam, but Pratt made it something even more memorable when, overcome with joy, he tackled Ventura between first and second base.

Ventura was called out for passing the base runner, but the winning run had already scored. With an assist from the backup catcher, Ventura would forever be connected with that oddest of game-enders, the grand-slam single.

The hit sent the series back to Atlanta, which had seemed virtually impossible just two days before. The impossible no longer seemed ridiculous, and it was no longer absurd to ask: Could the Mets come back from an insurmountable three-games-to none deficit?

Game six presented yet another opportunity for the team to give up early. Leiter started on short rest and was clobbered for four runs in the first inning. That score held until the sixth, when the Mets scored three off of Millwood, making the ball game a competitive one for the first time.

The wildness that marked the previous game then ensued. Atlanta scored three in the sixth, New York four in the seventh and one in the eighth to take the lead. The Mets were close to forcing a game seven, with all the momentum in their favor.

Franco, though, could not hold the lead, and allowed the Braves to tie the game in the eighth. As another game extended into extra innings, the Mets took a lead in the top of the tenth on Pratt's sacrifice fly, but Ozzie Guillen's RBI hit off Armando Benitez tied it again.

Kenny Rogers, the midseason trade acquisition, entered in the eleventh and allowed a leadoff double to Gerald Williams. After the runner moved to third on a sacrifice bunt, Valentine realized that a mere fly ball would end the series, so he made a bold and risky tactical decision.

Trying to set up a force-out at the plate, the manager called for intentional walks to the next two batters, Chipper Jones and Brian Jordan. The nightmare

scenario, then, became the possibility that Rogers would walk Andruw Jones and lose the game. He went to a 3-2 count and did just that, allowing a changeup to drift a shade outside the strike zone.

The Mets' cardiac run was over. They had failed to complete an unlikely comeback. At the end of a sorry decade, however, they had nearly reached the World Series once again, after landing in the postseason for the first time since the Strawberry-Gooden-Hernandez era. While the 1990s had begun with a decline, the decade ended with the Mets seemingly ascending toward a better place.

OPPOSITE: Robin Ventura's hit brings in the winning run in the fifteenth inning against the Atlanta Braves in game five of the 1999 National League Championship Series at Shea Stadium.

ABOVE: Robin Ventura (head down) is mobbed by teammates after his fifteenth-inning hit brought in the winning run against the Atlanta Braves in game five of the National League Championship Series at Shea Stadium.

MET MEMORIES

ANTHONY YOUNG

From May 6, 1992, to July 24, 1993, Met pitcher Anthony Young set a major league record by losing twenty-seven consecutive decisions.

My favorite is the first time I ran out there at Shea. I came in with the bases loaded, I'll never forget that. Shawon Dunston up to bat. I got him to ground into an inning-ending 6-4-3 double play. That's one of the best memories of my life. When that door opened, I don't remember the crowd or anything, I was just so focused. They played "Go, Johnny, Go" for Franco. I still don't know what song they played for me, I was so focused.

On the losing streak: I got a bad rap on that. I always said I didn't feel like I was pitching badly. I retired twenty-four or twenty-five guys in a row and losing. It just happened to me. I don't feel like I deserve it, but I wish it was forgotten. It was an eighty-six-year-old record and it might be eighty-six more years. People know me for it. Look at quality starts, my ERA.

I was twelve-for-twelve during the streak on saves. I was Pitcher of the Month. I had twentysomething scoreless innings.

Believe me, whenever I went out there, they were pressing so hard to break the record. Even the night I finally snapped it, I thought I was going to get another loss because Todd Hundley threw a ball away. We came back in the bottom of the ninth. I was like, here we go again.

GREGG JEFFERIES

A much-heralded prospect when he came up in 1987, Gregg Jefferies clashed with teammates who considered him spoiled and resented his phenom status. Although he enjoyed a decent career with other teams, Jefferies was gone from New York by 1992.

I do think about my career. I look back. There was some stuff I wished I could've accomplished if I stayed healthy. There was stuff I wouldn't have changed and stuff I would have. Do I feel I left stuff that I wanted to obtain? Yeah, without a question. I would've loved to have won the World Series. I was real spoiled on the Mets in '88, getting to the playoffs that early. We didn't have the wild card. I would've been happy to get back to the playoffs. I would've liked to stay healthy, that would've been nice. I broke in at nineteen, I had some immaturities. I had a temper and I wish I had learned to tone that down. I did later. I had a great time in New York. It gave me my name. People remember.

We were actually thinking of naming our little boy Shea and we opted for Luke. Took my wife back to New York two years ago and I was a little leery about the response, walking on the street. But it was great. I did leave some things there in New York. I wasn't sure about the response, but when I walked around, it was nice from the older guys. It was a nice response. I was recognized. I thought I'd go down the street, I thought I'd blend in and people would do double takes. It was pretty nice. We went to plays and they took care of us there and at some restaurants. I was pleasantly surprised.

On treatment from teammates: Yeah, it could've [changed things for him]. It was a veteran team. I blame nobody. I was a young kid, replacing Wally Backman after a World Series team. I could understand the resentment. When I got a little older and learned the game and put up some years, when I played against them, they were very friendly. I graduated high school at seventeen, got to the big leagues at nineteen. The veterans had their own pressures, I had to learn on the job by myself and that was fine, it took me a little longer to play the game. I turned the page on my baseball standards.

I had a temper, but I see some guys on TV now destroying bats. I really tried to stop. I struck out, bases loaded, lose a game, I was extremely mad. I stopped it for a while and then I got criticized for not caring anymore. I just kind of played the game. When I was in St. Louis and threw a helmet, it was—look, Jefferies cares. Once I got established, that helped. I was always very fiery, I had to be because I wasn't good enough to just throw the bat out there. Did it hurt me sometimes, being an emotional player? Yeah, but people tell me now that I always played hard, and we loved the intensity. It's always like that—the longer you're retired, the better player you were.

[His career] was cut a little short when I tore two hamstrings in the same leg. To this day, I still feel it in the same leg. I never believed when I heard people say it popped, but I believe them now. It was pretty pain-

Gregg Jefferies hustles around bases after belting off a homer at Shea.

ful. I tried to get back and I was in Texas, running before a game, and trainers told me that was it. It was a tough moment for me. Luckily, I got in early.

I remember teaching my son how to surf in the ocean. Kicking, I had to stop because I felt the pull in the same leg. I have to do elliptical instead of running. Can feel it up steep hills. I was playing softball for a while with my buddies and could never do a full sprint.

1990s

2000s

METS VICTORY SPECIAL

DAILY ● NEWS
New York's Hometown Newspaper

Tuesday, October 17, 200

www.nydailynews.com   50¢

BELIEVE!

Coming off a thrilling and disappointing NLCS the year before, the 2000 Mets had so much going on early in the season, it is perhaps a wonder they became the first Mets club to reach the postseason two straight years.

From an early smackdown by owner Fred Wilpon, who warned Bobby Valentine to stop discussing his contract status—the manager's deal was up after the season—to an international incident with Cub manager Don Baylor in Tokyo to the Wharton contretemps to a developing Rickey Henderson saga, the Mets had their hands full the first two months of the season.

Oh, yeah—Mike Hampton, the pitcher they traded for during the winter to anchor their rotation, got off to a poor start. And their starting shortstop, Rey Ordóñez, suffered a broken arm in late May that knocked him out for the season.

Still, Valentine's Mets were plucky, lethal, and good—they won nine straight in April, putting themselves in playoff contention early. There was plenty of other drama along the way, too, but it was ultimately one of the most memorable seasons in team history.

Hampton, who was 22-4 during the 1999 season, was acquired on December 23, 1999, from Houston for three players, including reliever Octavio Dotel and speedster Roger Cedeno, to fill one of three vacancies in the Met rotation. He lost on Opening Day in Tokyo, where the Mets and Cubs played a two-game series,

the first time regular-season games had been played outside North America.

The teams split the series, with the Mets winning the second game, on March 30, when Benny Agbayani hit a pinch-hit grand slam in the eleventh inning.

The real fireworks took place in the opener, however, when Valentine wanted to protest the game after Baylor handed in an incorrect lineup card. Valentine tried to withdraw the protest, but the seeds of ill will had already been sown. Baylor refused to shake Valentine's hand while delivering the lineup card.

"One thing I can tell you for sure: I don't cheat," Baylor said. "And people who cheat, they're always pointing at someone else. I know the things Valentine tries to do to disrupt other people. He's always done it. I played against him as a player. I know who his mentor is [Tommy Lasorda], so I take it with a grain of salt."

Al Leiter, who skipped the trip to Japan so he'd be properly rested for his start in the home opener, pitched well against the Padres, and Derek Bell hit an eighth-inning homer to lift the Mets to a 2–1 victory.

But Henderson was unhappy about not getting a contract extension. At the workout the day after the

2000s

home opener he said, "My mind ain't in it," according to Rafael Hermoso's story in the *News*.

Hampton flopped in his first start at Shea, too, giving up four runs (two earned) in 5 2/3 innings in an 8–5 loss to San Diego on April 6. Six days later, he lasted just three innings in Philadelphia, and his ERA was 6.59 after three starts.

"I feel there's pressure on me," Hampton is quoted assaying in Hermoso's story on April 13. "I know what I can do. I know what I need to do. I know what I'm here for as well."

On April 12, Valentine spoke to a group of graduate students at Penn's Wharton School of Business, and when word of his talk hit the Internet, the manager and the Mets were engulfed in controversy.

One listener—screen handle "Brad34"—posted what were allegedly Valentine's comments on a bulletin board on the Mets' Web site, and they were explosive. They did not stay online long, but the manager supposedly clipped ex-Met complainer Bobby Bonilla and took on Met management for, among other things, not pursuing John Olerud aggressively enough, trading Masato Yoshii, and giving Todd Zeile $6 million that could have been spent on a reliever such as Kaz Sasaki.

At one point during the mess, Leiter said, "I think I'm going to have to throw a no-hitter today to get the back page in New York with all the stuff going on."

GM Steve Phillips and Wilpon met and discussed firing Valentine, though that never gained much traction. There was talk that a videotape existed, but one did not surface. *Mets, Lies, and Videotape*, as Hermoso and Madden referred to it in a *News* story, sent Valentine around to each player's locker stall to discuss the incident.

Ultimately, "Brad34" admitted that much in his post had been fabricated, and the student apologized. Valentine was absolved, and the Mets tried to move past the controversy.

Of course, there was something else coming around the corner. Three days after Hampton finally got his first victory, on April 18, Baylor guaranteed that Valentine wouldn't bring out the lineup card when the Cubs visited Shea. Of course, Valentine delivered his lineup, and the two had an animated conversation at the plate.

Hostilities—the open kind, anyway—were snuffed. "I just wanted to make sure there wasn't a problem," Valentine said. "He indicated there isn't a problem and we indicated it's over."

Baylor shrugged, Hermoso wrote, and said, "Whatever." The Mets swept the Cubs in an April 22 doubleheader, giving them six straight wins, and they didn't lose again until the twenty-sixth, when knuckleballer Dennis Springer was clocked for eight runs and thirteen hits in a 12–1 loss to the Reds.

Two days later, in Denver, Hampton lost, and Piazza hyperextended his elbow, though he did not require a stint on the disabled list. Hampton lost again on May 3 in San Francisco in another outing stuffed with wildness.

On May 7, Henderson's unhappiness gained steam. The outfielder said Valentine used too many different lineups—twenty-one in the first thirty-three games—

and the lineup wasn't together enough. "If you're going to get a team in a rhythm to win ball games, you have to let them play," Henderson said. "If you believe in your players, you have to trust them. If you don't trust them, it's tough for the players."

The next day, Henderson passed through outright waivers, meaning the Mets exposed his contract to every other team, but no one took him.

The soap opera was interrupted briefly by Hampton taking a shutout into the ninth inning before giving way to struggling closer Armando Benitez, who saved a 2–0 win over the Pirates.

On May 12, the Mets lost for the eleventh time in sixteen games, dropping a 6–4 decision to the Marlins. But the big news came when Henderson hit a hard line drive he believed would be a home run. He started his home-run trot but was held to a single when the ball struck the wall.

According to Peter Botte's account in the *News*, Valentine called it "unacceptable." Henderson replied that his manager's opinion "doesn't matter, man. . . . I'm gonna do it again if I hit one like that."

The next day, the Mets released Henderson, with Phillips calling it "addition by subtraction" in Hermoso's story. Added Valentine, "I couldn't compromise my principles anymore. I'm perceived as an inflexible hardhead, but I felt I bent too much and I really wasn't having fun living with myself.

"I would never be the one to say any great player is done. I'm not that clever. He was done here."

At the time of his release, Henderson was batting .219 with just one extra-base hit in ninety-six at-bats. He didn't believe he was the problem, though. "I didn't cause them to lose," Henderson said. "Better look someplace else." Less than a week later, Henderson signed with the Mariners.

Hampton, meanwhile, beat the Marlins on May 14, 5–1, with help from a Piazza grand slam. After the game, Hampton talked in detail how two weeks

Mike Hampton pitches in game five of the 2000 NLCS.

earlier he had walked from Pac Bell Park in San Francisco, to the Westin St. Francis Hotel, where the Mets were staying, to do some soul-searching. He knew he was pitching poorly and tried to relax. Along the way, he saw some of San Francisco's homeless on the street and figured he was lucky. He ought to forget about his poor pitching and believe in himself.

"Sometimes you just have to sit back and think about stuff," Hampton said. "The best situation for me is to be off by myself."

Since his walk, he had toned down his wildness, which had been killing him. Including that San Francisco start, in which he walked six, Hampton had

2000s

Mike Piazza flexes for the fans following a Met victory over the Pirates.

issued thirty-six free passes in 38 2/3 innings, the most in the majors. Then he walked only one in the next 17 1/3 innings.

On the same day Henderson signed with the Mariners, Leiter beat the Rockies to improve to 5-0 and push the Mets one game over .500, at 21-20.

On May 21, the Mets got a lift from an unlikely source—Joe McEwing, called up only eight days earlier, doubled twice and homered off Arizona ace Randy Johnson. Then McEwing scored the winning run in the ninth on Derek Bell's single in a 7–6 victory.

Just over a week later, Ordóñez broke his arm tagging the Dodgers' F. P. Santangelo on a play at second. He was supposed to be out six weeks but his arm did not heal properly and he was out for the year, replaced at short by Kurt Abbott and Melvin Mora.

A few days later, on June 1, Piazza left the field

with blood pouring down his forehead after getting hit by Gary Sheffield's backswing in Los Angeles. He was diagnosed with a concussion, giving him three in three seasons, but returned to the lineup a few days later.

The Mets went into the first installment of interleague play with the Yankees at 34-26. Valentine, as Thomas Hill wrote in the June 10 *Daily News*, sat in the same room in which the previous year he had endured a press conference to detail several of his coaches getting fired, and talked about how he'd like to add another series with the Yankees to the schedule—a genuine Subway Series.

Whether he was prescient or simply prattling, who knows? But, Hill noted, he set the agenda for the rest of the season. "I'm sure there's not a person in the Mets organization who would be disappointed if we got to the World Series and the Yankees weren't there," Valentine said. "But if we had to write the perfect postseason, I think everyone in the organization would have the opponent be from the Bronx."

The Mets showed the Yankees their potential in the opener, pounding Roger Clemens in a 12–2 victory, the third time Clemens had lost to the Mets in two years as a Yankee. Piazza continued his superb hitting against Clemens by jacking a grand slam in the third inning, a blast to dead center that he—and everyone else at Yankee Stadium—knew was gone.

Leiter was terrific again, beating Clemens for the third time the pitchers met in New York. Clemens had a 13.18 ERA against the Mets.

The Yankees battered Bobby Jones the next day in a 13–5 victory, the same day it was revealed that the Yanks had dipped into the Mets'—and their own—past and signed Dwight Gooden to a minor league contract. The series finale was scheduled for the next night but was rained out, forcing the planning of a two-stadium doubleheader—one game at Shea, one at Yankee Stadium—on July 8.

On June 25, Hampton shut out the Pirates, his

first as a Met. It was the fourth in a streak of seven straights wins that brought the Mets to within two games of the Braves, with Atlanta en route to Shea for a four-game series. The Mets had been seven games back at the beginning of June.

It would be the first time the two teams played since the dramatic '99 N.L. Championship Series won by the Braves, and the first visit to Queens that season by big-mouthed Atlanta reliever John Rocker, who had dissed New York and its diverse population in a nitwitted, racist diatribe in a magazine article over the winter. The Mets pledged they were only concerned with playing baseball, but the rest of the folks at Shea were girded for more, particularly the beefed-up police force in the ballpark.

Rocker made an apology before the game that was broadcast on the stadium monitor, defusing some of the police-state tension, and later he threw a scoreless eighth inning as the Braves took advantage of multiple Met mistakes in a 6–4 victory. In the same game, Rick Reed suffered a broken wrist, putting him out indefinitely.

The next night, the Mets scored ten runs in the eighth inning to erase an 8–1 deficit. Piazza's three-run homer snapped an 8–8 tie. In the third game of the set, the Mets had a six-run second inning in a 9–1 victory. Piazza homered again, and Leiter earned the hundredth victory of his career.

"It's our year to give the Braves a run for their money," Jay Payton said in Hermoso's story in the July 2 edition of the *News*. "In the past, they may have been a little better than us, that's why they beat us. But this year, the way our team is right now and the way we're playing, this could be the year we give them a good run if not finally overtake them."

The Braves, however, weren't done. They clobbered the Mets in the series finale, 10–2, but the Mets retained their confidence. "Maybe we dispelled the myth that we can't beat the Braves," Todd Zeile said.

The Mets dropped two of three in Florida before their second series with the Yankees began, three-quarters of which took place at Yankee Stadium. The other game, of course, was at Shea, and it was part of a split doubleheader that had two teams playing two games in two ballparks on the same day for the first time in ninety-seven years.

In the Friday night opener, Orlando Hernandez threw eight terrific innings that were just a shade better than Leiter's terrific eight frames in a 2–1 Yankee victory.

The next day brought rage into the rivalry and forever changed its tenor. The Yankees won both games by identical 4–2 scores, and game one was marked by

Al Leiter uses some body language as he watches a play against the Arizona Diamondbacks in game four of the 1999 National League Divisional Series at Shea Stadium.

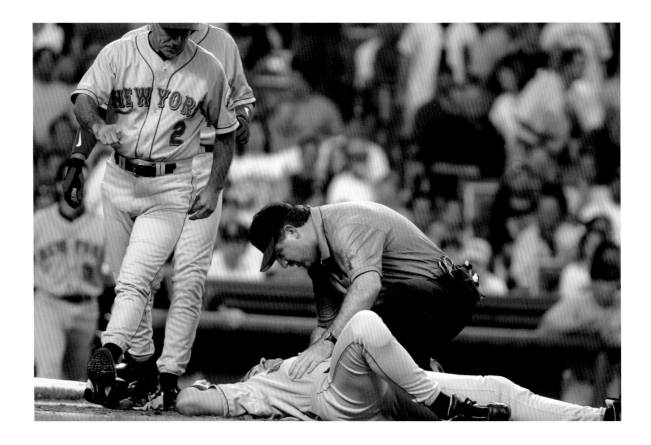

Valentine's ejection on an obstruction call and a solid start by a pinstriped Gooden. But the lingering image of the day came from game two—Piazza lying on his back at the plate, a dazed look in his eyes.

Clemens, the starter in the second game, beaned Piazza in the second inning, knocking the Met superstar out of the game with another concussion. He also threw close to two others. The Mets had hammered Clemens since he donned pinstripes, and Piazza was particularly successful against him, with a .583 lifetime average and three home runs.

"The guy is going to the Hall of Fame, he doesn't have that kind of bad control," Valentine said. "We handed his lunch to him every time we played him, so the first hitter he throws at his head. The second hitter he throws at his head. The fourth hitter he hits in the head. I guess he was just off a little."

While Clemens professed innocence, Met scoffing at his protests could be heard in all five boroughs. The Mets were so angry that Phillips banned the Yankees from the Mets' workout room and told Met players not to fly on the Yankee charter to the All-Star Game.

Backup catcher Todd Pratt said he "lost a lot of respect for Roger Clemens." Glendon Rusch hit Tino Martinez, the Yankees' first hitter in the second inning, and umpires warned both benches. But bad feelings simmered.

Pratt met with veteran players before the series finale, and sentiment was split over whether to retaliate again. Ultimately they did not, and Hampton was superb in a 2–0 Met win that staved off a sweep. He threw seven scoreless innings, and it meant that the Mets finished the first half at 48-38.

Benitez blew the first game of the second half in Boston, coughing up a lead in the bottom of the ninth. But the Mets got good news when Piazza's name was scrawled on the lineup card for the first time since the beaning—he had even missed the All-Star Game. The next night, Piazza blasted two home runs in a 6–4 win.

On July 21, the Mets arrived in Atlanta five games out of first and dropped two of three as the Braves extended their lead. Meanwhile, reporters were flying of the Mets trying to pry shortstop Barry Larkin away from the Reds in a trade or perhaps even Baltimore's Mike Bordick.

2000s

About a week later, the Mets did acquire Bordick, sending Mora and three minor leaguers to Baltimore for the man they thought would fix their shortstop issues. Bordick hit the first pitch he saw as a Met for a homer and kept a rally going in the eighth inning July 29 in a victory over St. Louis.

The Mets won sixteen of nineteen from July 25 to August 13 to pull within 1 1/2 games of Atlanta and even took over first place at the beginning of September, but they couldn't hold it. Darryl Hamilton returned after missing most of the season, too.

Piazza sloughed off a sprained left knee in early August to mount a compelling MVP campaign. On August 9 he came back from missing three days and homered, a 445-foot shot in Houston. The next day, he was four for four with four RBI in another victory.

The Mets returned to Shea the following night, and fans were chanting "MVP, MVP" at Piazza in a 4–1 victory over the Giants in which he hit his thirty-first homer.

Things were going so well for the Mets that when Agbayani forgot how many outs there were the next night and handed a souvenir ball to a kid in the stands when there were only two out, the Mets still won the game.

Hampton felt the flaring of an old high school football rib injury, but he beat the Diamondbacks on August 27, ten days after aggravating the injury swinging a bat.

A season that had started with what seemed like a new controversy per week was becoming low-key. The only thing that didn't go the Mets' way was that the Braves didn't stop winning, either. Even Valentine, who seemed like he might court trouble for his own job, got a vote of confidence from co-owner Nelson Doubleday, who said he wanted both Valentine and Phillips back.

But there was one more hurdle for them to overcome en route to the postseason: They lost seven of eight to

Mike Piazza shows he has the ball after tagging out the Arizona Diamondbacks' Tony Womack at home plate during a game at Shea Stadium.

the Cardinals, Reds, and Phillies from September 1 to 9, and their lead in the wild-card race dwindled to 3 1/2 games over Arizona. The next day, though, Leiter threw a five-hit shutout against the Phillies.

But Piazza slumped down the stretch and would finish third in the MVP voting. The Mets dropped two of three in Atlanta from September 18 to 20. Their division dreams were mostly dashed, but they were virtually assured of a postseason berth. When the Braves came to town with a four-game lead on September 26 for a three-game series, the Mets wanted to keep Atlanta from celebrating a clinching at Shea, but they failed.

The Braves won the series opener, 7–1, to clinch their ninth consecutive N.L. East title.

The Mets wrapped up their second consecutive wild card at 94-68, one game behind Atlanta, and quickly found out that they would face the Giants in the division series. The Giants, who had the National

2000s

League's best record, swept a four-game series from the Mets in San Francisco in May.

"We were struggling early in the year," Phillips said. "We were playing our worst baseball of the year. We've figured out who we are since then."

Certainly, the last time Hampton saw San Francisco, he was pacing its streets angrily after a poor start, refusing to take the team bus, and walking back to the hotel by himself instead. He won his next four days and gradually became the Mets' ace and choice to open the playoffs against the Giants' Livan Hernandez.

But the Giants scored five times against Hampton in game one, a 5–1 San Francisco win that put the Mets into quick trouble in the best-of-five series.

In game two, the Mets took a three-run lead into the ninth inning, but Benitez, the agita-inspiring closer, gave up a three-run homer to J. T. Snow in the bottom of the ninth inning. Even when Benitez was given a second chance—Jay Payton singled to knock in Hamilton in the tenth—Benitez still had Met stomachs churning. He gave up a single in the tenth and had to give way to John Franco, who finished the game by catching Barry Bonds looking at a third strike.

The Mets had tied the series, sure, but they had done even more, Piazza said. "We could have rolled over," the catcher said. "But we took a good punch and we came back."

The two teams played another close contest in game three, with the Mets tying the score at 2–2 in the bottom of the eighth inning against Giants' closer Robb Nen on a double by Edgardo Alfonzo. Benny Agbayani, who had lifted the Mets in the second game of the season with a grand slam across the globe, bashed a solo homer in the thirteenth to win the game and give the Mets a 2–1 series lead.

Agbayani was always an overachieving underdog. He was never supposed to make the Mets, and even when he did stick around, he wasn't supposed to be on the postseason roster because of a right hamstring injury. In the eleventh inning of game three, he had bungled two sac bunt tries that could have helped the Mets win earlier.

But there he was, mobbed by teammates at the plate after his home run.

"I couldn't hear anything," Agbayani was quoted saying in T. J. Quinn's story in the October 8 *Daily News*. "I just couldn't believe it."

Neither could the Giants the next day when Bobby Jones sent the Mets to the N.L. Championship Series by throwing the first one-hit shutout in the postsea-

son since 1967. The 4–0 victory, fueled by a Robin Ventura home run and a two-run double by Alfonzo, gave the Mets their second straight LCS berth and a date with the Cardinals.

Bobby Jones, "the man with the personality as exciting as his name," as Quinn described him, was 1-3 with a 10.19 ERA on June 10 and was sent to Triple-A to figure out his problems. He nearly was banished from the Met rotation, but now, even in the pitching-rich organization, he'll never be forgotten.

For years, the Mets and Cards were N.L. East rivals, but realignment took St. Louis out of the division. The teams had never met in the playoffs but battled through several bitter pennant races from 1985 to 1988, each winning the division twice.

Hampton had called himself the "weak link" in the division series. He was anything but that in the NLCS opener, throwing seven scoreless innings in St. Louis in the Mets' 6–2 victory.

The Mets took a 2–0 lead the next night with a 6–5

victory, taking advantage of then-pitcher Rick Ankiel's tragic wildness in the first inning. Ankiel, a promising young starter, had been bulldozed by a case of the yips in the division series against the Braves and they returned against the Mets; he got only two outs before he was taken out with the Mets up by two runs.

The Mets had a 3–1 lead in the third inning after Piazza homered, but the Cards kept scoring off Leiter. Alfonzo and Zeile hit RBI singles in the eighth, but Franco and Turk Wendell let the Cards tie it up in the bottom of the inning. Payton, who had looked bad at the plate and in the field during the game, saved the Mets with an RBI single in the ninth.

The Cards' Andy Benes made quick work of the Mets in game three, holding them to two runs over eight innings. Jim Edmonds hit a two-run double in the first inning off Rick Reed, and all the scoring in St. Louis's 8–2 victory was over by the fifth inning.

"It's just one of those days when it wasn't my day," Reed said.

Lenny Harris hugs teammate John Franco amid a shower of champagne in the Mets' locker room as they celebrate their victory over the San Francisco Giants in the 2000 National League Divisional Series at Shea Stadium.

2000s

It turned out that game three was the Cardinals' only day, even though Edmonds got St. Louis off to a strong start in game four by hitting a two-run homer off Jones in the first inning.

But the Mets established a record by hitting five doubles in the first inning, one apiece by Timo Perez, Alfonzo, Piazza, Ventura, and Agbayani, scoring four times. Cards' starter Darryl Kile was taken out in the fourth inning with the Mets ahead, 7–3, and Piazza homered off reliever Mike James. When Jones had trouble holding the lead, Glendon Rusch came out of the bullpen to throw three scoreless innings, and Franco and Benitez added one scoreless frame apiece.

The Mets were one game away from the World Series, which looked like it would be a Subway Series—for real, not this interleague stuff—because the Yankees were only one victory away, too.

Hampton, who had never won a postseason game before the series, threw a three-hit shutout in the Mets' 7–0 victory, giving them a 4–1 decision in the NLCS. "Mets Ride 7 into Series" read the *Daily News*'s headline over the game story and column. For his two wins and sixteen shutout innings in the series, Hampton was named NLCS MVP, but other Mets had shined, too.

Timo Perez, part of no one's plans mere months earlier, was a catalyst, batting .304 and scoring eight runs. Piazza hit .412 and homered twice, and Zeile had eight RBI. Alfonzo hit .444; Agbayani, .353.

"I'm very emotional," Perez said through a translator in the October 18 edition of the *News*. "I never thought about playing in a World Series. I saw one on TV—I can't believe I'm in one and I'm one of the leading guys."

The next night, the Yankees beat the Mariners in the ALCS, setting up the first Subway Series since 1956, when the Yanks topped the Brooklyn Dodgers. It may not have been what the rest of the country wanted, Series-wise, but the city was happy, if a bit divided. Even families were on opposite rooting sides as they sat on their sofas or in seats at Shea or Yankee Stadium.

The Mets, meanwhile, were still steamed at the

Daily News 2000
Subway Series pullout
featuring (left to
right) Luis Sojo,
Derek Jeter, Roger
"Batman" Clemens,
Benny Agbayani,
Mike Hampton, and
John Franco.

Yankees and Clemens for beaning Piazza earlier in the year, so this wasn't just a World Series. It was part grudge match, too. When someone suggested to Zeile that the beaning was ancient history, Zeile said, "Like hell it is. It's fresh."

Game one, at Yankee Stadium, was worth the forty-four years of waiting—the Mets rallied from a 2–0 deficit to take a 3–2 lead in the seventh inning

Met hopes were killed by three base-running blunders, and Perez made the most costly one. Perez was on base when Zeile hit a ball to left that both players thought was a home run. Both trotted instead of sprinted, and David Justice retrieved the ball and threw to Derek Jeter, whose relay easily beat the speedy Perez to the plate and a rally died.

Still, the Mets held a one-run lead entering the ninth, but Benitez failed to close the game. In a dazzling ten-pitch battle, Benitez walked Paul O'Neill with one out, starting a rally that would tie the score on Chuck Knoblauch's sacrifice fly. The Yankees won the game on a twelfth-inning single by ex-Met Jose Vizcaino, and the Mets were left with regrets.

No one remembered game one the next night, though—that's how bizarre game two was. Clemens started for the Yankees, and the renewal of hostilities between him and the Mets resulted in one of the craziest moments in World Series history.

In the first meeting since Clemens had hit Piazza in the head, he hurled the jagged barrel of a broken bat at the catcher after turning Piazza's bat into kindling in the first inning. Was it a spasm of lunacy, simple confusion, or intent to harm the pitcher's greatest tormentor? Everyone had their theories. The one thing for sure is that it was nothing anyone had ever seen before.

When the chunk of the bat came toward him, Piazza stopped and veered toward the mound. Clemens appeared to be yelling on television replays, "I thought it was the ball."

Clemens and Yankee manager Joe Torre denied there was any malice. Torre, his hands shaking with anger in a postgame press conference, bolted the room in protest of the very suggestion, but came back moments later. Clemens said he "had no idea Mike

2000s

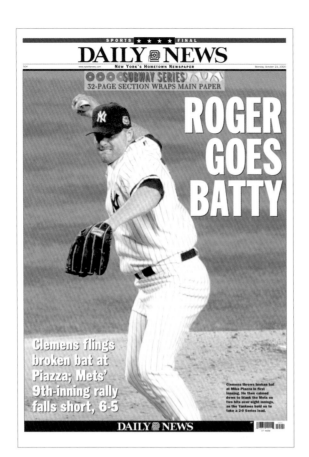

2000s

was running on the foul ball" when he flung the bat shard. "There was no intent there."

"When he threw the bat, I walked out to the mound to see what his problem was," Piazza said. "He really had no response. It was bizarre." The next day, Piazza said Clemens appeared "unstable."

Unfortunately for the Mets, he was also nearly un-hittable. Clemens was not bothered by the tumult, continuing a remarkable run of postseason pitching by throwing eight shutout innings. The Yanks took a 6–0 lead into the ninth inning, but the Mets scored five times against their bullpen, with Piazza hitting a two-run homer off Jeff Nelson and Payton slugging a three-run shot off Mariano Rivera. But Rivera struck out Kurt Abbott looking to save the 6–5 Yankee victory.

The Series switched to Shea for game three, and Agbayani rewarded Valentine's season-long faith in him with another big hit to snap the Yankees' record winning streak of fourteen straight World Series games. With the score tied 2–2 in the eighth inning, Agbayani delivered a tie-breaking RBI double off Orlando Hernandez, who had been unbeaten in the postseason, and the Mets went on to a 4–2 victory when Benitez threw a scoreless ninth. "Met Life" read the *Daily News*'s cover the next day.

"These guys had a big streak of World Series wins," Valentine said. "Maybe breaking the streak was some-thing special. Maybe we can ride a streak for a while."

But Met momentum was blunted quickly in game four. On an only-in-New-York kind of baseball day that started with George Steinbrenner ordering that plush chairs and couches be picked up from Yankee Stadium and delivered to the visiting clubhouse at Shea so his players could be more comfortable, Derek Jeter hit Bobby Jones's first pitch into the left-field bleachers for a leadoff home run. The Yankees won the game, 3–2, to move within one win of their third consecutive World Championship.

They even got help from ex-Met David Cone. Cone,

Managers Bobby
Valentine and Joe
Torre meet prior to
the start of the 2000
World Series.

OPPOSITE, LEFT:
The front page of the
Daily News following
the Mets' 4–2 win
over the Yankees in
game three of the
2000 World Series.

OPPOSITE, RIGHT:
Armando Benitez.

2000s

who had the worst year of his career, entered the game with two out in the fifth inning in place of starter Denny Neagle. Neagle was angry he was yanked just one out from qualifying for a World Series victory, but Torre had no faith that Neagle could retire Piazza, who had smashed a long, two-run homer off him in the third that brought the Mets within one run.

So Cone came in from the bullpen and got Piazza to pop up. "It was nice to get one out," Cone said. "Every out's a commodity in the postseason."

The Mets' outs were dwindling by the day. The Yankees had appeared vulnerable going into October after losing fifteen of their last eighteen games; Turk Wendell had even suggested that their reign would end. But maybe they were just being battle-hardened; they certainly seemed it by winning three one-run games in the first four of the Series.

Luis Sojo snapped a 2–2 tie with an RBI single in the top of the ninth inning, and another run came home on Payton's poor throw home. In the ninth, fans got one more moment of drama when Piazza faced Rivera with a runner on second and two out. Piazza

crushed a deep drive to center, but it wasn't quite deep enough—Bernie Williams caught it and the Yankees had won the Series, four games to one, though it seemed much closer than that.

"This, by far, was the best team we played in the five years I've been here," said Jeter, the Series MVP. "All five games could have gone either way. We were just able to come up with a few more runs."

The Mets lost, but the whole season was "just the thrill of a lifetime," pinch hitter extraordinaire Matt Franco said in a 2010 interview. "We had a great team, great group of guys. We were hot, man, tough to beat. We had a pretty easy playoffs, Giants and Cardinals, not too much stress there, and then the next thing you know, we were in the World Series against the Yankees.

"We should've won game one, had a late lead, we had a base-running error by Timo on Todd Zeile's ball. The Clemens-Piazza thing was crazy. I was right there in the middle of that. I still get asked about that all the time. People tend to remember that. That was a couple big boys out there getting ready to go at it. There was a lot of testosterone flowing around that night.

"We had a great group of guys. We just had a good mix—good pitching, bullpen, Mike Piazza was obviously our big horse. It was one of those special teams— lotsa guys going to dinner and lunch together. I think that kind of thing gets overlooked a lot. When guys are hanging out together off the field, it means good things on the field."

But after the 2001 season, the Mets would look back and realize that they perhaps had not added enough significant new pieces to their N.L. Championship team, something they'd regret in an 82-80, third-place season that was much more notable for the grace in which they handled the aftermath of the September 11 terrorist attacks than the way they played on the field.

But the Mets had chances to add big-time players. Alex Rodriguez, perhaps the game's best player at the time, was a free agent, and the Mets seemed to be his top choice. But Phillips quickly removed the Mets from consideration because the club had "serious reservations about a structure in which you have a twenty-four-plus-one man roster." Rodriguez, the Mets believed, wanted special treatment, includ-

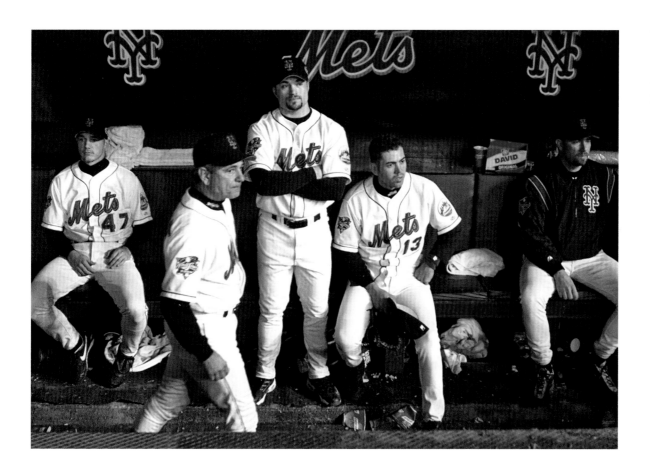

Manager Bobby
Valentine (front) and
Met players look on
as the Yankees, on
the field, celebrate
winning the 2000
World Series.

ing a tent to hawk "A-Rod" merchandise. He eventually signed a ten-year, $252 million contract with the Texas Rangers and later said he would've taken fewer years and less cash from the Mets.

They flirted with Mike Mussina and Denny Neagle, though Mussina proved impossible to pry from the Yankees. And the Mets and Dodgers talked about a Gary Sheffield trade in spring training that had the teams' GMs lobbing verbal unpleasantries at each other under Florida sunshine.

But Kevin Appier was the biggest name they got. The Mets signed the A's free agent one day before Mike Hampton's absurd eight-year, $121 million contract with the Rockies was announced. After one solid season, Hampton bolted as a free agent, signing with Colorado in part because he and his family believed in the Denver school system, something he'll forever be mocked about in New York.

Still, the Mets believed they were strong. They were operating, they said, with much the same team that had reached the World Series the previous year. And in their opener, in Atlanta, Piazza homered off

Tom Glavine in the first inning, and Robin Ventura hit two two-run homers—one off John Rocker in the eighth and the winner off Kerry Ligtenberg in the tenth—in a 6–4 victory.

On April 9, they got to raise their pennant and beat the Braves on the same day, and they took two of three from Atlanta in the series for the second time in little more than a week.

Subtle differences popped up, though. It was hard not to think of what might have been when the Mets went to Colorado in May. Appier got knocked out in the second inning, and Hampton shut out the Mets the next day. The Mets lost four of six to the Yankees in the annual series between the teams.

From April 7 to September 18, the Mets were under .500. From June 24 to August 29, they were double-digit games out of first place. They were simply not a good enough offensive team, despite Piazza's presence.

At the trading deadline, they swapped Rick Reed, who had signed a three-year, $21.75 million contract before the season, to Minnesota for outfielder Matt Lawton, hoping to gain some punch. The twenty-

2000s

Servicemen roll out a huge American flag on the field of Shea Stadium during a tribute to the victims of the World Trade Center tragedy, and a salute to its heroes, September 11, 2001.

OPPOSITE, LEFT: Mike Piazza pays tribute to members of the New York Police Department who were lost in the 9/11 terrorist attacks on the World Trade Center.

OPPOSITE, RIGHT: The Mets pay tribute to the victims of the 9/11 terrorist attack on the World Trade Center at their first home game since the tragedy.

2000s

nine-year-old was hitting .293 with ten homers and fifty-three RBI for the Twins, and the Mets believed things were looking up—Phillips even got a vote of confidence from Wilpon.

The Mets, hoping to get back in the playoff race, won six of seven before the world was interrupted by the death and destruction of the September 11 terrorist attacks. New York had a concrete scar where the Twin Towers once stood. Baseball was far from everyone's minds as rescue workers picked through rubble in search of survivors.

Baseball was postponed for eight days, and Shea became a staging area for rescue workers. The Mets visited hospitals and handed out relief supplies. They made a somber pilgrimage to Ground Zero and gave a day's pay to benefit victims' families. The team also donated $1 million.

After a visit to Bellevue Hospital Center, Piazza said, "Everyone was like, 'The Mets are here!' They looked at us like friends. The only thing we can do is get people's minds off it, get their minds off watching CNN twenty-four hours a day. They wanted to talk. We listened."

"We told the players they have got to do themselves proud, to do New York proud," Wilpon said. "New York needs an uplift and they can do that."

In their first game back, in Pittsburgh, John

Franco, a Brooklyn native, was the fitting winning pitcher. Franco, a proud New Yorker, always wore an orange Sanitation Department T-shirt under his jersey to honor his father, who had worked there.

"For three hours, I hope we gave some pleasure to the guys who have been working," Franco said. "We're not playing just for ourselves, we're playing for the whole city of New York."

The Mets swept the Pirates to move above .500 and were within 5 1/2 games of first on September 21 when they played the Braves in an emotional first game back in New York after the attacks.

It was a glorious night, but one rife with trappings of the times—bomb-sniffing dogs patrolled the ballpark, and every bag was inspected by security. The skies above Shea, famous for planes roaring overhead, were a no-fly zone.

Pregame ceremonies did not leave a dry eye in the house, whether it was the NYPD pipers playing "Amazing Grace" or the Braves and Mets, bitter rivals, shaking hands and hugging before taking the field. American flags flapped everywhere. Liza Minelli sang a wonderful rendition of "New York, New York" and planted a kiss on Jay Payton afterward.

Wearing caps bearing the logos of fire, police, EMS, and other rescue agencies, the Mets delivered a stirring salute to the city. A stirring game, too. Piazza crushed a two-run homer in the eighth inning, giving the Mets a 3–2 victory and continuing their remarkable run toward contention. Fans screamed deliriously, hugged strangers, wept.

"I felt like we were spectators tonight as everyone saluted fallen brothers and sisters," Piazza was quoted as saying in Roger Rubin's account in the next day's *News*. "I'm very sad for the loss of life but felt good we gave them something to cheer about."

"We came here and paid tribute to a lot of heroes," Valentine added. "One of the true New York heroes of the sports world put the icing on the cake."

The Mets won the next night, too, getting within 3 1/2 games of the Braves. But Benitez blew a 4–1 lead in the ninth inning of the finale of the series, and Brian Jordan blasted an eleventh-inning homer off Jerrod Riggan. Six days later, in Atlanta, Benitez could not protect a four-run lead in the ninth inning, putting the winning run on base, and Jordan homered off Franco, all but finishing the Mets' pennant fantasies. They beat the Braves the next day to move within four games with six to play, but the deficit was simply too much.

The Mets had been fourteen games under .500 in August, but had gotten into the playoff discussion, helping, perhaps, a wounded city along the way. But they also were not really good enough to go any further. They hit .238 with runners in scoring position, worst in the majors, and allowed seventy-one more runs than they scored. They also were hurt by injuries to Alfonzo, Piazza, Ventura, Agbayani, and others.

Still, it was a season to talk of with pride, as Valentine noted after it was done. "At the end of this disjointed season," he said, "we were there as a team."

Steve Phillips said he would not be fooled by the Mets' late-season run in '01 and stand mostly pat over the winter. The GM was not kidding. The Mets made major changes before the '02 season, and their $102 million team looked vastly different from the 2001 version, but that was not necessarily a good thing.

The '02 Mets stumbled to a 75-86 record and last place in the N.L. East. Though they had moments of early-season contention—they spent forty-two days in first and were there as late as May 29—they had

more chemistry problems than a high school fresh-man, lost twelve straight games from August 10 to 23, and saw Valentine fired.

So much for Fred Wilpon's lofty preseason expecta-tion: "My expectation is they'll be in the postseason," the owner had said in spring training.

Along the way there were scandals, from Piazza holding an impromptu press conference to address wild rumors that he's gay—"I'm not gay, I'm hetero-sexual," he said—to allegations that seven Mets had smoked marijuana during the season, to rifts between teammates and players sniping with Valentine and a seeming feud between Valentine and Phillips.

Before the season, Phillips and ownership worked feverishly to remake the team. The Mets acquired thirty-four-year-old Roberto Alomar to play second, which would move Alfonzo to third. They sent Kevin Appier, 11-10 in his only year as a Met, to the Angels for Mo Vaughn, who had missed all of 2001 after sur-gery to repair a torn biceps tendon.

They added pitchers Shawn Estes, Jeff D'Amico, and Pedro Astacio, and signed Roger Cedeno, their

former speedster, to a four-year, $18 million free agent deal and got slugger Jeromy Burnitz in a trade.

Gone were, among others, Robin Ventura, Todd Zeile, Benny Agbayani, Glendon Rusch, Matt Lawton, and touted prospect Alex Escobar. During the season they traded Jay Payton, too.

The Mets may have seemed better, but their aver-age age was now thirty-one. In addition, they lost John Franco for the year when he had Tommy John surgery on his elbow.

Nothing seemed to go right. Piazza lost his cool when the Dodgers' Guillermo Mota hit him with a pitch in spring training—the fourth time the catcher was plunked during camp—and Piazza grabbed Mota by the shirt after the pitcher came out of the game. No punches were thrown, but feelings were hurt, and Piazza was fined $3,000. "Why didn't he do that to Roger Clemens?" Mota said. "Roger Clemens hit him and he didn't do anything."

Alomar, long one of baseball's best players, had one of his worst seasons and saw his streak of twelve straight All-Star games end. He was clearly in a pre-cipitous decline. Vaughn suffered a broken hand three days into the season and seemed to have trouble figur-ing out which bat to use when he was healthy.

The Mets were tied for first on May 29, but 10 1/2 games out thirty-one days later. Second-half ral-lies had been a trademark of Valentine's tenure, but it wasn't happening this year. They were so bad that Wilpon, who bought out former partner Nelson Dou-bleday during the year, addressed the team himself on August 19, the first time he had done that since 1993.

Alomar supposedly didn't get along with Alfonzo and Ordóñez. Cedeno and Alomar had a confrontation in the dugout on June 26 over some joking gone wrong.

While all this was going on, Wilpon gave both Valentine and Phillips multiple votes of confidence, ensuring that both would be back in '03.

One of the Mets' best moments of the season, depend-

ing on your viewpoint, came during the June 14–16 Subway Series at Shea. After ex-Met Ventura stuck it to his old team with a game-winning, tenth-inning homer in the opener, Shawn Estes threw behind Roger Clemens in Clemens's first at-bat against the Mets since the Clemens-Piazza drama bloomed two years earlier.

Estes missed Clemens's rear, but hit him another way—Estes blasted his first hit of the season off the Rocket, sending a rocket of his own over the left-field wall in the fifth inning Then Estes threw seven shutout innings in an 8–0 Met victory. Piazza homered off Clemens, too.

In the finale, Vaughn smashed a three-run homer off David Wells, his ninth career homer off Wells, to give the Mets a 3–2 victory and a series win.

In August, Phillips said the team seemed stuck with "a feeling like we can't win when we go out there." Valentine didn't like Phillips' remark, and he added that some of the players "have been terrible." The manager also seemed to slight Alfonzo when he suggested that Alfonzo was distracted by being in his contract year.

"I think everybody has to be professional and mentally prepared," Alomar said. "Who is and who is not? I don't know. I know I am."

Late in the season, television analyst and former Met star Keith Hernandez irked Piazza when he wrote on msgnetwork.com, "The club has no heart; the Mets quit a long time ago. Bobby Valentine could've chewed this team out in June when this stuff started creeping in. He was quoted as saying, 'We brought veteran players in here who I felt were professionals, and I can be more hands off and they can police themselves. Obviously, I was wrong.' You can read between the lines there on what's going on in the clubhouse. It's not really finger-pointing, but Bobby has not been hands-on this year, and I think he has been disappointed with the leadership in the clubhouse."

Piazza called Hernandez "a voice from the grave" and added, "I just think it's disgraceful that people who used to play this game would smack anybody, whatever the case may be. The game has given a lot to you personally. I'm not saying we're perfect. No question we had a bad year. But this is a dog-pile situation.

2000s

Tom Glavine going after his three hundredth career win versus the Cubs at Wrigley Field.

Farts in the wind, just people trying to make a name for themselves."

By September, the team was lurching toward the finish. The Mets were embarrassed by accusations that at least seven players were smoking marijuana during the season and by an extortion attempt by a fan, whom pitcher Grant Roberts accused of giving a photo of him smoking pot to a newspaper after he refused to give her money.

Finally, Valentine was axed after the season, about a week after Wilpon said the manager would be back. "It was an agonizing decision," Wilpon said at a Shea news conference. "What made me change my mind was primarily the [team's] performance of the last two months. I didn't lie. I did change my mind."

Phillips kept his job because, Wilpon said, "We had very good players in place, but they did not play well. I clearly believe these guys are as good as we all thought they were when we got them."

The Mets quickly started working on who would

replace Valentine, dreaming about managers such as Dusty Baker and Lou Piniella. They had a lengthy negotiation that ultimately fizzled with the Mariners over compensation for being allowed to talk terms with Piniella and Seattle, and Tampa Bay agreed on a package and Piniella went back to his native Tampa to manage.

Met fans' appetites had been whetted for Piniella, so team brass stressed that they did not settle for their second choice when they made Art Howe their new manager in club history twenty-seven days after Valentine was fired.

"I know there has been criticism and . . . I think some of it is misguided," Wilpon was quoted as saying in Roger Rubin's account of Howe's introductory press conference. "Art Howe will be the guy who makes things click. He will be the glue that makes this team successful. . . . Regardless of any of the people who were available or could have been available, I think we have the right man for this job."

The Mets gave Howe a four-year contract worth

$9.4 million that they would quickly regret. The A's released Howe from the final year of his contract with them so he could become Met manager.

"He blew me away in a quiet, dignified, strong way," Wilpon said. "He reminded me so much of some great leaders. . . . Look at [Atlanta manager] Bobby Cox and my lifelong friend [Yankee manager] Joe Torre. They don't have to scream out at you, and this guy has that same quality."

So the Mets had reason to feel good going into the 2003 season. They had a new manager, the affable Howe, who had twelve years of experience as a major-league manager to go along with his solid, eleven-year playing career. They also had signed Tom Glavine as a free agent during the winter, adding an ace to their pitcher's park as well as taking him away from the Braves and keeping him from the Phillies, and added slugger Cliff Floyd, too.

There even was a potential feel-good story—ex-Met David Cone was attempting a comeback with the team.

But it didn't take long for this season to sour. The Mets were hammered by poor play and injuries and finished 66-95, 34 1/2 games behind the Braves. Cone's comeback didn't last. Mo Vaughn went on the disabled list in early May with a knee problem and never returned—in fact, he never played again. Mike Piazza suffered an awful groin injury that limited him to sixty-eight games, and Floyd had heel issues.

Perhaps the opener should have been construed as an omen when Glavine was battered in a 15–2 loss to the Cubs, pretty much the worst way to start the season after the '02 dud. Glavine, who couldn't get out of the fourth inning, allowed five runs.

"Obviously this team is fighting the stigma of what happened last year," Glavine said in Adam Rubin's story in the *News*. "I'm sure there's going to be a certain amount of, 'Well, same old Mets,' or 'Here we go again,' and all that stuff. But you know what? It's one game. I can guarantee you the players are not looking

at it any more than one game. A week from now we'll all forget about Opening Day."

Except it was the same old Mets and maybe worse. Closer Armando Benitez blew three saves in a week, and the Mets were 4-8. On April 27 they set a Major League record by striking out twenty-seven times in a doubleheader against Arizona. As the season moved into its second month, the Mets were already in crisis mode. Phillips, who had survived the previous season's purge, was put on notice that his job security hung by a gossamer-thin thread.

Jeff Wilpon, the team's chief operating officer and Fred Wilpon's son, told the *Daily News*'s Adam Rubin, "Fred and I are only as good as the info we get."

Rubin wrote, "If that sounded like Wilpon selling out GM Steve Phillips, well . . ." And Jeff Wilpon said, "You can read into it how you like. I'm stating the facts."

Jose Reyes gets the Mets started in game six of the 2006 NLCS versus the Cardinals with a leadoff home run in the bottom of the first.

2000s

There was more contretemps coming. The Mets had decided to talk to Piazza about making a part-time shift to first base, and it was revealed by Howe on a television program. The problem was, the Mets had not yet discussed it with their star player, who was "perturbed" and "confused," Rubin wrote.

The Mets were ten games out before mid-May. On May 13 they blew a seven-run lead in a loss at Colorado. Piazza blew out his groin on May 16. There was a brief scandal over accusations that infielder Rey Sanchez had gotten a haircut in the clubhouse during a game.

On June 10 there was some reason for excitement—Jose Reyes made his major league debut and went two-for-four with a double in a 9–7 loss at Texas.

But on June 12, the Wilpons signaled they'd had enough. Phillips, the architect of the Mets' 2000 World Series team, was fired after six years. The Mets were 28-35 at the time, but in second place in the majors in terms of payroll, at about $120 million. Jim Duquette, the assistant GM, took over.

"To date, this has been a very disappointing season," Fred Wilpon said at a press conference at Shea. "Our expectations over the last three seasons have not been realized. The team has not produced the results we wanted for ourselves or our fans."

That wouldn't change anytime soon. But the organization's philosophy got a makeover—Duquette came in with a mandate to trim underperforming veterans, so he quickly traded Roberto Alomar, Jeromy Burnitz, and Benitez for prospects, including a pitcher the Mets hoped could be a closer, Royce Ring. Ring was acquired from the White Sox, who got the disappointing Alomar.

Meanwhile, the product on the field did not improve. The Mets were swept by the Yankees in all six games of the Subway Series, including another two-ballpark, split doubleheader. Somehow they swept the Braves at Shea at the beginning of September, then lost sixteen of seventeen.

Piazza returned on August 13 with a home run and five RBI, but it was a lost season for him, though he did finally play one inning at first base, on September 25. On August 31, Reyes sprained his ankle and didn't play again that season. Floyd had heel surgery on August 29.

On September 14, a 7–3 loss in Montreal, everyone got a glimpse of how frustrating the season had been for Tom Glavine, who finished 9-14 and had massive problems against his old mates, the Braves. When Roger Cedeno botched two balls in the outfield, disgust was clearly visible on Glavine's face. He later apologized.

There weren't many highlights, but Steve Trachsel provided a few, going 16-10 with a 3.78 ERA in his finest major league season. He threw two one-hit shutouts, beating the Angels, 8–0, on June 15 and the Rockies, 8–0, on August 18. From June 15 to 17, the Mets were involved in three one-hitters: Trachel's, one by Florida's Dontrelle Willis, and a combined 1–0 victory over the Marlins thrown by Jae Weong Seo, David Weathers, and Benitez.

On Opening Day, the Mets unveiled orange-and-blue patches that read "Ya Gotta Believe" on their right sleeves to honor beloved reliever Tug McGraw, who had died the previous winter. For the Mets and their fans, though, the '04 Mets just brought more of the unbelievable.

The winter was sobering for the Mets, who planned to trim their payroll by about $30 million. They flirted briefly with Vlad Guerrero, the free agent slugger who eventually signed with the Angels, and saw Alex Rodriguez get traded to, of all teams, the Yankees.

The Mets' new players included Mike Cameron in center field and Japanese import Kaz Matsui, a short-stop whose signing forced the Mets to move Jose Reyes to second base. Improved defense up the middle was one

of their biggest concerns if they were going to play, as Fred Wilpon put it, "meaningful games" in September.

There was a whiff of first place—as late as July 15 the Mets were one game out of first and two games over .500, but then lost eight of their next ten. On August 21 they were 9 1/2 games back and lost nineteen of twenty-one and they finished in fourth place at 71-91, twenty-five games out of first.

The most memorable part of the season came with a flurry of deals near the trading deadline when the Mets and Jim Duquette, now fully vested as GM, sent top prospect Scott Kazmir to Tampa Bay for Victor Zambrano and then swapped Ty Wigginton, Jose Bautista, and pitching prospect Matt Peterson to Pittsburgh for Kris Benson and Jeff Keppinger.

The moves were pitched as a way to build while remaining in the race—the Mets were six games out before their game on July 30, the day the trades were made.

"This is a combination of building from within and acquiring players from outside the organization, and getting younger and transforming a roster that a year ago or two years ago was one of the oldest in baseball," Duquette said in Adam Rubin's story in the *News* about the deals. "Both these pitchers are [almost] twenty-nine years old. They'll have a lot of mileage ahead of them pitchingwise. It's a price we paid from within the organization, but we also feel like . . . we have replacements and reinforcements that are on their way that can actually within a year or so surpass a guy like Peterson or a guy like Kazmir."

Kazmir, a promising lefty whom the Mets had said they planned to build around, made the majors with Tampa Bay at twenty. At the time of the trade he said, "I'm heartbroken."

The next night, as if the baseball gods were commenting on the Mets' deals, Benson got rocked in an 8–0 loss to the Braves.

Injuries hampered the Mets again. A series of leg woes kept Reyes out of the lineup for most of the season, and he played in only fifty-three games.

2000s

Mike Piazza (center) is flanked by Hall of Fame catchers Gary Carter, Yogi Berra, Johnny Bench, and Carlton Fisk (left to right) during a pregame ceremony at Shea Stadium honoring Piazza for breaking the all-time home run record for catchers.

Floyd had injury trouble again, a strained right thigh muscle. Tom Glavine lost two front teeth in a taxicab accident. Zambrano made only three starts for the Mets before getting hurt, which made fans lament the Kazmir trade. Matsui, Piazza, and Cameron also missed significant stretches.

Late in the season, it became clear that Howe's job was in jeopardy, though he still had two years and $4.7 million left on his contract. His in-game moves puzzled his bosses, and the team was listing. Part of the problem was that Howe was "hired to be the anti–Bobby Valentine" and "went too far in the other direction," Rubin wrote. He was no communicator, which annoyed players.

Even his stock response to losses—"We battled"—became fodder for Met mocking.

On September 3 Piazza said, "We're a bad team right now," and Howe got a dreaded vote of confidence—of sorts, anyway—from Duquette.

"He's got two years left on his contract. I expect him to fulfill those two years," the GM said. "I also know how things work around here. He knows that. I

know that. We're all evaluated on a regular basis. That just doesn't go with myself and Art and the players. It's everyone in the office, all the way down to the entry-level positions. It's something that I know when the season is over we will reevaluate."

In the September 13 *Daily News*, Rubin wrote that the Mets' brass had decided in a meeting to fire Howe at the end of the season, but they were not going to announce it until then. Even though he was a lame duck, Howe agreed to finish the season as manager, perhaps a new low in a bad era for the Mets.

Not that there weren't highlights in '04. Matsui led off the season in Atlanta and homered in a 7–2 Glavine victory, offering a flicker of hope.

In a season in which he played sixty-eight games at first base, Piazza also became the all-time homer king among catchers. Piazza hit his 351st career home run as a backstop on April 27 in Los Angeles, tying Carlton Fisk's record for home runs by a catcher, and then topped Fisk with number 352 on May 5.

On June 18 there was a wonderful ceremony at Shea, with every living Hall of Fame catcher—Johnny

Bench, Yogi Berra, Gary Carter, and Fisk—along with Lance Parrish and Pudge Rodriguez in attendance.

"This is a real honor," Piazza remarked at the ceremony. "I just really appreciate it. But this is so much more a tribute to the game and especially the position of catching."

"This is a special occasion for us catchers," Fisk said. "Only we as catchers can fully appreciate what it takes to go behind the plate every day and also put some offensive numbers on the board. Mike has met that challenge for years now."

On May 12, Matsui again led off with a homer—this time off Arizona ace Randy Johnson—and Glavine beat the Diamondbacks, 1–0. Eleven days later, Glavine threw the twenty-seventh one-hitter in club history, losing a no-no when Colorado's Kit Pellow doubled with two out in the eighth inning.

The Mets also swept the Yankees at Shea from July 2 to 4, giving them a 4–2 victory in the season series, the first time they had won it.

At the All-Star Game, there was more Piazza-Clemens drama—would it ever end? Clemens was named to start the game for the National League, and Piazza was voted the starting catcher. The two tried to get along, and it was great theater for fans.

"I don't know if we're going to be playing golf anytime soon," Piazza said. "But we've got a job to do." Clemens was hammered for six runs in the first inning.

The best news of all may have come on July 21— David Wright's debut. The über-prospect became the

Catcher Mike Piazza shows the home plate umpire he still has possession of the ball after placing the tag on the Philadelphia Phillies' Pat Burrell, who was out at home.

2000s

129th third baseman in franchise history and quickly served notice that he might one day be the best. He went nothing for four in a 5–4 victory over Montreal in his first game, but batted .293 with fourteen homers and forty RBI in sixty-nine games.

After the 2004 season, circumstances aligned for the Mets to build another era of success. First, the team had two spectacular talents ready to emerge as young faces of the franchise, Wright and Reyes.

The Mets also were one season away from launching their answer to the YES Network, the Yankees'

ultraprofitable cable network. The 2005 Yankees were, as usual, a traveling All-Star show, featuring bold-face names such as Derek Jeter, Alex Rodriguez, Gary Sheffield, Randy Johnson, Tino Martinez, and Mariano Rivera. Over in Queens, the Mets knew they would have to raise their profile for their network to compete with YES.

As they had been upon promoting Steve Phillips and hiring Bobby Valentine in the late-1990s, the Mets were ready to spend, and seeking the right general manager to hunt for high-impact free agents and trades.

"With the network coming up, we knew at that time we had to invest in the team," assistant general manager John Ricco recalled five years later.

Fred Wilpon thought of Omar Minaya, one of the owner's favorites from his time in the 1990s as an assistant GM under Phillips, and now the GM of the Montreal Expos.

Minaya was born in the Dominican Republic and raised in Elmhurst and Corona, Queens, and his Horatio Alger story always appealed to the Brooklyn-born and self-made elder Wilpon. The Oakland Athletics made him a fourteenth-round draft choice in 1978, though his minor league career was shortened by injuries.

Minaya's time in scouting and development began in 1985, when the Texas Rangers offered him a job as a scout. In that role, Minaya gradually established a reputation as a keen discoverer and evaluator of talent, and recruited such future stars as Juan Gonzalez and Sammy Sosa.

His career launched by those years in Texas, Minaya came home to accept a position in the Mets' front office, eventually ascending to the position of assistant GM. He made history in 2002 when the Expos hired him away from New York and made him the first Hispanic general manager in baseball history. This was a pathbreaking event in a game that has been slow to diversify in leadership positions.

More than six decades after Jackie Robinson broke the all-white monopoly on the game, Major League Baseball is still run primarily by white men. For

decades, the game has been wildly popular in Latin America, but no Hispanic had been offered the chance to run a team until Minaya.

He was, however, presented with a flawed opportunity. The Expos were a franchise in decline, owned and operated by the league, and rumored to be headed for contraction. It was an odd situation with a limited budget, but Minaya attacked it with characteristic aggressiveness.

In 2004, when it appeared that the franchise would not exist in the near future, Minaya executed a trade that looked foolhardy in retrospect, sending Cliff Lee, Grady Sizemore, Brandon Phillips, and Lee Stevens to the Cleveland Indians for pitcher Bartolo Colon. Minaya still defends that trade, putting it the context of his extreme win-now situation in Montreal.

As it turned out, the Expos would not be contracted, but would move to Washington, D.C., after the 2004 season to become the Nationals. With all that upheaval coming, Minaya was in a vulnerable position—as were the Mets, who in 2004 had been both bad and boring. Ticket sales had been poor, and the boisterous Boston Red Sox, long-haired "idiots" such as Johnny Damon, Manny Ramirez, and well-trimmed but clutch-hitting David Ortiz, were threatening the Mets for back-page attention in New York after winning their first Word Series in eighty-six years.

The Mets knew they needed to forge aggressively forward. On September 27, 2004, Fred and Jeff Wilpon flew to Canada to speak with Minaya about the GM job. Though the Mets were in disarray, they presented far more stability than the Expos, who played half of their home games in a dilapidated stadium in San Juan, Puerto Rico. In 2004, MLB had not even allowed the Expos to make September call-ups because of the cost in travel and major league service time.

The Mets, though, did not represent an ideal situation, either. Fred Wilpon had actually tried to lure Minaya back to New York the previous year in a

power-sharing arrangement with Jim Duquette, but that had not appealed to Minaya. Even now, with Duquette set to be pushed aside, Minaya knew that Jeff Wilpon liked to remain involved in baseball operations, more so than some other owners.

Before accepting the new job and agreeing to return home, Minaya sought and received assurances from the Wilpons that he would have full control over baseball decisions. That concept is never fully attainable with the Mets, given the strong interest of ownership in the team, but Minaya was convinced he would be free to do his job. The whirlwind courtship and hiring were over.

"It was kept very private," Minaya told the *Daily News*. "And it happened very quickly, too—within seventy-two hours."

Duquette was a victim of the reunion that Fred Wilpon had long wanted. The GM had signed a three-year contract the previous winter, but that deal contained a fine-print clause saying that the Mets could change Duquette's title and significantly reduce his salary after one year. The club did not elect to go after Duquette's $450,000 paycheck, but they did demote him to senior vice president of baseball operations. He would remain with the organization for another season before leaving to work for the Baltimore Orioles.

During his first off-season running the Mets, Minaya moved to make bold changes to the team. While assessing the free-agent market, Minaya brought in a brash—some would say too brash—assistant GM, Tony Bernazard.

A former major league second baseman, Bernazard had worked for a long time at the Players' Association, where he had helped develop the World Baseball Classic. Ambitious and bold, Bernazard was well

2000s

Pedro Martinez shares a laugh with teammates during spring training.

connected in baseball, particularly within the Latin American baseball community.

In the fall and winter of 2004, Minaya deployed Bernazard to help him recruit one of the premier pitchers of his time, Pedro Martinez. Martinez had just won a World Series with the Boston Red Sox, and his former team did not appear overly motivated to re-sign him. Martinez had gone 16-9 in 2004, with a 3.90 earned-run average—his highest since 1996.

While he was showing slight signs of age and decline, Martinez was still an above-average pitcher,

and a marquee name. Because of those factors, and the Mets' tumble in recent seasons toward becoming irrelevant also-rans, Minaya was not overly optimistic about his chances of actually signing Martinez.

"I thought it was a long shot," Minaya said. "Why would a guy who had won the World Series, who is *the guy* in town, want to come to a last-place team, a tough town, not a great-hitting team? Why?"

The Mets' best chances were in appealing to Martinez's pride and his bank account. The latter factor is not unique; most modern ballplayers equate status in the game with dollar amounts in contracts. But the first factor, pride, was significant with Martinez.

One of the most outsized and complex characters baseball had seen for some time, Martinez always followed his own muse. Frequently late to team functions but willing to put in copious time mentoring younger pitchers. Humble and funny sometimes, rude and defiant on other occasions. Martinez was a mess of contradictions.

After years of enjoying life as one of the majors stars on the Red Sox, and certainly the undisputed leader of its pitching staff, Martinez was eclipsed in the 2004 postseason by new addition Curt Schilling.

Schilling, himself always needy of public attention, arrived from Arizona before that season, saying he wanted to end the Sox' long championship drought. He created an all-time visual when he pitched with a bloody (or red, at least) sock in the American League Championship Series as Boston made history by coming back from a three-games-to-none deficit against the Yankees.

With Schilling nudging his way into the spotlight in Boston, Martinez sought a new city for his outsized persona. As the Mets made overtures to Martinez and his agent, Fernando Cuza, Minaya and Bernazard's relationships played a significant role. The GM had known Cuza for years, while his new assistant had a long-standing relationship with Martinez.

By jettisoning a longtime stalwart, Minaya suddenly found a way to bring in Martinez without even having to expand the payroll a great deal. Al Leiter, though he had made an impact as a big-game pitcher during his early years with the team, had devolved into a five-inning nibbler, and a meddler in front office affairs.

Leiter and John Franco's close relationship with Jeff Wilpon helped lead to the trade of pitching prospect Scott Kazmir to Tampa Bay for Victor Zambrano. Kazmir had not been popular with some veterans, a view Leiter and Franco expressed to the young co-owner. It had particularly irked Leiter when Kazmir changed the music at the Mets' facility in Port St. Lucie, exposing the more senior members of the team to Eminem.

Minaya was not explicitly looking to change the tone of the clubhouse and team, but it was clearly time to sweep away the final pieces of the Steve Phillips–Bobby Valentine era (except for Mike Piazza, that is, who still had one season remaining on the seven-year deal he signed after the 1998 season).

The decisions to move on from Leiter and Franco made sense from a baseball perspective. Though Leiter had a 10-8 record in 2004, his outings averaged just 5 2/3 innings; he no longer had the fastball to overpower hitters, so he had to nibble at the strike zone rather than challenge them. Franco, forty-three in 2004, was baseball's all-time saves leader for a lefthander, but was 2-7 with a 5.28 ERA in 2004.

That winter, the Mets cut ties with both mainstays. Franco signed with the Houston Astros, who released him and ended his career later that summer. Leiter returned to the Florida Marlins, the team that had traded him to the Mets after winning the World Series in 1997. After a few months, Florida gave up on Leiter and shipped him to the Yankees, where he continued to demonstrate that he was mostly finished as a quality pitcher. The following spring, Leiter retired and soon launched a broadcasting career with the YES Network and MLB Network.

With the lefty gone from the Mets in 2004, Minaya suddenly had an easy way to make room in the budget for Martinez. Leiter had signed a one-year, $8 million contract with Florida. Minaya reasoned it would take about $11 million per year to lure Martinez—just $2 million more than the Mets would have needed to re-sign Leiter.

In a Thanksgiving Day lunch in Santo Domingo, Dominican Republic, Minaya again appealed to Mar-

Al Leiter pitching in game five of the 2000 World Series.

Carlos Beltran slams a two-run homer to right field in the sixth inning of game one of the 2006 National League Championship Series against the St. Louis Cardinals at Shea Stadium.

a baseball sense—Martinez won fifteen, nine, three, and five games in his years with the Mets—it served to inject instant energy in and credibility to the franchise. Just as the Yankees' signing of free-agent pitcher Catfish Hunter in 1975 amounted to one terrific season and several years of physical decline—but showed that the owner, George Steinbrenner, was ready to revive the franchise—the Mets' pursuit of Martinez made a statement. It gave them more credibility for their next two pursuits, outfielder Carlos Beltran and first baseman Carlos Delgado.

Beltran was coming off a spectacular postseason with the Houston Astros, who had rented him the previous summer from his longtime employer, the Kansas City Royals. Knowing that the fabulously talented Beltran would command huge money on the free-agent market, the Royals had conceded.

As expected, the bidding for Beltran was intense. The Mets first focused on Delgado, a slugging first baseman formerly of the Toronto Blue Jays. But the strategy of appealing to their shared Hispanic heritage backfired this time on Minaya and Bernazard when Delgado called Bernazard "the highest-paid translator on the planet."

Delgado eventually signed with Florida for less money than the Mets offered, and the team turned its attention to Beltran. The outfielder was impressed by Fred Wilpon, who made a recruiting visit to Puerto Rico, but encouraged Beltran to do what was right for him.

"He was saying if you wanted to play for a big market team, New York was the right place to be—Mets or Yankees," Beltran later said. "That was something [with] an owner you don't see happen. You don't see a guy going to Puerto Rico to recruit me, and at the same time he's giving me options to go other places. That sounds funny. But at the same time, that's what he was doing, and that's why I'm here."

Wilpon's unusually open advice impressed Beltran, but not enough to prevent the outfielder's agent, Scott

tinez's pride. The GM framed the two as Davids to the Goliaths of baseball—Martinez had grown up impoverished in the Dominican Republic, while Minaya was raised on the streets of Queens. Both men had risen from modest beginnings in the same country, and Minaya stressed that connection.

In the end, money and length of contract allowed the Mets to trump the less-motivated Boston in pursuing Martinez. While the Red Sox offered three years and $40.5 million, the Mets went to four years and $53 million.

While the contract did not entirely work out in

Boras, from making a last-minute call to the Yankees to offer Beltran at a discount. Focused on acquiring Randy Johnson from Arizona, Yank GM Brian Cashman declined, and Beltran signed with the Mets for seven years and $119 million ($19 million more than Beltran's final proposal to the Yankees). Also important to Beltran, the Mets offered a full no-trade clause, granting him control over his career. The Astros, another aggressive bidder for Beltran, would not do the same for him.

Beltran and Martinez provided Met fans with two players to be excited about, but they were not the only significant additions that off-season. After Art Howe had failed to inspire his team or the public, the Mets turned to a New York icon, hiring longtime Yankee player and coach—and childhood Mets fan from Brooklyn who had finished his career with the team in 1992—Willie Randolph to manage. Minaya, the first Hispanic GM in baseball history, brought in the first black manager in New York fifty-eight years after Jackie Robinson debuted in Flatbush.

The new cast created a dramatic change in image for the team, and some white fans resented the heavily Hispanic composition of the roster under Minaya and Bernazard. That segment was surely not pleased when the team held dual press conferences to announce the signings of Beltran and Martinez—one in New York for both players, and one in San Juan for Beltran and in Santo Domingo for Martinez.

It would became a controversy throughout Minaya's reign, the so-called Los Mets. The roster provoked a xenophobic impulse among some white fans and led to stereotyping of Reyes, Beltran, and other Hispanic players as lazy, selfish, and flashy.

Before the 2005 season, though, most fans were simply excited to watch a team that seemed to be trying again. The exciting era of Piazza and Valentine brought the Mets to the World Series but flamed out abruptly. Now the team was prepared to be relevant again.

It did not immediately work out. Although the Mets were much improved in 2005, winning eighty-three games, they were not ready to contend. In a strong year for the National League East in which no team finished with a losing record, the Mets landed in fourth place. Beltran endured a disappointing debut season, batting just .266 with sixteen home runs, and suffering a concussion after a gruesome head-on collision with Mike Cameron in the outfield of San Diego's Petco Park.

Wright enjoyed an excellent rookie season, knock-

Shortstop Jose Reyes (7) and center fielder Angel Pagan (16) celebrate a Mets win.

2000s

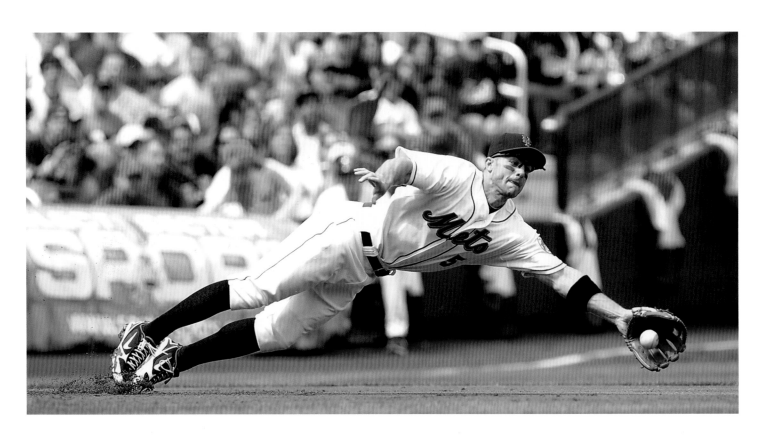

ing twenty-seven home runs, but Reyes batted .273 and clearly needed further development. Doug Mient-kiewicz, the plan B at first base after negotiations with Delgado soured, was a disaster, batting .240 with eleven home runs. Left fielder Cliff Floyd, however, had remained healthy and productive, hitting thirty-four home runs.

In Piazza's final year with the team—his contract up and his skills declining, he would sign with San Diego in 2006 and Oakland in 2007 before retiring—he hit nineteen homers. Martinez, at 15-8, and Kris Benson, at 10-8, were the only two starters with winning records, and Braden Looper was an adventure as closer.

The winter after that season, as the Mets prepared to launch the cable network SportsNet New York, Minaya and ownership realized they were still several big moves away from serious contention. With Piazza leaving and Floyd always an injury risk, the young Wright needed more support in the middle of the lineup.

Facing a hole at second base and seeing the Florida

Marlins once again ready to reduce payroll, Minaya again targeted Delgado. This time he would not need the player's consent. On November 23, 2005, the Mets finally reeled in a player they had coveted for more than a year, acquiring Delgado for young first base-man Mike Jacobs and three other minor leaguers.

One more weak spot on the roster needed to be addressed. In 2004, Looper was inconsistent as the Mets' closer, and was far less appealing after the season than the player they eventually targeted, hard-throwing lefthander Billy Wagner. Formerly of the Philadelphia Phillies, Wagner was a top closer—and wanted to be paid accordingly. The Mets obliged, giving the alpaca farmer from Virginia a four-year, $43 million deal. They also provided him and the rest of the pitching staff with an experienced catcher to replace Piazza when they acquired Paul LoDuca from the Los Angeles Dodgers.

With the refurbished roster complete—and a broadcast team of Gary Cohen, Ron Darling, and Keith

2000s

The New York Mets
celebrate on the field
at Shea Stadium after
defeating the Florida
Marlins, 4–0, and
clinching the 2006
National League
East title.

Hernandez assembled for the new network—the Mets were set for a strong season. From the very beginning, their American League–style lineup dominated the National League. They rolled through April, going 16-8 in that opening month. The middle-of-the-lineup trio of Wright, Beltran, and Delgado gave the team impressive power, and the pitching was good enough.

The Mets were never more than half a game out of first place that year, and the summer evolved into nothing but an anxious wait for the playoffs. The Mets had the offense, but strong starting rotations are often key in October. With Martinez, Tom Glavine, and Orlando "El Duque" Hernandez three of the team's key pitchers, fans and teammates hoped the trio could remain healthy long enough to guide their team to the World Series.

After a mild September swoon, they clinched their first National League East title since 1988, and first postseason appearance since 2000, with a win over Florida on September 17. They ended up finishing twelve games ahead of the second-place Phillies and eighteen ahead of the third-place Braves. It was a rare and sublime summer of domination for the Mets, but the team's fears heading into the playoffs were being realized; before beginning the division series against Los Angeles, the Mets learned they would be without the injured Martinez and Hernandez.

Martinez had learned he would be lost for the post-season after a dramatic month of dealing with calf and arm issues. On September 15, when he left a game in Pittsburgh and appeared to weep on the dugout bench, Martinez said, "Everybody is human and everybody has weak points. Today was one time where I would snap on anybody after I came out of that game because I knew I didn't achieve what I was looking for and I didn't feel the way that I was hoping to."

The team soon discovered that Martinez would be lost for the entire postseason, and resorted to naming the aging (though, because of a famously disputed birth

2000s

2000s

With Jeff Kent on second base and J. D. Drew on first, Russell Martin sent a line drive past Met right fielder Shawn Green. The ball made it all the way to the wall, where Green retrieved it and fired it to second baseman and cutoff man Jose Valentin. Seeing Kent dash home and Drew round second, Valentin fired home, where LoDuca tagged both runners in succession.

"It was out of a movie," LoDuca later said. I knew we had Kent. Everybody said they were screaming at me, but I was waiting for [umpire John] Hirschbeck to call him out, and then I turn around and all of a sudden I saw J. D. Drew. I didn't even hear anybody. It was weird. They almost caught me sleeping."

Carlos Delgado and David Wright were among the Mets who drove in runs that day, thrilling the raucous crowd of more than fifty-six thousand people. The Mets were relieved to have taken a series lead despite assigning the game to a rookie starter. In game two, Tom Glavine drew on his years of postseason experience with the Atlanta Braves, and pitched six scoreless innings to help defeat the Dodgers, 4–1.

With the series going to Los Angeles, the Mets were one win away from advancing to the next round. They scored three runs in the first inning off future Hall of Famer Greg Maddux in the first inning, but Steve Trachsel, in his first career postseason start, gave two of those back in the fourth.

Randolph managed that series with supreme aggressiveness and a very quick hook, unwilling to allow his hobbled rotation to sink the team. After all the injuries, the Mets' bullpen that year was superior to its starting pitching, and Randolph handled the games accordingly. In this case, the move just barely worked, as reliever Darren Oliver got Andre Ethier to smack a sharp liner back to him. A few inches in another direction, and the game could have turned, but Oliver snagged it and fired to Wright to double Wilson Betemit off third base.

Though Los Angeles scored three times in the fifth

year, it was unclear just how aging) Hernandez their game one starter. Even that shaky backup plan fell through, though, as Hernandez injured his own calf jogging in the outfield the day before the series began.

That left rookie John Maine to open the team's long-awaited return to the playoffs at Shea Stadium. Maine fared well on a short leash, allowing just one run in 4 1/3 innings, and the 6–5 Met win was most memorable for a strange moment of Dodger base running in the second inning.

ABOVE: The Cardinals' J. D. Drew is tagged out at home by Paul LoDuca for the second out of a bizarre double play in game one of the 2006 NLCS.

BELOW: Met players celebrate joyfully on the field at Dodger Stadium after beating the Los Angeles Dodgers, 9–5, in game three of the 2006 National League Divisional Series to sweep the best-of-five series.

2000s

to take a 5–4 lead, the Mets charged back. The piled on runs in the sixth and eighth en route to a 9–5 romp, a sweep without two of their top starting pitchers, and an invitation to play the St. Louis Cardinals in the National League Championship Series. The Yankees had lost their division series matchup against Detroit, and for the first time since 1988 the Mets played deeper into October than their crosstown rivals.

Game one, at Shea Stadium, pitted Glavine against Jeff Weaver, and both were excellent. Glavine pitched seven shutout innings, and Beltran's two-run home run off Weaver represented the sole Mets runs. That swing was enough to give the team a 1–0 series lead and to crawl to within three wins of the World Series.

They very nearly took an intimidating two-games-to-none advantage, but Wagner squandered a ninth-inning lead in game two. John Maine survived another playoff start, and the Mets actually led Cardinal ace Chris Carpenter 5–4 after five innings. When looking back on lost series, teams can always point to several early pivotal moments. Though the series would extend all the way into a seventh game, the Mets wasted success against their opponent's top pitcher—a difficult mistake to overcome in a short series.

Delgado did all he could, with two home runs and four runs batted in, and Wagner jogged out from the bullpen to the loud strains of "Enter Sandman," seeming ready to seal a most important win.

Cards reserve outfielder So Taguchi led off the ninth by homering on a 3-2 pitch. "Once he got me to 3-2, I was just really trying to get the ball up, get him to pop it up," Wagner said. "He just got the head [of

the bat] out. He's a good fastball hitter. I know that. Tonight he won the battle."

The Cardinals scored three runs in the inning, presenting the Mets with their first playoff loss of the year and sending them to St. Louis disappointed with a 1–1 split in their home ballpark. If that late loss spoiled the positive vibrations, a dead-energy defeat in game three made the Mets situation seem suddenly dire.

Trachsel started and exited in the first inning after being hit by a line drive. This left the Mets and their tired bullpen deep in an early hole, and they did not emerge. Though the Cardinals did not score after the second inning, the Mets did not score at all, and Jeff Suppan and his team cruised to a 5–0 win and a 2–1 series advantage.

For a pivotal game, the Mets next turned to left-hander Oliver Perez, acquired from Pittsburgh in July. The talented but inconsistent Perez was 3-13 between the two teams that year, but he performed well enough in game four. Although he ended up allowing five runs in 5 2/3 innings, Perez survived enough to support another big home run by Delgado, and a Met offense that exploded for twelve runs. The 12–5 final score evened the series. Glavine lost game five, which sent the teams back to New York with the Cardinals leading three games to two, requiring just one win to end the series.

That meant that the Mets' entire season, their most exciting and hopeful in several years, depended on John Maine. He responded by pitching 5 2/3 shutout innings, and tipping his cap to a wildly appreciate Shea Stadium crowd upon leaving in the sixth.

David Wright celebrates with champagne and a cigar as fans at Shea Stadium show their appreciation after the Mets clinched the 2006 National League East title.

2000s

After Jose Reyes led off the first with a home run, the Mets enjoyed a lead all night. Though Wagner surrendered a run-scoring double in the ninth to So Taguchi, he managed to survive this threat.

Game seven, on Thursday, October 19, 2006, would become one of the most thrilling and heartbreaking in the history of the franchise. Perez started, and again kept his team in the game. The man who several years later became a team pariah might well have been the hero, but his gutsy performance was overshadowed by two fly balls by Cardinal hitters—one that did not clear that fence, and one that did.

With the game tied 1–1 with two out in the sixth inning, St. Louis third baseman Scott Rolen hit a long fly ball to left, where Endy Chavez was playing in place of the injured Cliff Floyd. It appeared a certain home run, but Chavez tracked it, leaped, and snagged the ball in the tip of his glove, pulling it back from over the fence. It was one of the most spectacular catches in postseason history.

As Gary Cohen described it on WFAN radio:

"Perez deals. Fastball, hit in the air to left field—that's deep. Back goes Chavez, back near the wall . . . leaping . . . and . . . HE MADE THE CATCH! He took a home run away from Rolen! Trying to get back to first, Edmonds; he's doubled off! And the inning is over! Endy Chavez saved the day! He reached high over the left-field wall, right in front of the Mets' visitors' bullpen, and pulled back a two-run homer. He went to the apex of his leap, and caught it in the webbing of his glove—with his elbow up above the fence. A miraculous play by Endy Chavez, and then Edmonds is doubled off first, and Oliver Perez escapes the sixth inning. The play of the year, the play—maybe—of the franchise's history for Endy Chavez! The inning is over!"

A team that received a catch that good seemed destined to win the series, but two quick moments that same night initiated a decline that continued for years.

Endy Chavez making a spectacular catch of Cardinal Scott Rolen's deep drive in the sixth inning of game seven of the 2006 NLCS.

2000s

In the top of the ninth, light-hitting catcher Yadier Molina stunned the Mets with a two-run homer.

The team had just a half inning to recover from the shock, and they loaded the bases against rookie closer Adam Wainwright. Beltran batted with two out and the chance to send his team into the World Series. He fell behind 0-2 in the count, then watched as Wainwright's best pitch, the curveball, sailed low and away but remained in the strike zone. The team's ninety-seven-win season ended with a called strike three.

"Sometimes you have to live with good memories in this game of baseball, and sometimes you have to live with bad memories. Today was bad," Beltran said after the game. "I was trying to put the ball in play and just couldn't do anything with it. I tracked it all the way to the glove, and I was hoping the umpire called a ball or something. It was a strike. Game over."

The only consolation for the Mets, after they lost that stunning NLCS in 2006 on the Molina home run and Beltran strikeout, was that the future seemed bright. With Beltran, Wright, and Reyes as their young core, the team seemed poised to contend for years. In the off-season Minaya added veteran left fielder Moises Alou, who seemed a perfect, power-hitting complement to a team that came within one inning of a World Series.

When the Philadelphia Phillies' shortstop said in spring training that he played for "the team to beat" in the National League East, the Mets scoffed. They had earned that distinction, and Jimmy Rollins and the Phils would have to prove otherwise.

For most of the 2007 season, the Mets seemed unperturbed by the previous October's disappointment. The rotation continued to be shaky, with no major additions and Glavine, Martinez, and Hernandez all a year older. The Mets hoped that an infusion of youth in the pitching staff, led by surprise play-off performers Maine and Perez and including rookie and former top draft pick Mike Pelfrey, would provide a lift. The bullpen also was also shakier than the year before, after Darren Oliver, Chad Bradford, and Roberto Hernandez all departed as free agents.

Further complicating the issue, Minaya executed several moves that appeared, in retrospect, to be ill-advised. He swapped relievers Heath Bell and Royce Ring to San Diego for minor leaguers who never contributed, and watched over the next few years as Bell became an elite closer. He moved so-so starter Brian Bannister to Kansas City for reliever Ambiorex Burgos.

The organization was excited about Burgos, thinking he had a live arm and could become a late-inning threat, but the pitcher ended up being charged in 2010 with attempted murder for allegedly forcing his ex-wife to eat rat poison. The Mets also signed free-agent reliever Scott Schoenweis, who would struggle mightily in 2008. The bullpen ultimately became a major factor in the unraveling of that era, and those issues began in earnest after the 2006 season.

Still, 2007 began well, with a three-game sweep over the Cardinals in St. Louis. Maine was undefeated

2000s

in April and earned Pitcher of the Month honors, helping to mask deep season-opening slumps by Wright and Delgado. The Mets won nineteen games in May and ended the month 4 1/2 games ahead of second-place Atlanta. Unlike the previous spring and summer, though, issues were clear, and threatened to undermine the team's success.

The offense was aging, and Alou would have difficulty remaining on the field. Pelfrey struggled and was demoted to the minor leagues, replaced by veteran Jorge Sosa. Sosa began with four wins and one loss, propping the team up on the illusion that he could remain effective indefinitely.

Despite a few losing stretches in the summer—including six consecutive series losses against winning teams—the Mets remained the class of their division into September. There were ominous experiences, such as a four-game sweep in Philadelphia August 27–30 that shaved their lead to two games, but the team showed resilience in winning nine for its next ten.

*S*even games up with seventeen to play. The phrase has infected nearly every big-picture conversation about the Mets since 2007, when they gave away a substantial September lead to the Phillies. As the season grew late and the Mets kept losing, that futility came against woeful teams, including the last-place Washington Nationals, who took five of six games from the Mets that September. The Phillies, meanwhile, continued to win.

A September 28 loss knocked the Mets into second place for the first time since May, though a win the next day lifted them back into a tie. Tom Glavine prepared to take the ball on the final day of the season against the Marlins. If he and the Mets won, and the Phillies lost, New York would win the division and reduce the September losing to a footnote. If the Phils won and Glavine lost, the collapse would be complete. If both teams won or both teams lost, they would meet in a one-game playoff the next day.

Glavine's start, his last as a Met, was an unmitigated failure. He allowed seven runs in the first inning, and the team showed no life after that. As they lost 8–1 in Flushing, reliever Brett Myers closed out the Phils' win over Washington in Philadelphia, tossed his glove in the air, and dove into the crowd. Power in the National League East had shifted dramatically, and the Wright/Reyes/Beltran era was forever tarnished by one of the most severe collapses

ABOVE, LEFT: Tom Glavine is all smiles after finally recording his three hundredth career victory, an 8–3 win over the Chicago Cubs, August 5, 2007.

ABOVE, RIGHT: David Wright and Carlos Beltran show off their Gold Glove trophies.

2000s

Johan Santana.

to the blockbuster acquisition on January 29, 2008, when the Mets traded for Johan Santana, who had won two American League Cy Young Awards while pitching for the Minnesota Twins. Santana signed a six-year contract extension, and the Mets had added one of the game's top pitchers.

Santana pitched well that year, but drama created during the 2007 collapse followed the team into the spring. Ownership had elected to retain Randolph after that debacle, but the manager's status was obviously shaky. On June 17, 2008, with the Mets 34-35, the team fired Randolph and handled the transition in a way that inspired a great deal of criticism.

As he saw the end approaching, Randolph asked the team to fire him before flying to Anaheim for a West Coast trip on June 16, if indeed they planned on cutting ties. Instead, the Mets sent Randolph to California, watched him defeat the Angels, and informed him afterward that they were replacing him with bench coach Jerry Manuel.

The news broke at about midnight in California, three hours later back in New York; the time zone difference ensured that the move would forever be known as a 3:00 A.M. firing. Randolph, for one, was angered by the team's handling of his dismissal.

In an article coauthored by Wayne Coffey in the *Daily News*, Randolph recounted the incident, which began when Bernazard popped into the visiting manager's office at Angel Stadium after the game:

"'Omar wants to see you in his room when you get back to the hotel,' he said.

"'Okay,' I replied. There had been a slew of stories in recent days that a couple of my coaches were about to be fired. All the stories were leaked by 'Met front-office sources.'

"It got to the point over the last month or so that whenever I saw the word 'sources' in a story, I knew either me or someone on my staff was going to be declared on the verge of unemployment.

in baseball history. The team had fallen far and hard from the ninth inning of the 2006 NLCS, when they were a Carlos Beltran hit away from the World Series.

And then, unbelievably, it happened again. Minaya tweaked the roster in the off-season, trading for catcher Brian Schneider and outfielder Ryan Church. Those moves were minuscule compared

"Anyway, when I walked into the room Omar asked me to sit down. He sat right across from me. He started talking about how the team was underperforming, how it needed to turn around.

"He said it was time to make some changes, and I waited for him to talk about whacking Rick and Tommy, but he just kept talking, for a minute or two, maybe longer, about how the team was better than it was playing, about all the stories that were out there and the cloud hovering over the team.

"As Omar went on and on, looking very uncomfortable, this weird chill started to course through by body. I could feel myself going cold. He kept talking, almost stammering, and the chill got worse.

"Suddenly, it occurred to me that maybe he was talking about me. Maybe I was the one about to get whacked.

"Finally, I stopped him. I looked right at him.

"'Omar, are you firing me?' I asked. He looked away for a minute and then met my eyes. 'Yeah, I'm going to make a move,' he said. 'It's a hard decision, but I have to make it.'"

It was the premature end to what had seemed so promising in 2006. The city's first black manager, a popular figure in New York baseball for decades, was gone. Manuel took over, and kept the team in contention for most of the year.

But no manager could have overcome the health and bullpen issues that led to a second consecutive collapse. Ryan Church began the season as a reliable hitter and right fielder for the team, but suffered two concussions in the early part of the year. The Mets several times asked him to pinch-hit and travel with the team, further setting him back. Church attempted to return several times, but never again showed the power and potential he brought to the team.

The relievers, meanwhile, were abysmal. Wagner was spottier than in previous years, and his setup men—Aaron Heilman, Schoenweis, Joe Smith, and others—provided the shakiest bridge the team had had in several years. In September, Wagner discovered he needed reconstructive elbow surgery, finishing him for the season and most of 2009. With no one prepared to assume his role, the team continued to sink.

Once again, the Phillies were charging. And once again, the Mets lost to the Florida Marlins on the final day of the season—and the final day of Shea Stadium,

ABOVE, LEFT: New Met player Willie Randolph shows off his jersey.

ABOVE, RIGHT: New Met manager Willie Randolph answers reporters' questions in 2004.

2000s

Met players watch
another late-season
collapse unfold in
2008.

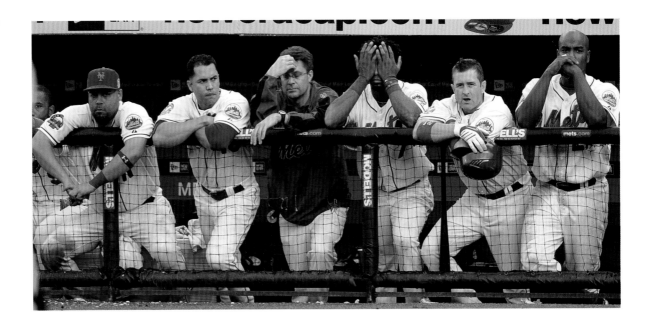

as they prepared to move into Citi Field next door—allowing Philadelphia to slip into the postseason.

David Wright, who went nothing for four in the final game and made an out in the ninth inning, later reflected on the two collapses.

"It was supposed to be a storybook ending, going to the playoffs in the last season at Shea. [The collapse] was a feeling I can't begin to describe. Anger, disappointment, frustration. Individually, and as a team, we failed."

After the Mets lost that day, Wright returned alone to his Manhattan apartment. For several days, he kept mostly to himself. At night, he replayed at-bats in his mind, obsessing over the individual pitches he might have swung at but didn't. During the day, he tried to process the setback.

"I'm very emotional," he said. "I hate losing, I'm desperate to win, and I have a pure hatred of failure. But I deal with frustration a little differently than most people. I like to be by myself a lot, just reflect on what I could do better."

He couldn't believe that the same end had befallen his team two years in a row.

"I've always been the type, you make a mistake, you're supposed to learn from that mistake," he says. "You don't know how many opportunities you're going to get. The first year, we couldn't stop the bleeding. It was like a snowball. This year, we knew what to do, we thought [going into the final weekend] that there was no way we weren't making the playoffs . . . and we just couldn't get out there and perform."

In the two seasons that followed those collapses, the Mets entered another dismal era, this one without even a World Series visit. Manuel remained the manager in 2009 and watched helplessly as nearly every regular player—Reyes, Delgado, Santana, Beltran, Maine, Perez, and others—saw his season ruined by an injury. The first year at Citi Field could hardly have been less inspiring to a fan base worn out by two years of unexpected losing.

Trying to fix the situation single-handly, Wright instead failed to match his performance in other situations. The third baseman hit just ten home runs, and suffered a concussion when a fastball from San Francisco's Matt Cain hit him on the head in mid-August.

The Mets finished 70-92, in fourth place in the N.L. East. Looking to stabilize the next season, they instead drifted further into an unpleasant circus.

Perez, who signed a three-year, $36 million contact after the 2008 season, had mysteriously lost his fastball. The Mets asked him to accept a minor league assignment but Perez refused, exercising his right as a player with more than five years of service time. The Mets then placed him on the disabled list with a knee injury, prompting a suspicious Major League Baseball to investigate the team.

Maine suffered from the same mysterious malady, unable to elevate his fastball to a velocity that would make him effective. In a May 20 start against the Nationals in Washington, Maine could throw in the low eighties, prompting Manuel to remove him from the game for precautionary reasons. In the clubhouse after the game, Maine erupted, ripping his manager and team.

"Me throwing eighty-five miles per hour I don't think is a good explanation to be taken out of the game," Maine said. "It was the first batter of the game. Cut me a little bit of slack. The last couple pitches started getting back to normal. . . . I'm sure he doesn't have any confidence in me. Whatever. Whatever Jerry does, Jerry does."

Maine would later have season-ending surgery, effectively ending a Met career that had seemed so promising during the 2006 postseason. Those on-field issues seemed quaint later in the summer, when Santana and closer Francisco "K-Rod" Rodriguez created headlines with their alleged misbehavior and misbehavior, respectively.

In late June, details surfaced of a rape investigation the previous fall in Florida involving Santana. Though the Mets' ace was ultimately cleared by police,

he admitted to cheating on his wife, and was later named in a civil suit by the accuser.

Then, in August, Rodriguez stormed into the family lounge at Citi Field after a Met loss and allegedly punched his girlfriend's father, with the wives and children of many teammates watching. Rodriguez was arrested, charged with assault, and confined in a ballpark holding cell until his arraignment the next day. The Mets later placed their closer on the disqualified list and sought to avoid paying him for the season. The union filed a grievance.

Somehow, without experiencing the glory of the 1980s, the Mets had managed to become a mess yet again. Failing to make a playoff appearance after the disappointment in 2006 (and failing again in 2010), the team headed once again for a period of change and rebuilding. The goal would be sustained success, a pleasure that had eluded the franchise since its inception in 1962.

But despite the long periods of failure that bookend a year or two of winning, the team has never failed to be interesting. Whether starting as a woeful but lovable expansion team, emerging as an unlikely champion just seven years later, cloaked in scandal, or basking in victory, the New York Mets have always entertained.

2000s

ABOVE Construction workers at the new Citi Field take in the game at Shea Stadium during their lunch break.

BELOW: Citi Field sparkles during a night game, 2009.

A rainbow appears over Citi Field as the game begins after rain delayed the start of the Mets' game against the Diamondbacks, July 31, 2009.

ACKNOWLEDGMENTS

I thoroughly enjoyed telling my half of all this, and am deeply indebted to Kyle Finck and Deanna Harvey, whose comprehensive research made this book possible.

I would also like to thank Ruby Rosser, Ray Martino, Jeannie Martino, Olivia Martino, Teri Thompson, Jim Rich, Bill Price, Sandy Padwe, John Harper, Bill Madden, Mike Lupica, Peter Botte, Anthony McCarron, Roger Rubin, Kristie Ackert, Sean Brennan, Robert Lipsyte, Jim Cohen, John Quinn, Jim Salisbury, T. J. Quinn, Leon Carter, and Jay Horwitz.

—*Andy Martino*

Delving deep into the days I remember growing up was a treat. So was looking back at the 2000 Mets, which is when I first started working regularly around the Mets. But writing my share of this book wasn't easy and I had plenty of help.

I'd like to thank my darling wife, Judy Battista, for allowing me to colonize the kitchen table for weeks on end, and for her good counsel, understanding, and love. I'd also like to thank my wonderful daughter, Grace, for her sweetness and inspiration. The memory of my lovely parents, Bob and Mary, is something I hold dear every day.

Thanks to Kyle Finck and Deanna Harvey for their research. Jay Horwitz, as usual, was helpful.

Thanks to Teri Thompson, sports editor extraordinaire, as well as Jim Rich, Eric Barrow, and Bill Price. Thanks also to *Daily News* baseball teammates Bill Madden, John Harper, Andy Martino, Mark Feinsand, Kristie Ackert, Peter Botte, Roger Rubin, and Sean Brennan, who are irreplaceable.

—*Anthony McCarron*

BIBLIOGRAPHY

Goldman, Steven. *Forging Genius: The Making of Casey Stengel*. Dulles, Virginia: Potomac Books, 2005.

Golenbock, Peter. *Amazin'*. New York: St. Martin's Press, 2002.

Herman, Bruce. *New York Mets: Yesterday and Today*. Lincolnwood, Illinois: Publications International, Ltd., 2010.

Klapisch, Bob, and John Harper. *The Worst Team Money Could Buy: The Collapse of the New York Mets*. New York: Random House, 1993.

Pearlman, Jeff. *The Bad Guys Won!* New York: HarperCollins Publishers, Inc., 2004.

Rubin, Adam. *Pedro, Carlos and Omar*. Guilford, Connecticut: Lyons Press, 2005.

Ryczek, William J. *The Amazin' Mets, 1962–1969*. Jefferson, North Carolina: McFarland, 2008.

PHOTO CREDITS

INDEX

READY TO RUMBLE

Mets serenade fans with "I Love New York" during pre-series workout at Shea Stadium yesterday.

COMPLETE COVERAGE ON PAGES 2-7 & IN SPORTS

DAILY NEWS
NEW YORK'S HOMETOWN NEWSPAPER
50¢ — nydailynews.com

IT'S OUR TOWN!

Mets battle Cards for pennant

24-page playoff preview wraps the paper

BOSS KEEPS TORRE INSIDE

DAIL
New Yo

FAN-

BOSS KEEPS TORRE

COMPLETE PLAY

METS PLOT PLAYOFFS

Met-Amour-phosis

There's nothing like being a winner to make you a hit in society. And these loyal members of the New Breed are after the Schaefer. They're literally engulfing Gate 8 at Shea Stadium but right to be among the first when Mets' playoff tickets go on sale today. Tickets are only for grandstand, however, as fans and reserves reage sell through the mails. Lion was headed by Mark Cohen, 11, of Brooklyn. —Stories p. 96; other pics centerfold

Report Joe Louis Has Breakdown

Story on Page 111

AWE-MAZIN'

Met fans cheer grand new home, new era

PAGES 23 SPORTS

150 years standing tall.

Today, New York Community Bank and the entire NYCB Family of Banks are celebrating 150 years of strength, stability and service to our communities.

NYCB 150 FAMILY

SHOWTIME!

Andy Pettitte — Al Leiter

Yanks and Mets face off in Game 1

DAILY NEWS

FOR

Bobby Valentine and Mets take field in Pitts N.Y. Police Department and Fire Departmen

NFL, REFS AGR
Officials expected bac

OUTRAGE!

DAILY NEWS
NEW YORK'S PICTURE NEWSPAPER ®
Saturday, June 19, 2010

HERE COMES LEFTY

Mets roll in Bronx for eighth win in row

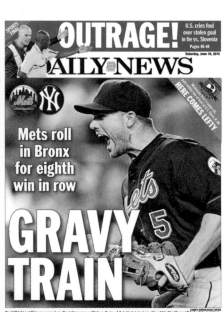

GRAVY TRAIN

David Wright and Mets are pumped up after taking opener of Subway Series, 4-0, behind six innings of four-hit ball by Hisanori Takahashi last night at Stadium, running their winning streak to eight and extending Yanks' skid to three.
Subway Series coverage, Pages 40-44

METS ARE NO. 1

Big Hits by Donn, Ron, Weis Leave Birds for Dead, 5-3

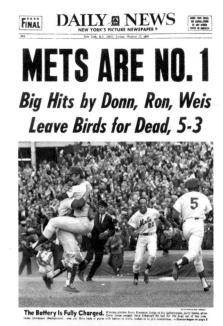

The Battery Is Fully Charged. Winning pitcher Jerry Koosman leaps on his batterymate, Jerry Grote, after Cleon Jones snagged Dave Johnson's fly ball for the final out of the game. Jerry Christensen, near you. Mets back a purse with homer at each, rushes in to join celebration.—Stories begin on page 3

Franco bails out Benitez in 10th, Mets tie series

SAVIOR

John Franco is all pumped up after striking out Barry Bonds to close out Mets' 5-4 victory over Giants in San Francisco last night after Armando Benitez allows three-run homer to J.T. Snow in ninth to tie game. Jay Payton knocks in winning run in 10th, Game 3 is tomorrow at Shea. 14 pages of coverage begin on page 96

EL DUQUE, YANKS LIKE HOME EDGE — PAGES 104-109
CARDS TAKE 2-0 LEAD ON BRAVES — PAGE 102
ERASMUS HAS AL DAVIS ON SIDE — PAGE 116

W

David Wright comes through in big spot, driving in at 1-1. Wright gets help from starter Mike Pelfrey - rum. Tonight it's a battle of aces as Johan Santana